D1433254

ECONOMIC PHILOSOPHY AND AMERICAN PROBLEMS

ECONOMIC PHILOSOPHY
AND
AMERICAN PROBLEMS

*Classical Mechanism, Marxist Dialectic,
and Cultural Evolution*

Floyd B. McFarland

Rowman & Littlefield Publishers, Inc.

ROWMAN & LITTLEFIELD PUBLISHERS, INC.

Published in the United States of America
by Rowman & Littlefield Publishers, Inc.
8705 Bollman Place, Savage, Maryland 20763

Permission by Harvard University Press to quote from *The Entropy Law
and the Economic Process* by Nicholas Georgescu-Roegen is gratefully
acknowledged.

Library of Congress Cataloging-in-Publication Data

McFarland, Floyd B.
Economic philosophy and American problems : classical mechanism,
Marxist dialectic, and cultural evolution / Floyd B. McFarland.
p.   cm.
Includes bibliographical references
1. Classical school of economics.
2. Marxian economics.
3. Institutional economics.
4. United States—Economic conditions.
5. United States—Economic policy.
6. Comparative economics.
I. Title.
HB94.M365   1991   330.1—dc20   91-17868 CIP

ISBN 0–8476–7670–6 (alk. paper)

Printed in the United States of America

 ™ The paper used in this publication meets the minimum requirements of
American National Standard for Information Sciences—Permanence of
Paper for Printed Library Materials, ANSI Z39.48–1984.

The import of the conclusion that economics cannot be a theoretical and at the same time a pertinent science may seem purely academic. Unfortunately, this is not so. For the tenacity with which we cling to the tenet that standard theory is valid in all institutional settings—either because its principles are universally valid or because all economic systems are mere mixtures of some invariable elements—has far-reaching consequences for the world's efforts to develop the economy of nations which differ in their institutions from the capitalist countries. These consequences may go down in history as the greatest monument to the arrogant self-assurance of some of science's servants.

Nicholas Georgescu-Roegen,
The Entropy Law and the Economic Process

Contents

Preface

The completion of a manuscript is a culmination of effort, but frequently it also brings recognition that new beginnings and further work are implied. Both principles apply in the present case. When the central view is evolution and change, the work is never done. I have demonstrated, or at least have argued, that in the economic thought of the past two centuries there are only three basic paradigms. Unfortunately, all three are inadequate. A paradigm is a model plus the setting and the philosophy appropriate for it to make sense or seem tenable.

The oldest of the paradigms is Classical Mechanism, formalized by Isaac Newton, in which the central idea is equilibrium of forces, with possible growth but no genuine qualitative change in the nature of society. All economists are aware of this fact of historical antecedents, but rarely is the full philosophic significance recognized. A staunch commitment to the laissez-faire, self-adjusting, maximizing model derives straightforwardly from Newton, as does emphasis on individual decision-making and decentralized, individualized property forms. Demand and supply, pleasure and pain, are the two functional relationship patterns in human affairs that are methodological equivalents of mass and motion employed in Newtonian science. The empiricism of science derives as much from Newton the Model Scientist as from the epistemology of John Locke the Model Philosopher. In addition to firm insistence on empiricism or reliance on sensed experience, Locke, a personal friend of Newton, brought us the full statement of English Natural Rights philosophy that includes the Labor Theory of Value and the corollary doctrine of property rights as the logical derivative of the right of the laborer to the fruits of his work. Economists are fully aware of, and quite proud of, the fact that data abound in our realm of science, and in macro studies we employ data regularly. But in the micro sphere measurement has proved insuperably difficult. Economists long have resorted by default to the convenience of Cartesian forms of mechanism because of Descartes's insistence that knowledge both derives from and rests solely upon operations within the mind, a phenomenon totally distinct from matter. The only way this is operationally possible is via the use of mathematics, which requires no data. Because of our awareness that many data are potentially available in economics, however, we economists are only half-hearted or "default Cartesians."

The greater proportion of standard economics is contained in the body of thought known as microeconomics, which can be presented as a purely logical construct, devoid of any trace of data or real information whatsoever. In "theory of the firm" treatises, the firm can be wholly imaginary, and this student, for one, had the good fortune to take the microeconomics graduate course with a professor who made the point at the outset that the material could more readily be comprehended if we students realized that we were dealing with imaginary constructions. The core models are powerful and compelling, but they make no necessary contact with our experienced real world. Facts or data merely get in the way and cause confusion for the beginner. Thus the transition from positive arguments and proofs to normative policy conclusions—which must be accomplished, even if by default—is an enormous leap, whereas it "needs to be" almost a continuum. It is with respect to law and the entire issue of proper role for government that the leap from positive analysis to normative policy is broadest.

With poor understanding of Newton and consequent distortion of his model and methodology, Adam Smith brought mechanistic equilibrium into service as the paradigm for economics. Since qualitative change in beliefs, knowledge, wants, societal influence, and resources in fact occurs, that world-view is not fully appropriate for social science. The greater the passage of time, the greater the change, and hence in all likelihood the greater the inappropriateness of mechanistic theoretical formulations. The best that can be said of traditional Classicism is that it involves useful tools, such as mathematics and modeling, which establishes its value as high indeed. It is, in fact, indispensable. However, the tools are completely independent of the paradigm. Dogmatic allegiance to the Classical world-view necessarily distorts effort at scientific application of valuable tool concepts.

A second paradigm is the Marxist dialectic, which had its origin in efforts to transcend the static and apologetic forms of Classicist equilibrium. Use of the dialectic shunted Marx's efforts into nonscientific forms of determinism, unfortunately. Although it has strengths, Marxism is a mixture of untenable mechanism with untenable dialectic. It focuses attention upon critique of capitalism, which is enormously useful. Thus it must not be "tossed into the dustbin of history," but Marxism neither tells effectively how to reach postcapitalist society, nor how to operate such society, nor enables essential critique of socialist or communist forms of society. The doctrine of "class struggle" as an inexorable aspect of history long ago proved to be virtually devoid of scientific merit. Since the world keeps changing, socialism is no more nearly "the answer" to social problems than is capitalism, and Evolutionary Socialism would be decidedly non-Marxist.

The third paradigm is cultural evolution, which is so poorly developed both theoretically and with respect to potential application as to be of limited use. Darwin and Lamarck, contemporaries of Marx, were forerunners, but both of those bodies of theory require serious modification. It was Thorstein Veblen, at the end of the nineteenth century, who made the best start at development of evolutionism in social science. Unfortunately, his efforts succeeded much better in the task of critique of Classicism than in formulation of positive theory. Work by Nicholas Georgescu-Roegen and others in the past three decades has advanced the evolutionary approach in some important respects.

Although numerous, the majority of publications under the rubric of evolutionary thought have been boringly repetitious of doctrines of the group, and therefore superficial and of little genuine merit. The writers have lacked a firm grasp both of where they came from and where they were going, and clear recommendations for evolutionary programs have been almost nonexistent. Whatever their possible commitment to deep-reaching socioeconomic change, in practice and preaching almost all Evolutionary or Institutionalist economists during the second half of the twentieth century have been status quo conservatives. "The philosophers have only *interpreted* the world, in various ways; the point, however, is to *change* it." This Eleventh of Marx's *Theses on Feuerbach* carries a rebuke to Institutionalists just as pointed as for Classical Traditionalists. Because it transcends the positive-normative distinction, but at its best does not subscribe to a deterministic reliance on either history or technology, of the three paradigms it is only Cultural Evolutionism that virtually forces attention upon the necessity for positive, interventionist programs.

More than a century has passed since the appearance of the first publication by the founding philosopher of Evolutionism or Institutionalism, Thorstein Veblen. Veblen's contemporary, John Rogers Commons, saw the necessity of programmatic formulations and did more to change society along the espoused lines than the combined efforts of all later Institutionalists. Careerist conservatism, the bane of creative exploratory work throughout social science academia, has dominated the scene since World War II and the rise of Cold War academic timidity. Nowadays no group is more institutionalized than the Institutionalists.

Hence this book presents and critiques the three paradigms and outlines a program of evolutionary reforms that, in combination, would be of revolutionary impact, but which of necessity are presented in impressionistic and sketchy outline form. An additional volume would be required for development of implied promises of cultural evolution as a paradigm for social science, but hopefully it is clear that we have tried to go beyond mere philosophic chitchat. It seems likely that international decline of the United States in recognizable degree will be required to make possible much real change. Now is the time, however, to work out broad outlines of programs, and in orthodox form neither Classicist capitalism nor Dialectical socialism is suitable. What can an evolutionary perspective offer?

The major part of the book was written while in Spain on sabbatical leave, for which support I wish to express appreciation to the Oregon State System of Higher Education. The first section of chapter 3 was written during two weeks in Wales, United Kingdom, a trip that was funded in part by Oregon State University Foundation.

I have inherited most of the ideas of the book from various economists, most notably Adam Smith, Karl Marx, Thorstein Veblen, J. M. Keynes, and Nicholas Georgescu-Roegen. They have been my best teachers, and I thank them. Also I wish to thank my wife, Beverly, and our three children for their support of the project. Needless to say, I have only myself to blame for shortcomings.

1

Concept of Mechanism

What do economics professors profess? If one takes fully into account the many branches and ramifications of the field, there can be no short answer. However, if one considers the core theoretical framework to be what is taught and required in most economics curricula, the answer is both manageable and meaningful. Economics professors profess Classical mechanism, a model still based in some important ways upon seventeenth-century natural science. This model is commonly referred to as Classical mechanism because it partakes of the mechanistic imagery of natural science synthesized by Isaac Newton and his predecessors such as Galileo, Kepler, and Descartes fully three hundred years ago. The model made possible some important advances in economic thought, but it preserves several assumptions and methodological positions, especially those derived from Descartes, that are not fully valid or adequate. This fact parallels the inadequacy of classical physics subsequent to the work of Einstein. Economists should lay bare these assumptions and advance to new methods, visions, and values.

In economics the central concept of mechanism is the working of forces of supply and demand in equilibrium in a private property setting. Competition insures an outcome treated as both equitable and efficient, and any form of socialism or economic planning is seen as disruptive of natural forces. Many economic relationships are perceived as too complex for efficient centralized management. This view may well be correct, but a conclusion that laissez-faire is adequate is a non sequitur. The argument is shaky that Smithian-Ricardian economics was indeed based on Newtonian Mechanism, but the Marginalist Revolution of the 1870s brought a new paradigm bearing the label

1

Neoclassical Economics. Smith and Ricardo were weak as mathematicians, and their supply-side Labor Theory of Value approach did not serve well for Rationalist no-data mathematical model building. However, Newton's great invention, calculus, could be brought into service with subjective, introspective demand and marginal utility as the focal point of theory. Realization that the concept of the margin involves derivatives opened an entirely new subset of Newtonian mathematics for exploration, and unmeasurable utility could be debated but never proved wrong. Newton is known mainly as a scientist; it was the philosopher Descartes who provided the methodology for new developments via his position that total abstraction—hence mathematics—was the one reliable way to knowledge. Facts or the senses were untrustworthy.

We economists need not attempt to prove that our mechanistic model brings near-ideal results because there is at all times less than perfect competition in the economy. We endeavor to be positive, scientific, objective, and value-free, but it is clear that for some of us the attachment to Classicism is subjective. We do not prove the near-perfection results. Instead we assume them. Given an approximation of conditions requisite for perfect competition, the outcome might be what we long have argued it would be. It need not matter to economists whether "the real world" is noticeably similar to our models. Consistency of mathematical logic from stipulated assumptions is what counts, and all that counts, to sustain or to falsify the models, and apparent data can be debated as to authenticity, can be time-lagged, respecified, or another sample drawn or alluded to, etc., to support a theoretical construction. Anyone who can believe Rational Expectationist arguments and thereby conclude that governmental fiscal policy is impossible can believe anything. It is revealing, moreover, that this school of economists have picked for themselves a nametag or label that serves to put them on the very side of the angels. Who would choose opposite views, and thereby be labeled "Irrational"? Some critics go too far and pronounce the word econometrics as "economy tricks." The idea of measurement of economic interrelationships is of course critically important.

Many economists agree that the wealth and income distribution patterns that result are embarrassingly top-heavy and concentrated. One can argue, however, that some people own better minds and bodies than do others, and that these inexorable facts account for natural and proper income and wealth differentials. What results from operation of the unimpeded market forces is the best of all possible worlds, and the route to improvement is held to be the reduction of impediments. The message is taught as gospel, not merely pondered. The entire subject reeks of ideology, and embodies an extraordinarily conservative and defensive position to be taken in a time when evidences of social malaise crop up almost daily. Physician, heal thyself!

Chapter 2 sketches the historical origins of Classicism, and lists Marxism and Darwinism as alternative modes of science. The rigid Marxist model with its minor variations, as taught or preached in the Soviet Union, is by far the most clearly structured alternative. Its performance has not been good, but we need to see the weaknesses of our market model equally well. Soviet social scientists are fully as normative or committed before investigation of facts begins as are their counterparts in the capitalist world. As is the case with the United States, the world-view and assumptions with which Marxist scholars begin determine the general form of conclusions that will be reached. Their view is that human reality is a historical process in which forces dialectically work their roles toward the determinate end—Communism. Class struggle is the mode of operation of economic forces, and although battles will be lost by the underlying labor class, the war will be won by "labor" because the struggle of workers against their capitalist oppressors necessarily goes on until the workers win and destroy or "expropriate the expropriators."

Other views of economic science and how economies might be run, for example, via either cooperatives or public-private partnerships, are greatly overshadowed by the two major dogmas and are perceived as soft-headed and temporary at best. Thorstein Veblen rejected both the Marxist and the Classical models of economic thought, but he did not clearly formulate an alternative. Veblen died in 1929, less than three months before the collapse of the American stock market and the onset of the Great Depression. We will argue that several important things were learned during the decade of the 1930s that strongly support Veblen's critical view of Classicism. In like manner, history has not been kind to Marxist theory in an objectively convincing way. Capitalism has its deep-seated problems, but this does not mean that Marxism brings definitive solutions, as continues to be argued in much of the world. Hence it is easy to point out that neither capitalist nor Marxist societies function particularly well, but formulation of an alternative remains problematic. Whatever is suggested will be ignored or attacked as utopian, unrealistic, or unworkable. We will offer suggestions, falling back on the position that we are trying to stay within the framework of an evolutionary paradigm.

Chapter 2 also is an effort to demonstrate that orthodox mechanism is a conception of certain facts of science, a view of how the world works, and a theory of methodology of science. The father of modern capitalist-world economics is Isaac Newton, not Adam Smith. It is essential that this fact be understood and kept in mind in an effort to understand our modern situation because Classical economics is still with us, necessarily so the way things have come about, and it is the same body of doctrine as Classical physics. The Darwinian revolution might have hit economics with force equal to its impact in biological sciences and in religion and theology, except that economics was never identified with biological science and did not have to give up equilibrium for evolution as its central viewpoint.

The Darwinian revolution in ideas has its critical flaws when transposed directly to social theory, as noted by many writers, because Social Darwinism is a thoroughly unscientific path. What evolve in society are tradition and know-how, which are acquired rather than innate or genetic traits. To this day Newtonian-mechanism science is satisfactory in many spheres of study, for example, civil and mechanical engineering and double-entry bookkeeping.

Rudolf Clausius, a German physicist, developed the central concept of the Entropy Law, the Second Law of Thermodynamics, at the same time Darwin was synthesizing the ideas and facts available in support of the doctrines of evolution in the biosphere. Darwin's evolution of species demonstrates as biological fact the occurrence of qualitative change in the universe. New species differ from previous species. The Entropy Law likewise demonstrates qualitative change. As per the First Law of Thermodynamics, mass-energy is conserved, and there can be neither creation nor destruction in a net sense in the universe. However, the Second Law enables us to see that when we burn a mere bit of coal, for example, the universe is qualitatively changed. That bit of mass-energy structure no longer exists in that form, but is instead ash, dust, heat, and other radiation diffused in space. Classical mechanism ignores qualitative change, and when set into place dogmatically as the essence of science, leads to denial of qualitative change as a phenomenon that must be confronted. In updated and modified Classical physics, which continues its role of most common model of science, history has no particular role. Gravitation is not merely universal, it is timeless. The entire universe could just as well run backward as far as our theories were concerned until the Entropy Law brought us Time's Arrow, the direction of continuous and unidirectional qualitative change.

The Adam Smith doctrine of self-regulating society that must be left free of intervention for proper functioning is a subset of Newtonian mechanism. Classical economics was not totally devoid of concern for history, to be sure, but the view intrinsically was that forces of history had brought us to market capitalism. Adam Smith had brought the first clear rays of modern light. Slavery, tribalism, feudalism, and mercantilism, which preceded the market system of unfettered supply and demand, were facts, of course, but regrettable mistaken arrangements. Once explained, laissez-faire principles would be seen as timeless and valid forever.

Karl Marx, Prussian by birth and brought up within the *Weltanschauung* or world-view of Hegelian dialectics, had his attention focused on questions of qualitative change. Marx accordingly saw the laissez-faire model as a naive and self-serving view, explicable by taking mechanism as the essence of science. If, to the contrary, the Hegelian dialectic is the authentic essence, then history has had its struggles that have indeed brought us market capitalism, but the clash of capitalists with labor dictates that another, classless or one-class, stage of society necessarily lies ahead. Marx "found Hegel standing on his head" in Idealism, he asserted, and set him upright in Materialism. Veblen appreciated the Marxist rejection of Classicism, but held— as he had been taught in graduate school—that Darwinian evolution was a better mode of approach to explanation of qualitative change in human social affairs when interpreted as he saw fit.

In Veblen's 1899 *The Theory of the Leisure Class*, there is embodied a fragmented and outdated anthropology. Involved is a strong emphasis on evolution, and we will need to inquire more deeply into the bases of culture and of human behavior he perceived. A one-sentence summary is that humans engage in conspicuous consumption that is a zero-sum quest for status. More generally, we must inquire whether behavior is primarily learned, or whether it is significantly derivative from and based upon innate drives. Cultural patterns of a group or society impose a frame of reference upon what is to be taught. However, all or most animal species have behavioral characteristics that involve something innate. Anyone who chooses to argue that we humans have entirely escaped our genetic-instinctive heritage must make that case. That we have not fully escaped is the default position.

Human culture clearly has overshadowed instincts, but remnants remain. In a context presuming evolution of both the natural and cultural worlds, survival value remains a crucial element of explanation of the continuation of behavioral patterns. With respect to customs or institutions, "whatever is, is right or nearly so" is the basic conservative view, implying that the tests of time have eliminated ill-suited ways of doing things, and only the fittest have survived. Veblen, to the contrary, was certain that many customs were strongly resistant to change, with the consequence that there was not nearly enough institutional fluidity to warrant the "whatever is, is right" dictum.

Returning to our previously mentioned issue of conspicuous consumption, we note the meaning to be purchase or possession of commodities that are conspicuously visible, to the end that the status of the owner-consumer is enhanced. At this initial point we note that Veblen parted company with orthodox or Newtonian "economic man" philosophy and methodology because status-conscious behavior intrinsically is group behavior. Status is ranking of position in society. Historically, and strongly at present, economists relegate such theoretical approaches to the world of sociology. Veblen's group-centered theory is not strictly compatible with the idea of utility maximization via individual choices. Conspicuous consumption, or conspicuous investment, accumulation, or any other deliberately conspicuous behavior, is group activity and is of the nature of a zero-sum game. If someone gains in status or rank, necessarily someone else loses rank. One consequence is that game theory of some type, as well as differential or "felicific" calculus, emerges as a basic analytical tool. Another consideration is that national total production, and even per capita, could rise substantially while as large a portion of the population would be in conditions of poverty as before. In a strongly status-conscious society, whatever its advantages, the poorest or lowest-income quintile, say, of residents will be in a state of poverty, and the condition will not be subject to abolition. One cannot lift the log one is standing upon.

At the moment only the briefest mention will be made of relationships between status behavior and what is called imperialism, or even the euphemism, national aggrandizement. Success in life, including reproductive success through millions of years of evolution, has involved forms of cooperation, but also interpersonal rivalry, struggle, and competition. Indeed, the ill-conceived idea of a *social contract* is a venerable theory of the state. It implies that society consists merely of a collection of autonomous individuals who after rational calculation have concluded that they have a clear option but will contract into an agreement to enter the group. Life does not permit that option, however. Virtually all large and powerful nations throughout human history, whose populations had no real choice as to membership, have been self-aggrandizing imperialists. Viewed in this status-centered perspective, efforts to argue that it is Capitalism or Communism or some other such -ism that underlies and causes imperialistic domination of one nation over others can simply be set aside as ill-based.

Chapter 3 is a historical sketch of efforts by economists to apply the mechanical model to the behavior of individuals as consumers. It seems clear that all such efforts have failed. Individual behavior is a subset of what is called microeconomics. We also criticize as inadequate another part of microeconomics known as the theory of the firm, competitive and imperfectly competitive, in a later chapter. Toward the end of the first section of chapter 3 we pull out from standard doctrine a few ideas or principles that we think are valid enough to be useful in our later recommendations. Formal game theorizing is an example of this. The second part of the chapter critically evaluates intermediate-level macroeconomics, and the case is made that much of what is taught is "blatantly contrary to fact."

Chapters 4 and 5 present our interpretation of the basic ideas of Veblen. His ideas are summarized by the title of his first book, *The Theory of the Leisure Class*, perhaps better understood as the privileged class. A theoretical frame of reference is set forth that permits an unusual understanding of the United States. Concern with predatory or exploitative social structures and behavior on both the domestic and international scenes—called Imperialism in the latter setting and involving a continuous thrust toward militarism and war—were hallmark features of Veblen's body of thought.

Imperialism has been accompanied by a widening gap between well-being in poor countries and levels of living characteristic of industrialized societies. Moreover, the well-being gap has widened within the United States in recent years in the sense that the rich are getting richer, while the poor are remaining poor, relatively beyond question but absolutely in the case of millions of families. Meanwhile, our economic base of natural resource potentials plus man-made apparatus and know-how has become inordinately productive. These factors include technology and science. They are not the considerations that cause poverty as much as do the factors Veblen called social institutions. The latter meant habits of thought and action, custom, or the entire philosophy of life or theory of "how things ought to be and ought to be done." Technology may be seen as a major productive factor, but for the most part it is not holding us back. Institutions or roughly what Marx called the relations of production are the source of much of our human troubles, and thus are where emphasis for change

must be made. This line of thought of course underlies what is meant
by saying Veblen was an Institutionalist or Evolutionist.

The institutionalized ideas that are involved in the theory of life and
how it ought to be are deeply bifurcated or dualistic in most instances,
notably so for the United States. We will list a few of these contrasts,
citing the socially serviceable first, the disservicable second:[1]

Evolution versus Creation;
Darwinism (modified) versus Newtonism;
Empiricism (matter-of-fact) versus Animism;
History-rooted theory versus Taxonomy;
Impersonalism (what one does) versus Personalism (who one is).

For the most part, derivative from and resting upon these considerations, we have such contrasts as:

Industrial occupations—Pecuniary occupations;
Engineer or Technician—Businessman or "Captain of Industry";
Scholar—"Captain of Erudition";
Science based on "idle curiosity"—Pragmatism as expediency.

How could the second-listed, socially disserviceable institutional
bits be dominant in a modern, technically and industrially advanced
society? One key to understanding this paradox is Veblen's master
institution, the Leisure or Privileged Class. Society does not genuinely
split into laborers versus capitalists, or poor versus rich. Much more
nearly the case is a hierarchy of wealth, income, power, and influence,
with people at all levels emulating or mimicking persons higher in the
hierarchy. To appear to have wealth and influence is, in many instances, of greater importance than the fact, even if false appearance
can hardly be continued for long. Consequently, there results an
unremitting struggle, not for survival, not labor against capital, but for
social rank and showmanship across many sociological lines. In the
idiom of today, our society has become more and more a "rat-race."
The Great Crash of the 1930s stunned our Captains of Industry and
politicians enough so that for a few years it appeared that genuine
institutional change along the ill-defined lines of New Dealism might
be accomplished. But in efforts to fulfill opportunities brought by
World War II, we turned to imperial expansion to replace the broken
power of European nations throughout the Third World. This movement has been coupled with anticommunism related to the idea that if

we did not imperialize the world that was available for grabs, the Russians certainly would. And this view has been coupled with the discovery that giant-scale governmental spending could be done interminably to insure prosperity of the rich via militarism. These considerations, along with a few lesser arguments, killed New Deal welfarism by the middle 1960s. What has resulted is a predatory and violent society, to be called civilized only through a somewhat loose usage of language.

It seems quite impossible that such social ills as homelessness, poor nutrition, poor health care, racism and sexism, unequal opportunities, grossly warped educational standards, alcoholism and other drug use, violence and other symptoms of social dissatisfaction and malaise, can be overcome without institutional change of profound nature and extent. Can revolutionary social and economic change be accomplished without bloody revolution? We economists usually assert that those are not our problems. We properly are concerned with the functioning of market forces and the economic growth that always results and with very little else. Other concerns would be "normative" or judgmental, which is declared to be unscientific.

Do institutions determine or influence societal norms, or do institutions comprise the norms? We will take some of both as an adequate position for trying to understand our society. Norms or values and institutions are closely interrelated, and definitions continue to be thoroughly imprecise. The job of the economist *as social scientist* includes critique of these norms-institutions and recommendations for change. Mere rationalization of the status quo is evasion of important issues and responsibilities. We try to state our values forthrightly, and draw conclusions as seems appropriate. Everyone else likewise is normative; may we all take care to tell it like it is!

There are three approaches to resource allocation that we wish to emphasize as moderately distinct choices. The first two are drawn from orthodox theory, while the third poses challenges that an evolutionary perspective would need to confront.

First, consider the approach employed by standard microeconomic theory at intermediate levels of analysis. Given and limited *means* confront given but limitless *ends*. Economics thereby is defined as rationing. How both means and ends historically rise and fall is outside the scope of concern. Let market forces of supply and demand interact so that "what is desired" is produced. This means production of whatever commodities persons with purchasing power want, with demand not dependent upon authentic needs, however imprecisely construed. Low incomes result in almost zero impact upon decision making. What goes to the poor has trickled down. Whatever is desired is desirable, bypassing questions of distribution of income, wealth, or power. An important and equally illogical corollary is not mentioned: What is respected is respectable. If mentioned, who would believe it? As Joan Robinson commented, we are no more aware of our own ideology than we are of our own bad breath!

Second, one may ponder the relevance of a modification of orthodox mechanism developed by David Ricardo shortly after the work by Adam Smith. Reference is to comparative advantage, which fully internationalizes the scope of market forces. Nations should specialize in the commodity production for which they are comparatively well-endowed regarding overall resource inputs, taking into account international dimensions of supply and demand. Construed in static terms, the intrinsic nature of the Classical mechanism model admonishes "hewers of wood and drawers of water" to specialize in supply of raw materials to exchange for manufactured goods, a process that may continue world without end. Progress must come via a trickle down of technology from advanced country investments into poor countries. Such a degree of internationalization of economic activity carries with it a corollary with ominous overtones for workers in high-income nations: Why should they be paid more than workers in Third World countries? With more than two billion adults as potential industrial and services workers in backward areas, and the numbers rapidly growing, universalized free trade means subsistence wages, as Smith and Ricardo saw quite clearly. The model is highly nondevelopmental except with satellite status for underdeveloped nations, and hence commonly is rejected in the Third World. Moreover, proponents of mechanistic equilibrium theory are due for a shock if and when workers from the wealthier countries organize in demands for protection from internationalization of wage rates. Thus far they passively accept the benefits coming to them as consumers.

Third, if a role for the positive state can be effectively defined—not a mere matter of asserting "socialism in lieu of capitalism"—then emphasis can be shifted to use of resources to produce what humans need, partially bypassing manipulable market forces: food, clothing, shelter, medical services, basic education, social security protections, opportunity for self-expression of potentials, etc. Basic needs are well-established as matters of scientifically demonstrable fact. The emphasis would shift from maximization of GNP to achievement of high levels of well-being or welfare, which is not the same thing. Although

Germany and Japan have serious politico-economic problems, they are examples of capitalist nations that have deep-seated, thoroughly institutionalized positive roles for the state, using large proportions of total product. We believe that the absence of Newtonian mechanism as a dominant factor in the philosophical and institutional traditions of these two nations serves to explain their ability to incorporate the state positively and effectively within a system of capitalism. Communist countries have problems deriving from the nature of the philosophy involved. Within the capitalist world, the English-speaking peoples may have the most difficult problem of facing up to the inexorable fact of cultural evolution because we are the direct heirs of Classicism. An equilibrium-centered philosophy tends to emphasize getting things right, once for all, and then "conserving" what is right. Change, being outside the framework of what is proper and decent, is alluded to but stubbornly resisted.

Since the advent of Smith's application of Newton's mechanism-in-equilibrium, economic science has deliberately been patterned after what is perceived as the foundation model of science. Classical physics, with "simple location" in Whitehead's language,[2] using Euclidian geometry and Newtonian calculus, Cartesian and other *a priorism*, still has its place, but it is no longer so much foundation of physics as parts and tools. The same is true for economics in certain respects. Orthodoxy involves useful tools, such as calculus and double-entry accounting, and until they may be transcended by new understanding of human behavior, the tools are crucially important. However, since mechanism cannot possibly cope adequately either with qualitative change or human behavior, it most decidedly is not appropriate as the foundation of economics. Mechanism is desirable as a source of tools, but not as the essence of science.

Adam Smith had achieved fame as professor of moral philosophy before he enlarged the scope of his studies to focus on concern with man's worldly goods. He developed the method of perceiving humans as analogous to atoms, so that behavior could be analyzed as a quest to gain pleasure and avoid pain. Hence questions of values or what ought to be could be dropped and attention instead focused on interpretations of what people in fact do. Individual gain was thus enthroned, and self-aggrandizement has been either tolerated or endorsed ever since. Utilitarianism and hedonism are two common labels for the philosophy involved. A common justification is that humans by nature are greedy and hence self-aggrandizement is necessary to motivate people to peak performance. Enough is *not* enough.

But do we have innate traits within the standard framework? Standard theoretical formulations rely instead on "revealed preference" of various types. It may be clear that we cannot forever finesse the questions of values and what "ought to be." For reasons of philosophical understanding and matters of habit and emotion, religious beliefs and other bases of ethics persist, and modern societies confront uncertainty concerning legitimization of some of our most pronounced displays of greed and materialist excesses. It seems apparent that we moderns must come more fully to terms with our past.

Chapter 6, "Evolution and History: Modern Germany and Russia," applies some of Veblen's ideas on the nature and importance of institutions and change to those two cases. Veblen long had been a sympathetic critic of the German Historical School of economics, which was decidedly non-Newtonian in its philosophy. He traveled in Germany, and his book *Imperial Germany and the Industrial Revolution*[3] contains some of his most insightful writing, especially on change and development. He wrote only a few articles about the newly formed Soviet Union, in which he made use of the ideas on Germany and his conceptions of institutions and change. The final section of the chapter, "USSR: Failure of Dialectical Socialism," is based in part on his wary appraisal of Marxism in his 1906 Harvard lectures, reprinted as two articles.[4] Veblen differentiated Socialism from Marxism, favoring what he vaguely called an evolving "industrial democracy" that somewhat resembled the old Guild Socialism.

Chapter 7 is "Three Thirds of the Twentieth Century," in which we observe that this century divides for analytical purpose into three time segments of almost identical length, especially with reference to the United States. The First Third was characterized by general institutionalized acceptance of laissez-faire capitalism, in which business and money making dominated outlook and activity. Hence the orientation was strongly supply-side. From the early 1930s until the late 1960s—the Second Third—New Dealism and Keynesian thought were dominant. The core concern was manipulation of demand as the adequate route to growth and prosperity. This third of a century was almost precisely definitive of the time boundaries of The Age of Keynes.

The Final Third, beginning in the late 1960s, has seen the emergence of faults and failures in our peculiar American formulation of Keynesian doctrines. In this chapter we insist that Keynes should be interpreted quite differently.[5] Events have occurred in such fashion that environmental problems, sociopolitical protests, and stagflation define or highlight our contemporary difficulties. The Reagan 1980s, especially, have witnessed a predictable attempt to return to the First Third supply-side orientation, but both "sides," supply as well as demand, failed in their respective eras, and cannot succeed long term in reincarnation. In this Final Third orthodox economists deny a demand-side label but have turned to demand expansion via debt creation at a frenzied and foolish pace. Our debt-to-income ratio is rising at an unaccustomed rate, and such rise absolutely cannot be sustained forever. The debt-ratio rise is driven by high interest rates—rates which formerly closely matched the economic growth rate but now exceed it by a factor of more than two. Simple algebra brings the debt and interest problem sharply into focus.

It is certain that we as a nation do not know what to do. Serious collapse or "twist" is predictable, with basic change implied virtually to the point of certainty. Shall we say that economics needs three "sides," not just demand and supply? A new system would have to embody revolutionary changes.

We have previewed the conceptual framework of the book. The final chapter restates the main lines of thought of the book and attempts to make the conclusions specific enough to constitute the basis of a program of revolutionary reform.

As an appendix to this introductory chapter, we present an outline or schematic statement of some basic principles of ontological systems. The entire book is an effort to demonstrate that neither Materialism nor Idealism-Spiritualism is an adequate base for economics and social science, however decisively that issue may possibly have been laid to rest in the physical sciences. As Marxism is overly Materialist in emphasis, so orthodox economic thought is overly Idealist-Spiritualist. What philosophers in this context call Realism is a much more satisfactory ontological position.

Ontological Systems, Materialism vs. Idealism

"In general, the ontological position of a school of philosophy may be appraised in terms of materialism, idealism, or realism. Materialism holds that all being is ultimately matter; idealism maintains that mind and spirit are all-important; and realism asserts that no monistic formulation explains the ultimate nature of being."

[*Columbia Encyclopedia*, p. 1443]

MATERIALISM	REALISM	IDEALISM
Darwin, Evolution	"habits of thought"	God, creation
man created God	Veblen's *Institutions*	God created man
	Data-plus-theory based history	.

The "Real World"	The Imagined World
The sense-experience world	The make-believe or theoretical
The Material World	world, the world as a logical
The world of physics, chemistry, geology, etc.	construct
"Efficient cause"	"Sufficient reason"
Push of the past	Pull of the future
Behaviorism	Rationalism
Determinism (very complex)	Free-will (at individual level)
History as uninterpreted folklore	Deductive logic as model-making
Examples: Marx, Skinner, Darwin (each somewhat different)	Examples: all orthodox economic theory is primarily rationalist and based on "economic man" assumptions

Notes

1. Stanley M. Daugert, *The Philosophy of Thorstein Veblen* (New York: King's Crown Press, 1950), 50.

2. Alfred N. Whitehead, *Science and the Modern World* (New York: Macmillan, 1925).

3. Thorstein Veblen, *Imperial Germany and the Industrial Revolution* (New York: Viking Press, 1954).

4. Thorstein Veblen, *The Place of Science in Modern Civilization* (New York: Russell and Russell, 1961).

5. Victoria Chick, *Macroeconomics After Keynes* (Cambridge, Mass.: MIT Press, 1983).

2

The Rise of Capitalism and Classical Theory

Economists regard Adam Smith as "the first economist," but such a view is quite misleading. There is no more such a thing as the first economist than there is a first physicist or a first physician. Smith made a giant step forward with application of post-Copernican philosophy to social affairs. The central figure in late seventeenth century world vision was Isaac Newton, however, and the intriguing fact is that the system of science and philosophy he devised, Classical mechanism, was applied to "the world politic," as Newton called it, long before Smith was born in 1723. Newton participated actively in this application as we will detail later.

Smith's *Wealth of Nations* is indeed a masterpiece that required a decade to write. Before its publication in 1776, Great Britain, Smith's home territory, was already the world leader in both commerce and industry. Thus Smith's ideas did not underlie the "Greatness" of Great Britain. The British had defeated the Spanish Armada in 1588, broken the power of the Dutch during the 1600s, and defeated the French—temporarily of course—by 1756. For a leading power, a doctrine of laissez-faire, no trade barriers, or "each man for himself, cried the fox in the henhouse," was appropriate, since the British could outdo just about everybody else. Free trade capitalism came into place slowly, over many protests and many dead bodies, and with it British power grew.

Mercantilism, state-run privileges, monopolies, rules and red tape, plus state managed construction of infrastructure, establishment of laws and protections, and standardization of measurements had been

15

the economic system under which the British had thrust themselves ahead. To a great extent they did not have to "save" gold or any other form of capital—they contrived possession of much of what the Spanish had looted out of the Americas. Smith's book can be interpreted as a demonstration, via mountains of detailed bits of historical information, that mercantilism had once played a necessary role, but was by his time obsolete and a hindrance to progress.

The more common interpretation of Smith, however, is that he was the sage who brought the light into a world of confusion and muddled thinking. This is a comfortable and safe view, since it implies that progress is in some sense linear, that Smith was helping mankind to "zero-in" on scientific truth, and that laissez-faire truth is valid forever.

To admit the relativity of economic doctrine, that mercantilism had been appropriate during a specific period, is a dangerous line of thought. Feudalism may be seen as having preceded mercantilism and free market capitalism as, in turn, replacing mercantilism. Thus, might some other system inexorably replace market capitalism? Marx, of course, so argued not much later, but in the Western world he remains an underground figure of ill repute. Smith cautioned against conspiratorial monopolies of businessmen who scheme and plot against the public. Competition, properly kept in place, would block the efforts at monopolization. The other threat to progress was government interferences, the mercantile system we have already identified as obsolete and corrupt.

A long list of physiocratic and mercantilist theorists preceded Smith. A member of the former group, François Quesnay, had even worked out a *Tableau Economique* that was shockingly similar to the later Input-Output table of Wassily Leontief, which work won for him the Nobel Prize for economics in 1973. Quesnay had shown the *Tableau* to Smith, who thought it of little merit and did not use its concepts. Hence it is strange not to acknowledge at least that Quesnay was an economist, and obviously prior to Smith, but ideology intervenes, and in the capitalist view, the first economist must have been the person who brought us the light of capitalism. Labeling Smith as "the first economist" defines economics as the study of the market system. Smith was in fact the first person to demonstrate clearly and convincingly that market forces of supply and demand could give expression to the quest for individual self-seeking and bring order out of social chaos. He was the first person effectively to make those arguments, which leads into a neat tautology. So long as we regard this paradigm as "The Truth," Smith remains the first economist. Scientific objectivity has little chance against ideological necessity.

Religion Alongside the Rise of Capitalism

The career that made Smith famous was that of professor of moral philosophy at the University of Glasgow. His 1759 book, *Theory of Moral Sentiments*, became a classic, and his fame was merited thereby.[1] It was this scholarship and the issue of morality that brought him into economics, that is, man's handling of matters of material goods. The language itself, "goods" instead of "bads," points to the question of ethics. Accordingly, *The Wealth of Nations* may be constructively viewed as Volume II of "Smith on Ethics."

What were the characteristics of feudalism and mercantilism that provided the background for Smith's treatises on ethics in 1759 as well as 1776? The accepted idea of feudalism is that of a rigid social class system that was almost a caste structure that sought continuity of customs and tradition rather than change. The two major economic classes were manor lords and serfs, with royalty, clergy, merchants, warlords, and military functionaries as auxiliary classes that were usually politically dominant and in league with wealth-holders. There was at all times in some places in Europe a class of traders and financiers, and trade is one of the crucial factors that forced change and eventually brought the downfall of feudalism.

The Emergence of Protestantism

For a millennium or more, Roman Catholicism had been the focal point of social and cultural life and the framework of morality, but from the sixteenth century on, Protestantism made inroads. Protestant individualism and the quest for grounds on which to oppose the Catholic church had developed into a "Protestant ethic" that was at least congruent with "the spirit of capitalism." We must resist the urge to delve at length into the arguments of Tawney's *Religion and the Rise of Capitalism* or Weber's *The Protestant Ethic and the Spirit of Capitalism*.[2] Yet the repeal of the law of usury, the abolition of purgatory, as Bertrand Russell appraised it,[3] and direct communion with God by individual prayer, were novel features of Protestantism. These facts were of enormous importance in the rise of industry, science, capitalism, and commerce prior to Smith. Martin Luther lived from 1483 to 1546, and John Calvin from 1509 to 1564. Calvin thus died in the year of birth of Shakespeare and Galileo, a significant year in another context to be introduced shortly.

The Protestantism-and-capitalism thesis became a major issue in theology, sociology, and general history, but we need not take sides, because the validity of the thesis depends heavily upon how one specifies it. Weber and Tawney both were careful to point out that they were considering only certain manifestations of capitalism, not all forms in which it had ever existed. They saw the capitalists of their models as driven by, or acting as if driven by, a "calling" of religious dimensions, to accumulate and become ever wealthier. A quest for the pleasures of high consumption was no part of their behavior patterns. Wealth, power, and demonstration that they could, in fact, become wealthy, whereas lesser folk could not make it, provided justification or reward. In a Calvinist interpretation, one's eternal fate or destiny was predestined, and demonstration of ability to gain great wealth and power was the means of knowing whether or not one was well regarded in the eyes of God, and hence whether one's name was written in "the Lamb's book of life." (The dozen articles, including the introduction, comprising Robert W. Green, *Protestantism and Capitalism: The Weber Thesis and Its Critics*, have served as a major source of ideas.)[4]

The greater degree of individualism embodied in Protestant doctrines and theology, and the correspondingly less restrictive conception of what comprises religious heresy, accorded well with the relaxation of the long-standing prohibition against the taking of interest at whatever rates. Powers of science, experimentation, and technological change were crucial ingredients of progress, we may aver, and these powers had grown from the relative freedom of thought, speech, writing, research, personal movement among locales and trades in Britain in contrast with the inquisitorial powers of the Catholic church on the continent. Magna Carta, 1215, and the founding of Oxford University Press, 1478, are both substantive and symbolic examples of the factors underlying the development of know-how, production, and commerce in Britain. Spain, on the contrary, established its Inquisition in that same year, 1478. However, it appears that Christian religious forms were more a passive or permissive factor in the cultural and economic development of Britain and of capitalism, than an active *sine qua non*.

The Protestant "Glorious Revolution" and "Newtonians"

Britain was involved in scientific revolution throughout the seventeenth century of such scope and profundity that the philosopher

Alfred North Whitehead, among others, refers to this as "the century of genius."[5] What is perhaps equally true is that it was the scene of political, social, and religious upheavals of matching importance.

Our primary concern is with the "Glorious Revolution" of 1688–89 and its aftermath. James II, a Stuart, reigned over England after 1685 but was dethroned and forced to flee to France in 1688. William III and his consort Mary II, Protestant daughter of Catholic James II, were invited from Holland and succeeded him on the throne. The Declaration of Rights, 1688, and the Bill of Rights, 1689, redefined the subject-monarch relationship, and barred future Catholic succession to the throne. The triumph of parliament over "divine right" of kings has endured to the present.

Within the Anglican church there was a group that included Robert Boyle, famous for his "Law of Gasses" and other scientific work, and Isaac Newton in certain degree, although he was Arian rather than Anglican. Newton's religious views changed during his lifetime, and reflected his views on the interrelations among God, the world natural, and the world politic. His biographer Westfall noted that he was an Arian, a religious cult that dated from the fourth century, but was during Newton's time so small in numbers that

> No one considered Arians a threat to the state. They were a threat rather to the moral foundations of society. Newton was well aware that the vast majority of his compatriots detested the views he held—more than detested, looked upon them with revulsion as an excretion that fouled the air breathed by decent persons. . . . Newton did not worship in an Arian church. None such existed. As long as he was willing occasionally to take the sacrament of the Church of England, the law required of him nothing at which he need balk. Only on his deathbed did he venture finally to refuse the sacrament. Nevertheless, Newton had moved a considerable distance since 1674. In that year, he had prepared to vacate his fellowship rather than accept the mark of the beast in ordination.[6]

Further, it is interesting to note that Newton served in the Glorious Revolution Parliament that dealt with William and Mary and established the principle of parliamentary preeminence over the throne. "There is no way to pretend that Newton played a leading role in its deliberations. According to a story that rests solely on anecdotal authority, he spoke only once; feeling a draft, he asked an usher to close a window" (Westfall 1980, 483). These giant figures of the world of science were deeply religious and found interpretations of their

scientific discoveries that did not present insuperable contradictions of
science and religion. Boyle was active in bringing the major findings of
Newton's incredible work, *Mathematical Principles of Natural Philosophy*, 1687, into the comprehensibility of church and lay leaders.[7]
Newton's message was clear and simple:

> I received also much light in this search [of the Scriptures] by the
> analogy between the *world natural* and the *world politic*. For the mystical
> language was founded in this analogy and will be best understood by
> considering its original.
> The whole *world natural* consisting of heaven and earth signifies the
> whole *world politic* consisting of thrones and people, or so much of it as
> is considered in the prophecy; and the things in that world signify the
> analogous things in this. For the Heavens with the things therein signify
> thrones and dignities and those that enjoy them, and the earth with all
> things therein the inferior people, and the lowest parts of the earth, called
> Hades or Hell, the lowest and most miserable part of the people. . . .
> Great earthquakes and the shaking of heaven and earth [stand] for the
> shaking of kingdoms so as to overthrow them. The creating a heaven and
> earth and their passing away, or which is all one, the beginning and end
> of the world—for the rise and ruin of the *body politic* signified thereby. [8]

Hence, to Newton the *world politic* closely paralleled the *world
natural*. They were created; they get their driving force from God,
who intervenes on rare occasion only, for example earthquakes; they
involve a careful, God-ordained balance of forces or equilibrium; there
is a hierarchy of God-established rank or ordering, everything in its
place and time; and, having been created, both worlds are timeless and
eternal.

The "new science," as it was called, involved the rejection of the
ancient Aristotelianism that still dominated thought in many universities and learned circles, and Cartesian and Hobbesian mechanical
philosophies as well. Why did these liberal churchmen choose this
science over the older teachings? They had little apparent interest in
explanatory or predictive power of science as we construe those terms
today. But these churchmen, called the Newtonians or the Latitudinar-
ians, held vested interests in the parliamentary government and Anglican religion of the era following the Glorious Revolution proper. They
had social position and wealth that they wished to protect. They
strongly detested popery and absolutism. They were able to see that
to preserve their religion they needed to find accommodation to the
ideas and insights of the new science. They were both ideological and,

at the same time, pragmatic in their actions. The ideas of Boyle, and especially those of Newton, were exceedingly useful to them because the philosophical views were highly compatible. If a God-ordered society that was intrinsically "natural" was what they were *for*, Hobbesian atheism was one of the things, along with popery, instability, and disorder, that they were *against*. Newton's science of the *world natural* was materialist in pronounced degree, but he was pious and held to the concept of a motive force emanating only from God. The materialism of Hobbes was far more radical and dangerous to their interests because it envisioned man as just another creature of nature, drawing motive force from nature, not God. As a man, Hobbes professed a religion, but his philosophy was strongly atheistic and hence had to be opposed.

Jacob summarized the issues:

> This social explanation for the triumph of Newtonianism in the late seventeenth century stresses what previous commentators have ignored— its usefulness to the intellectual leaders of the Anglican church as an underpinning for their vision of what they liked to call the "world politick." . . . Stability was possible without constant divine intervention; the spiritual order could be maintained; the church was necessary and essential; yet at the same time men could pursue their worldly interests. That, briefly stated, was what the world natural, explicated in the *Principia*, meant to churchmen who were primarily interested in promoting their vision of the "world politick." [9]

Moreover, "Darwin's science was lethal to religion only because in the second half of the seventeenth century a particular explanation of the natural order had gained acceptance as an indispensable support for liberal English Protestantism."[10]

Before moving on, we will interject the thought that since what is called Classical or neo-Classical economics was part and parcel of this seventeenth century intellectual movement of the Newtonians, the proper label would be "Newtonian economics." It is supremely ironical that the foundations of economics escaped destruction by the Darwinian "earthquake," whereas religion did not. The escape, in large part, is attributable to the fact that economists always have been unaware of the true nature and extent of the anchorage of economics in Newtonian cosmology, and instead have stubbornly insisted that Adam Smith is its founder. Smith thought and wrote in terms of a "natural order," but since he was neither physicist nor biologist nor theologian, it has been possible to evade the thorough-going association of *world natural* with *world politic*.

There is a vast literature of studies on seventeenth century England, and a sizeable body of materials, both documents and commentary, on the "Newtonians." The central world view was of a created, nonevolutionary, well-ordered, hierarchical society of individuals who seek expression of their desires and self-interests through the wealth form of private property, while simultaneously observing the moderation and respect for certain rights of others that God-fearing Protestantism had long emphasized. Balance or equilibrium of forces was requisite to keep this *world politic* from flying apart. Except for such details of refinement as decision making at the margin, Newtonian theory and practice captured the spirit and employed the vision that have held throughout modern neo-Classical economics. This was three quarters of a century before the written elaboration of precisely these same ideas in *The Wealth of Nations*. Smith's contribution was not nearly so much that of originality of ideas as that of serving as "the great communicator." He cited Newton only once, that being in connection with a statement from Newton's 1717 *Representation to the Lords of the Treasury*, that "in China and Japan the ratio [of the value of gold to that of silver] is 9 or 10 to 1 and in India 12 to 1, and this carries away the silver from all Europe." [11] It is not common knowledge within the economics profession that Newton wrote anything concerning social affairs or participated in the movement that Jacob described.

Adam Smith's earlier treatise on morals was true to its title, that is, it was specifically concerned with the quest for a suitable basis for ethics. Smith was far too clever to be totally misled by religious narrowness, and thereby forced to choose among competing religious doctrines extant in the world. The book was far more agnostic in tone than religious, or it may be seen as more a scholarly venture in the sense of academic freedom of inquiry and expression than reflecting the confined scope of perspective one would find in the literary products of the various priesthoods of the day. By the time of his second major book, Smith had altered his Newtonian approach to ethics, to such character that the self-regulating society solves its ethical problems without even admitting or seeing that such a thing is occurring. Society is "led by an invisible hand" of the Natural Order of both *world natural* and *world politic* to promote ends that were no part of anybody's intent.

Newton's Doctrine of Mechanism and Smith's Merger of Ethics with the New Science

Smith's problem of ethics, centering on the question of what constitutes moral behavior, found an intriguing answer in the proposition that the scientific way to get at the question of what humans "ought" to do was to drop the word "ought" entirely and observe what they in fact do. The Newtonian–Cartesian cosmology and epistemology thereby came into play with an authority and precision rarely seen before or since. One did not suggest how atoms or planets ought to behave; one observed them. If God hurled them into boxlike space, then motion and mass interact through the mysterious ether to result in universal gravitation, and the Laws of Motion were precise and final, created by the wish of God and of course could only be ended in the same manner. This was entirely a creational view of cosmology or reality: all phenomena were at essence locomotion of particles in motion in fixed space and could hardly be construed as anything else. There was thus no such thing as change other than locomotion-location, which hardly merits the label. The principles of maximization-minimization were intrinsic in such a view, so inherent they would be impossible to doubt or challenge. Mass and motion simply did whatever it was they did, and the Laws as a mathematical description of what is going on could be formulated in procedures approaching what was meant by saying they were "waiting to be discovered."

In an article written for the occasion of his receipt of the Nobel Prize for economics in 1970, Paul Samuelson repeated some of the best-known cases of maximization in Classical physics. For example, "let us consider how light is reflected when it hits a mirror. You may observe and memorize the rule that the angle of reflection is equal to the angle of incidence. A neater way of understanding this fact is by the least-time principle of Fermat, which was already known to Hero and other Greek scientists."[12] The details involved we need not present, but properly expanded they have relevance to economics: "If an increase in the price of fertilizer alone always increases the amount the firm buys of caviar, from that fact alone I can predict . . . [that] . . . an increase in the price of caviar alone will increase the amount the firm buys of fertilizer" (1972, 253). This idea has great importance and is stated in a charming form of stark analytical clarity. Also of importance is the issue raised in the finale of the paper. "I have tried to understand what it is that Adam Smith's 'invisible hand' is supposed to be maximizing."[13] Samuelson then endorsed the idea known as Pareto optimality with an apparent concern for what may be called democratic operational procedure: "it seemed to me that precisely in a society grown affluent . . . there arises an especial importance to the notion of giving people what *they* want."[14] This is a clear example of assuming that what is desired is thereby desirable, but that involves a logical fallacy, as we detail elsewhere, and what is to be maximized remains an open question. We do not solve our problems of morality by ceasing to ask how things ought to be.

The *First* Law of Thermodynamics accords well with such a view of Samuelson and the Classicists and pronounces that mass-energy are conserved, not lost or created. Such a view has led many a person, including the eminent Buckminster Fuller, to utter what are seen as bits of foolishness when the *Second* Law of Thermodynamics is also taken into account: all motion involves unidirectional net diffusion of mass-energy, which is a net increase in entropy. What the First Law seems to promise (that resources are infinite) the Second Law takes away. Fuller wrote, "Science's Law of Conservation of Energy states that 'energy cannot be created or destroyed.' The first constituent of wealth—energy—is therefore irreducible. . . . Energy cannot decrease. Knowledge can only increase. It is therefore scientifically clear that wealth which combines energy and intellect can only increase, and that wealth can only increase with use and that wealth increases as fast as it is used."[15] As someone long ago said, a little learning is a dangerous thing. Classical physics when overdosed or misapplied is disastrous, and in fact we all make our mistakes. Thus humility is called for.

Classical physics, based upon nomological—law-based—conceptions, is better perceived as a collection of pronouncements than as hypotheses when thrust into a realm of social affairs such as economics. Here charity of statement and objectivity run in harness: while carefully formulated laws of classical physics are true and correct, their truth inheres in their tautological nature. God is outside, above, Newton's universe; within the bounded space are only mass and motion, and these were not perceived as manifestations of one and the same thing until Einstein.

How did Newton, who made "the greatest discovery that ever was made by man," Smith wrote in eulogy, in fact lay the basis for solving Smith's problem of ethics or morality? Smith described Newton's method as that of laying down "certain principles, primary or proved, in the beginning, from whence we account for the several phenomena, connecting all together by the same chain."[16] Gravity, he observed, constituted the "chain." In view of the crucial role of sympathy for other persons in *Theory of Moral Sentiments* and that of self-regard in *Wealth of Nations*, it is clear that Smith made deliberate attempts to apply the Newtonian method. Although it was Jeremy Bentham who formalized this corollary, behaviorism imbued with hedonism became the psychology appropriate to Smith's Newton-influenced morality. Each person acts so as to maximize pleasures and minimize pains, to be treated as a net resultant, the maximization of pleasure. This truism cannot be falsified. Whatever one does maximizes pleasures, or else one would not do it. This is the tautology of tautologies, but it is regularly passed off as science. We cannot and need not know just how the mind functions to accomplish the outcome—thus the advent of behaviorist, revealed preference psychology.

The appropriate view of "social" behavior in this philosophy is to deny its scientific validity. Do the planets socialize? Of course not, but do humans socialize? Here Smith was forced to set aside his entire philosophy with one of the greatest finesses in human history: *obviously*, we must have social interaction (as government) to enforce contracts and protect property of individuals. The nose of the camel was thus slipped under the tent. Moreover, we will require national defense, roads, and harbors, and so on, to the total *dénouement* accomplished by the United States constitution—of Smith's time and philosophy—"to promote the general welfare." Until the present, the finesse is treated as merely an obvious corollary. We humans see things as we choose; mind and senses are connected in a mysterious way! Here the senses are merely bypassed. *Homo sapiens* has to give himself up to his mental creation *homo economicus* to accept the Smithian finesse.

The group-government finesse or effective denial of a major role for what we may call the positive state is not the only disaster of Smith's philosophy however. A greater claim must be reserved for the utter denial of genuine change derived from Newton's view and transferred to the Smithian cosmology. Smith observed that capital formation, and along with it enlargement of know-how and skills of labor, have silently accumulated through time. But if so, it is in spite of his philosophy, not because of it. To him, technology mainly was a given. It was not explained, nor could it be, except by the ruse that men come up with new contrivances because of their quest for greater individual benefits. Humans as rationalistic "felicific calculus" individuals, as Bentham furnished the language, have neither antecedent nor consequent, neither history nor future, that bear on behavior. Scientific research and planning, in their twentieth century meaning, which involves immense concern for group phenomena rather than pure individualism, are totally beyond the pale of Smithian-Newtonian philosophy.

Also, explicitly, are externalities. How does one envision the influence of one planet upon the "environment" of another planet? Universal gravitation via that mysterious postulation, the ether, is all there is or needs be. Concepts of planetary externalities apply only in the world of science fiction where one might contemplate or assign meaning to such an expression as "drop dead, Venus, I prefer the shifted orbits that would result." To acknowledge that one human may demand of another, "stop that silly construction you have begun, because it would impede my view," is to acknowledge that Newtonian philosophy is not suitable for application to social affairs.

Two Post-Religion Rationalizations of Capitalism: Newtonian Mechanism as Science and Darwinian "Survival of the Fittest" Evolution as Science

The philosophy of economic man, Georgescu-Roegen noted:

strips man's behavior of every cultural propensity, which is tantamount to saying that in his economic life man acts mechanically. . . . The whole truth is that economics, in the way this discipline is now generally professed, is mechanistic in the same strong sense in which we generally believe only Classical mechanics to be.

Orthodox economics is a subset of mechanics, and:

In this sense Classical mechanics is mechanistic because it can neither account for the existence of enduring qualitative changes in nature nor accept this existence as an independent fact. Mechanics knows only locomotion, and locomotion is both reversible and qualityless. The same drawback was built into modern economics by its founders, who, on the testimony of Jevons and Walras, had no greater aspiration than to create an economic science after the exact pattern of mechanics.[17]

The Smith–Newton–Descartes views, however antithetical, are of creation, not evolution. Only in the latter case is there change, but the issue is not that of one philosophy being correct and the other incorrect. One can assert that there is no greater figure in the history of science than Isaac Newton, and then say the exact same thing about Albert Einstein, while maintaining total credibility in noting that both Einstein's science and philosophy are thoroughly revolutionary in their impact upon Newton's views, although we note that both men were firmly committed to democracy.

In the Newtonian world there was only repetition, not change—world without beginning or end except by the hand of God. This was the true, unchanging world of mechanics, and there was little to astonish us on realizing that Newton required a full twenty years to publish his *opus magnum* after having formulated his central perception of how to synthesize the works of Copernicus, Tycho Brae, Galileo, and Kepler. However, he had to apply his great invention, calculus, to properly substantiate his findings. That was a fair piece of work, spread over many years! Actual work on the book itself required only two years. Calculus and its forerunner, analytical geometry, thrust ahead by Descartes, admirably served the needs of mechanics. Political or social philosophy and ideology need not intrude because there is only creation followed by repetition, not evolution and change. "The logic is perfect: man is not an economic agent simply because there is no economic process. There is only a jigsaw puzzle of fitting given means to given ends, which requires a computer not an agent."[18]

Within the purview of Classical, Newton–or–Descartes mechanics, there could be little authentic argument or quarrel with the assertions or conclusions because everything was immanent in the postulates and world-view. Descartes, Newton, Smith, LaPlace, LaGrange, and on through Walras, Jevons, Marshall, and Pareto—the founders—are not "wrong." However, they are largely irrelevant to the study of economics perceived as something that "real" humans do.

"The Mecca of the economist," Marshall admitted in his prefatory remarks (but did not develop as *his* Mecca), "lies in economic biology rather than in economic dynamics."[19] What had happened in the world of science, we may ask, that made it apparent to Marshall by 1890 that economics properly conceived was a branch of biology? Two considerations seem overwhelming, although he made no such acknowledgment. In 1859 Charles Darwin's *Origin of Species* was published. A few years later the Entropy Law, the Second Law of Thermodynamics, was formulated on a basis of physical facts, not mechanistic mathematical operations or statistical probabilities, by the German physicist Rudolf Clausius. Separately as developed, or jointly as we now are able to see, these principles or perceptions thrust change, in the sense of irreversible alteration of conditions, circumstances, agents, or envi-

ronment, into the equations of whatever is called reality. The fact of
change, meaning qualitative differentiation of present from past, not
merely location, was recognized as inexorable. The rate, nature,
extent, and location of change are subject to modification or influence
from human action. Human behavior becomes a process, complete
with propensities, motivations, frustrations, neuroses, and other mad-
dening complexities. It is not merely a feat of equilibration. Descartes
suffered his period of psychological crisis and came forth with the view
that scientific thought immersed totally in the seas of mathematics and
logic was our only means of certainty or avoidance of being proved
wrong. Newton invented calculus, as did Leibnitz (with different
notation), and he synthesized and improved the Laws of Motion. His
system of thought became the "gospel" until Einstein came along.
Adam Smith demonstrated that "leave it alone" individualism applies
those principles to the question of moral behavior. Classical mechanics
in social science is the result, and it is never wrong in terms of its own
logic. But its relevance becomes nil in relation to an evolving universe,
evolving life forms, evolving cultural propensities, values, and know-
how, and the inexorable fact of entropy. In sticking firmly to the
cosmology, world-view, and methodology of Classical mechanics,
economists have made model mongers of themselves.

Cause-effect are seen as a totally determinative, reversible sequence,
with equilibrium central to the view, a framework long recognized as
comparative statics. There simply is no change other than locomotion,
which is change of mass and/or motion. Hence there is no dialectics or
"overlapping," that is, there is no qualitative change. All science has,
properly elucidated, a nomological basis. All theory properly developed will be axiomatized. These laws are to be discovered, not merely
imputed, and are to be quantified, using algebra, geometry, calculus,
and other forms of mathematics. Hence future events are not to be
predicted so much as calculated. An entire paradigm for economics,
indeed for all social science, is envisioned. "Atom" Smith made the
application, copying the idea that individual desires would soar to the
forefront of free behavior. The argument then requires validity of the
principle that "whatever is desired is desirable." John Stuart Mill
actually accepted this strained bit of logic in his book entitled *Utilitarianism.*[20] In 1945 Bertrand Russell, who, in spite of serious errors, was
one of the eminent logicians of the twentieth century, pointed out the
logical impossibility of concluding that something is desirable just
because it is desired.[21] The free market brings economic advice, and

apparent difficulties definitionally, by assumption, and by postulation, must result from interferences with market forces.

Our argument is that standard economics of the Western world indeed employs the Classical paradigm, and this application is obtusely outdated and hence thoroughly unscientific, with results that are nothing short of disastrous when taken as social policy, especially long term. Accordingly, an alternative must be in part contrary to "what is," must be speculative, and must rest on value judgments of what "ought to be" as in some sense the way forward. Social sciences intrinsically are quests for advice and direction, and this involves a definition or perception of science that is nonmechanistic. It was the adoption of a hybrid mechanics from Newton and Descartes that we see as the basis of the social science disaster.

Let us therefore speculate a bit as to possible alternate courses of events, beliefs, theories, and paradigms had the scientific discoveries that we think render Newton's an invalid model for economics come early enough. It is tragic that Darwin's ideas and those of Clausius were not on the scene prior to the laying of the foundations of mechanics by Newton and others. Darwin is regarded as the father of the principles of biological and other evolution, and Rudolf Clausius was the formulator of entropy as a physical fact. His perception of entropy was that of an undeniable fact of qualitative change in nature, the Second Law of Thermodynamics.

Let us illustrate with a game of make-believe. William Shakespeare and Galileo Galilei both were born in 1564. We will then speculate concerning the possible course of events had Darwin and Clausius also been born that year, and achieved their basic work by the end of that century. Galileo died in 1642, the year that Newton was born, so the timing involved in our speculations is easy to keep in mind. Let us state overtly our speculative assumption that the groundwork for the ideas of Clausius and Darwin was in place by that time, and that by the time of Newton's major publication, 1687, the Clausius–Darwin ideas were thoroughly established and accepted as solid science. Thus, our scenario is to pretend for a moment that the ideas of evolution were invented earlier than the ideas of universal gravitation and all the Newtonian "laws," or, more precisely, their formulation by Newton.

Darwin's ideas hit religious dogma hard. Evolution involves a perception that the universe began with a "Big Bang," or other event-as-process, and has been changing ever since by laws, mutations, and novelties via combinations beyond the necessity for postulation of a God of any ordinary sort. Because the planet and life forms evolve, so do the societies and cultures of *homo sapiens*. Anthropology, especially cultural anthropology, grows out of Darwinism. Later we will discuss the dangers and limitations of the use of Darwin's ideas in application to cultural evolution. A conception of evolution at our projected early date would have undercut religion far more than subverting capitalism. Human control over human affairs, subject to evolutionary laws and facts of nature, would have weakened the power of the clergy and have provided a scientific instead of theological, a natural instead of a supernatural, rationale for capitalism.

Both the Newtonian world-view or system of thought and that of Darwin are scientific. Perhaps this is paradoxical, for the implications of the one differ sharply from those of the other. However, we cannot simply assert that the one system is science but the other is not. Science is indeed "a many splendored thing." The appropriateness or relativity to a given context is the issue and the distinguishing criterion. The Newtonian view is of a *created* nature; the Darwinian view is of an *evolved* nature. Darwin-based cultural anthropology sees man as having created God, rather than God having created man, and thus the gods vary greatly in their perceived forms and powers. "Survival of the fittest" was an essential foundation of Darwin's work, and it is certain that this doctrine would be available, past and present, to rationalize the *status quo* of capitalist societies.

There is a trap hidden in all this. Evolution via capitalists, a class that is open to whomever can make it, involves change as its very essence, and change of the most unmistakably qualitative type. Evolution has never been perceived as merely a more-of-the-same, quantitative change, growth phenomenon. The stronger the degree of acceptance of evolution, mixed with pragmatism and theology, at the time Smith dropped the bombshell of application of Newtonian mechanics into human behavior, the less the Newtonian impact would have been. Mechanics might never have become dogma. Pragmatism, dead-hand custom, theology, evolution, and mechanics would have been set to simmer in one pot, even if early arrivals had pride of place. Prior to Isaac Newton, capitalism had no firm claim to scientific validity as a natural phenomenon, that is, implied by nature, a part of the workings of nature. That such a claim at any time is spurious is not the entire point. High prices in circumstances of scarcity and low prices in conditions of abundance had been a common occurrence for centuries, even though religious and other protests against price gouging had been legendary. The entropy law in place by 1600 would seemingly have had little direct bearing on the question of legitimacy of capitalism. It could instead have provided firm support to the claim to validity and scientific standing for the concepts of evolution. Darwinism has always been construed as fundamental in the biosphere, whereas Clausius's Entropy Law is primarily of the realm of physics.

With the forms of mathematics thus far invented, enunciation of a "foundations of economic analysis," as begun by Walras, et al., furthered by Samuelson, and epitomized by Debreu, necessarily involves question-begging as to the suitability of mathematics as its foundation. "If humans behaved like this, they would behave like this." Even if taken as "survival of the fittest" dogma, the concepts of evolution would have been a much weaker form of dogma for economics than has been the mechanism dogma based on illicit application of Newtonian principles into the realms of biology.

Had the doctrines of evolution and entropy been firmly in place, and with more than a century of standing, would Adam Smith still have made his Newtonian application? We assume so for the possibility was still there, but the claim of scientific legitimacy would have been different. Economics as a science would have been in trouble had its scientific servants tried to opt for either mechanism or evolution, with no attention to the other domain. Ignoring evolution ignores or question-begs man as a biological form, to be characterized as having behavior. Furthermore, to leap to the mechanism horn of the dilemma would leave open the charge: Does not economics require to be axiomatized to make good a claim to scientific standing? We suggest that both bases of scientific foundation of necessity would have been adopted, somewhat in parallel to the physics of today with its admission that light for some purposes has to be treated as waves, and for other purposes has to be perceived as quanta. It is important to remember that no one has yet accomplished Einstein's goal of establishing a Unified Field Theory in physics, and certainly not elsewhere.

In the vision of Newton-Smith, malfunctions such as poverty, unemployment, inflation, and the like still occur, but must be caused by interferences with God's natural and obvious system of liberties. Labor unions, governmental taxes and regulations, foreigners, Communists, and Liberals must be the roots of the interferences. Apparently one is free to choose the *bête noir*. Overall, use of the Newtonian model to solve the ethical problems fails badly. We cannot get past the question of what ought to be by simply ceasing to ask the question, and instead observing what is human conduct. What is desired is merely desired, but is not thereby desirable. The latter is the central issue, and it persists.

Use of the Newtonian model throws an aura of scientific objectivity over the entire issue, and leads unmistakably to the conclusion that if self-interest and private property are left alone, whatever may result can be called the natural outcome, the best possible world, a scientific result not wisely tampered with. That the phenomenon called government must exist in order to protect individual interests, but must do little more, can only be seen as a great finesse. Since there is not, nor could there be, anything analogous to authentic government in the Newtonian particles-only model, nor is there anything that even approaches mind, freedom of action, or profound decision making, nor is there change as contrasted to locomotion, it is painfully obvious that Newtonian classical mechanics is an inappropriate analog for economics or any other social science. Its continued use as the foundation of our economic ideology can only be for the rationalization of the *status quo ante*. Insistence that social science can only rationalize what *is*, obviously the status quo, without making value judgments, which strip away the claim to scientific validity, is a preposterous exercise that our ideology has permitted us to accept. Rationalizing the status quo by refusing sharply critical comment or refutation of the way things *are* quite clearly involves a value judgment acceptance of *what is*. In economics it remains a matter of no little appeal and importance that use of mathematical technique, without facts from measurement, for analysis of utility underlying demand and disutility underlying supply, means that the model is never wrong in its own internal logic. What a magnificent façade to present to ourselves and to the public! Mathematical use of pseudo-data that has always supported "The Truth" enables us to take seriously the comical view that in economics we are "zeroing in on the truth."

All resource factors of nature obviously may be perceived as free of cost to the humans who use them, except for the cost or bother of the human effort involved in securing, shaping, transporting, and otherwise handling materials, even if the entropy law may imply the *desirability* of caution in resource use. However, parsimony of use of our common earthly dowry of natural resources thus far is not what is *desired* by a great many people. Greedy desires stemming from short, human lifetime planning horizons are what enter into the market system of consumer sovereignty signals of supply and demand. It is thus far impossible objectively and scientifically to measure either the pleasure benefits or the pain costs. Even aside from evolutionary change, this immeasurability means that we cannot validly derive an analog from Newtonian mechanics because his system has measurability and data.[22] Since what is desired is subject to influence from habit, emotion, sales promotion, and the like, to follow market signals dogmatically is a social procedure of no greater scientific validity than the old adage to "follow your nose."

What we are acknowledging is only that economists as logicians have done a fine job of specifying the requisite conditions. But where does one find such practice? In the long run we are all dead, but in the short run we live in "the real world," not the world of *homo economicus*.

Is the "Neo-Classical Economics" Label Appropriate?

We noted in the Preface that all economists are aware to some degree of the Newtonian Classical mechanism origins of what is called modern economics. In the orthodox view, however, during the 1870s there occurred what is called the Marginalist Revolution, which broke sharply with the extant Classicism and brought into being what, reassuringly, is regarded as a new departure and a new paradigm. While it is obvious that pronounced change occurred, it is much the better interpretation that what resulted merely constituted further development of Newtonian Classicism. The Classicists proper had developed, and then become enslaved by, several varieties of the antiquated Labor Theory of Value. It was a highly supply-side, cost of production affair, having only a minor active role for demand. Since costs were viewed as an objective phenomenon, it was assumed that all good theory would rest on facts that had to be made ready to hand so writers could check and criticize each other's work. Ricardo and Malthus, as is well-known, maintained a relationship of sharp critique and disagreement for many years. Malthus argued that landlords were fully worthy of their hire, or income, because they performed a thoroughly useful function, that of high levels of consumption. Ricardo, to the contrary, and Smith along with him on this, regarded landlords as a pesky class of parasites, whose high incomes were unearned. Their monopolistic seizure of rental income permitted food prices to remain high, which forced industrial capitalists, the real wheels of progress, to pay increased wage rates. This in turn restricted profits and limited the prospects for progress. Moreover, Karl Marx before the 1870s had made a rather "unsportsmanlike" use of the venerable Labor Theory of Value to argue that capitalists exploited workers of the profit portion of value that laborers had created.

The Marginalists, Jevons in England and Menger and others on the continent,[23] escaped from those perplexities by making the shift to as full a degree of emphasis on demand as the received theory had used supply. Measurement is nice and proper, but utility or want-satisfaction as the basis of demand offered no clear method or indeed even a unit for measurement. As we develop the thought at length in chapter 3, the assumption was made or merely was "in the air" that later scholars would find solutions to the measurement problems. Demand based on utility brought with it an utterly fascinating concept, a good one, of utility at the margin—from a bit more of this, a bit less of that. The truly revolutionary impact, to be sure, derived from the fact that marginalism makes it possible and necessary to use the derivative, a mathematical concept stemming directly from Newton's calculus but never employed in the Labor Theory of Value approaches formerly used. Was there a Marginalist Revolution? Most scholars say yes, while a few say no.[24] It depends in great part on how one chooses to use language; words over time can only mean what we say they mean.

We prefer not to call the work of the Marginalists a revolution because it seems quite clear that their use of the derivatives of Newton's calculus constituted far more a great triumph for his work than a shunting aside of his methods. It is almost enough merely to recall the name of Newton's major work, *Mathematical Principles of Natural Philosophy*. Particularly since the Marginalists, all treatises in economic theory, and especially the heart of it, microeconomics, could well bear the title "Economics Regarded as Mathematical Principles of Natural Philosophy." What greater tribute to Isaac Newton would be possible by our profession? Moreover, the pronounced allegiance to Positivism on the part of economics during the past century or more squares fully with Newton's continuous concern for empiricism or facts-data-information in sharp contradistinction to Cartesianism and its primary reliance upon purely mental operations.

It is certain that both physics and mathematics have seen extensive development since the time of Newton. Economics, of course, has made applications right along, but surely no one who knows anything at all about the life and work of Isaac Newton would fail to recognize his acknowledgment of his predecessors and his concern that further work be done. As mentioned above, Paul Samuelson, in his Nobel Prize recipient address, utilized conceptions from Classical physics as the heart of his presentation.

A further thought leads to perplexity. Suppose we grant the thesis of a Marginalist Revolution; that gives us "neo-Classical" economics.

But by 1890, Alfred Marshall in his *Principles*[25] carried the day with the new insistence that value is determined in effect "by the blades of a scissors," both supply and demand, not just demand as argued by the Marginalists. Marshall ruled the world of English-speaking economists right up until the 1930s. Shall we label his work "neo-neo-Classical economics"? Furthermore, early in the 1930s several varieties of imperfect competition or monopolistic competition theory were devised, with firm insistence that some markets were highly competitive but others were not.[26] The body of theory had to be split. Do we at this stage say "neo-neo-neo-Classical"? A bit later, John Maynard Keynes demonstrated that the main body of then-current theory was a matter of a special case of assumed full employment of resources, whereas *The General Theory of Employment, Interest and Money* was a separate and distinct situation.[27] How many times must we say "neo"? Keynes had the good sense to lump all his predecessors into one category that he called the Classicists. We share the view, but know full well that one "neo" will continue as standard usage.

An Important Scream of Protest: Karl Marx

By 1848, Karl Marx, along with Fredrich Engels and some others, had the basic structure of Marxism well in place with the publication of *The Communist Manifesto*.[28] By 1859 Charles Darwin had published *The Origin of Species*, and Rudolph Clausius had worked out the central meaning of entropy as a sharp departure from Classical mechanics. Evolution and entropy shattered the Classical world, even if a few physicists and nearly all economists to this day deny or ignore the significance of the revolution.

What if Darwin and Clausius had been even two decades earlier, or Marx had been two decades later? Marx, to be sure, had known about Darwin's work with change, had been keenly interested, and had tried to dedicate his greatest work to Darwin but was rejected. Also in 1848 there appeared John Stuart Mill's *Principles of Political Economy*,[29] which was destined to run through six editions, surviving Marxist Materialism on one side and Jevons–Menger Rational Idealism on the other. Mill's book served as the bible of the English-speaking economists all the way to another Britisher, Alfred Marshall, and his great book in 1890. Newtonian science was as firmly, and as disastrously, entrenched in social science as in physical science. We now see that neither Darwin, nor Clausius, nor Einstein, nor anyone else is going to save us from the tragedy of Newtonism as social science. But suppose Darwin and Clausius had come much earlier, somewhere between Copernicus and Newton? Classical mechanics, in all likelihood, would have emerged, but not as dogma underlying all of science.

At some point we must raise the question: Would the work of Karl Marx have been what it was, had the 1600 publication of the major works of Darwin and Clausius actually occurred? To confront the question we must make at least a few crucial assumptions. Would economic developments in the world have gone along about the same as they actually did? We assume so. Capitalism was growing and developing rapidly both before and after Adam Smith, and we assume that any cautions about resource use that might have been stated would have been ignored. After all, note how lengthy the time was between Smith's great book, 1776, and the actual repeal of the Corn Laws, a flagrant violation of basic ideas of free trade, 1844–45. Likewise, Darwin-based recognition of qualitative change and our assumed work by anthropologists concerning the variety and relativity of social customs and mores would have brought recognition in some quarters that capitalism was not genuinely a "survival of the fittest" phenomenon, and there was not much reason to think that nature leads to capitalism. At least those philosophers and anthropologists of strong religious persuasion could have continued to oppose both capitalism and evolution. The scientific standing of capitalism accordingly would have been much more confused, and probably weaker, than it actually was.

Thus Marx might well have proceeded on his chosen path. But a major interruption must be made: Would Hegel have adjusted *his* philosophy in a world that included Darwin? Darwin and Clausius were pointing to the scientific facts of qualitative change, and that was Hegel's forte, the core of the dialectic. A central part—and the strength—of dialectics is to point up and explain qualitative change. State of Being X differs from State of Being Y, either currently or later, although they came from a common origin, ultimately the "Big Bang." Vital characteristics overlap during change, and at various points. This overlap Georgescu-Roegen calls a penumbra, a word put to good use much earlier by Veblen. Darwin's change, which we may label dialectic, was of a materialist *genre*. Earlier, Hegel had made his dialectics a matter of spirit or ideas. What if dialectical materialism had come earlier than dialectical idealism, and specifically via Darwin? Such a suggestion is not farfetched because Darwin acknowleged that his work with evolution had drawn inspiration from Malthus's work on population theory, only a quarter century after Smith's *Wealth of Nations*. Malthus's lifespan (1766–1834) overlapped that of Hegel at both ends (1770–1831).

Hegel was highly deterministic as to the outcome of history as process. Man's self-realization of spiritual essence as a real oneness with God was the teleological goal or end. Darwinism does not yield much at all in the way of determinate ends. Evolution, with struggle and survival of the temporarily fittest or the strongest via mutation and adaptation, just goes on. Some species and some customs become extinct, which fate might well befall man, who has some degree of influence over his transactions with nature. That Hegel, writing two centuries subsequent to our assumed 1600 publications, would have been uninfluenced by so major a work of dialectical impact as that of Darwin, seems entirely unlikely. However, it is perhaps as likely that a different Hegel would have strengthened Marx's hand as well as weakened it. So we must leave to Marx a firey denunciation of capitalism from his use of the labor theory of value and his development of his own theory of the value of labor. His "laws of motion of capitalism" formulation is nearly pure Newtonism. The class struggle, revolution, replacement of capitalism by socialism, and the transition to communism are Marx interpreting Hegel to suit Marx's own purposes.

How valid, scientific, correct, verified, or falsified is Marxism? There is no chance for agreement on the answer, but some things can be said. First, it is true and crucial that the basic structure of Marxism is of two parts: an inverted Hegelianism that becomes economics or materialist based instead of spiritualist or idealist in the sense of being totally mental, rational, or abstractly logical at any first formulation. A dialectical perception of qualitative change is retained, however. The other foundation stone is Classical economics, based on Newton and adapted by Marx for his purposes. Herein arises a superb irony. Marx was openly and honestly striving to be scientific. The epitome of science, even more in his day than now, was Newtonian mechanics. He was thus forced to the techniques and methods of Smith and Ricardo in this regard. Marx made a thorough study of the basic tool of mechanics-as-science, in which effort:

> he produced about 1,000 handwritten pages of mathematical manuscripts from about 1858 to his death in 1883. About half of these materials deal with differential calculus. Although he may originally have written many of the concepts in *Capital* in terms of differential equations, he apparently

believed that the calculus was inappropriate for his type of historical
analysis, and it does not appear in the published work. Toward the end of
his life, Marx became interested in finite mathematics, which would have
been more applicable.[30]

To be regarded as scientific, Marx had to take the calculus-of-
mechanics paradigm, and although he backed off from publishing in
the notation of differential calculus, the damage was done in the sense
that his thinking and analysis proceed that way. Marx was wary, but
he had to confront the Classical economists on their own terms.

Georgescu-Roegen pulled several points together nicely:

> It is thus that economics is reduced to "the mechanics of utility and
> self-interest." Indeed, any system that involves a conservation principle
> (given means) and a maximization rule (optimal satisfaction) is a mechan-
> ical analogue. . . . [Many economic models] consist of a system of
> equations which has a quite special structure: they involve only analytical
> functions. Now, the peculiar property of an analytical function, $f(x)$, is
> that its value for *any x,* is completely determined by the values $f(x)$ has in
> *any interval, however small.* The reason why we use only such functions
> is obvious. Without analytical functions we would not be able to extrap-
> olate the model beyond the range of past observations. But why should
> economic laws, or any other laws for that matter, be expressed by
> analytical functions? Undoubtedly, we are inclined to attribute to reality
> a far greater degree of orderliness than the facts justify.[31]

Rapid qualitative change in our economic conditions renders our
mechanistic measures and statistical tests frequently of dubious validity. So we are playing games. He continues:

> if one formula does not pass the test, we can always add another variable,
> deflate by another, and so on. By cleverly choosing one's chisels, one can
> always prove that inside any log there is a beautiful Madonna. . . .
> [Furthermore] the very idea of a mathematical (read arithmomorphic)
> relation between pseudo measures, like those used in economics, is a
> manifest contradiction in terms.[32]

Pondering these various considerations, we see that Marx had the
defects of his great strengths. He learned the Classical calculus well,
and he selected his functions carefully so that no one can point out
that his assumed relationships are clearly wrong or inferior to those of
the Classical "model chiselers." His chosen functions lead inexorably

to the collapse of the capitalist system, no doubt of that. Then the peculiar assumption of a form of hedonic logic imputed to laborers, or "labor," causes them (it) to self-servingly rise up and overthrow the capitalists and their system, and institute a system of socialism in which workers transcend their selfish hedonism. Marx was not Darwinian however much he admired Darwin. He was Hegelian, and it is impossible to be both Hegelian and Darwinian. He would have no part of qualitative change coming merely in bits and pieces, such as labor union gains for workers or governmental fiscal or welfare programs that would shift his functions and send him back to the drawing boards to see if collapse was still inevitable. As a Hegelian, he could envision only a minor role for such patchwork changes, and as the collapse comes, so does revolution (bringing into play the laws of the new stage of history) from feudalism, to various types of capitalisms, to socialism. Laws of each stage necessarily have analytical functions as their foundations, even if Marx was wary enough not to write it all out as mathematical notation.

Since nineteenth century science was overwhelmingly a virulent form of Classical mechanics, what was Marx to do? He wanted a better, more appropriate mathematics, but we can hardly fault him for failing to invent it since no one to this day has invented a mathematics that copes with the qualitative change that is required. Indeed, we credit Marx for seeing the problem. He insisted on building qualitative change into social science, and thus the study of history, and he turned to what was at hand, which was Hegel. The dramatic collapse and revolutionary change to a new stage of history are no more foolish than the mechanical model in its insistence on keeping science free of qualitative change. Marx used functional relations that lead to collapse and revolution. In part the developments of history that he foresaw have not come about in the fashion he calculated because of man-made policy tinkering with the functions. Can the tinkering go on forever and the system still be called capitalism? Marx saw the question, and answered negatively. Orthodox economists for the most part cannot even admit the question. A few decades back, for example, they watched New Deal reforms being patched into place, and later they turned viciously against the reformers and insisted that science demonstrates that reforms caused the problems in the first place by interfering with the ideology and practice of free-market self-adjustments. Clearly, we must perceive the ongoing scheme of mechanical science in application to human affairs as a form of religion, as did the "Newtonians," and of a peculiarly mystical sort. Marx tried to solve the problem of qualitative change by way of the unsatisfactory Hegelian dialectical apparatus, but perhaps we should note that, as Robert L. Heilbroner informs us, it was the modern philosopher Fichte who coined the expression "thesis, antithesis, synthesis," not Hegel, Marx, or Engels.[33]

Notes

1. Adam Smith, *The Theory of Moral Sentiments* (New York: Augustus M. Kelley, 1966).

2. Richard H. Tawney, *Religion and the Rise of Capitalism* (New York: Harcourt, Brace and Company, 1926); Max Weber, *The Protestant Ethic and the Spirit of Capitalism* (New York: C. Scribner's Sons, 1956).

3. Bertrand Russell, *A History of Western Philosophy* (New York: Simon and Schuster, 1945), 523.

4. Robert W. Green, *Protestantism and Capitalism: The Weber Thesis and Its Critics* (New York: D. C. Heath, 1973).

5. Whitehead, *Science and the Modern World*, 57–82.

6. Richard Westfall, *Never at Rest: A Biography of Isaac Newton* (New York: Cambridge University Press, 1980) 486–87.

7. Isaac Newton, *Mathematical Principles of Natural Philosophy*. Great Books of the Western World, vol. 34 (Chicago and London: Encyclopaedia Britannica Inc., 1952).

8. Margaret C. Jacob, *The Newtonians and the English Revolution, 1689–1720* (Ithaca, N. Y: Cornell University Press, 1976), frontispiece; also cited on 137 n.; here slightly rearranged and with emphasis added.

9. Jacob, *Newtonians . . .* , 18.

10. Jacob, *Newtonians . . .* , 16.

11. Adam Smith, *The Wealth of Nations* (New York: Modern Library, 1937), 207 n.

12. Paul Samuelson, "Maximization Principles in Analytical Economics," *American Economic Review* (June 1972): 251.

13. Samuelson, "Maximization . . . ," 253.

14. *Ibid.*

15. R. Buckminster Fuller, *Utopia or Oblivian: The Prospects for Humanity* (New York: Bantam, 1969), 288.

16. Adam Smith, *The Early Writings of Adam Smith*. Edited by J. Ralph Lindgren. (New York: Augustus M. Kelley, 1967) 78.

17. Nicholas Georgescu-Roegen, *The Entropy Law and the Economic Process* (Cambridge: Harvard University Press, 1971), 1.

18. Georgescu-Roegen, *Entropy . . .* , 343.

19. Alfred Marshall, *Principles of Economics* (London: Macmillan, 8th ed. 1920), xiv.

20. John Stuart Mill, *Utilitarianism, On Liberty, Essay on Bentham and John Austin*. Edited by M. Warnock (Cleveland: World Publishing, 1962).

21. Russell, *A History* . . . , 778.

22. Georgescu-Roegen, *Entropy* . . . , 95–113.

23. William Stanley Jevons, *The Theory of Political Economy* 4th ed. (London: Macmillan, 1924); Carl Menger, *Principles of Economics*. Translated by P. Dingwall and B. Hoselitz. (New York: New York University Press, 1981).

24. See discussion in Philip Mirowski, *Against Mechanism: Protecting Economics From Science* (Totowa, N.J.: Rowman & Littlefield, 1988), ch.1, 11–56.

25. Marshall, *Principles* . . . .

26. Joan Robinson, *The Economics of Imperfect Competition* (New York: St. Martin, 1969); Edward Chamberlin, *The Theory of Monopolistic Competition* (Cambridge, Mass.: Harvard University Press, 1962).

27. John Maynard Keynes, *The General Theory of Employment, Interest, and Money* (New York: Harcourt, Brace, 1936).

28. Karl Marx, *The Communist Manifesto*. (1848); reprinted in *A Handbook of Marxism*. Edited by Emile Burns. (London: Victor Gollancz Ltd, 1935) 21–59.

29. John Stuart Mill, *Principles of Political Economy*, 5th ed. (New York: D. Appleton, 1891).

30. Leon Smolinski, "Karl Marx and Mathematical Economics." *Journal of Political Economy* 81 (September-October 1973): 1189–1204.

31. Georgescu-Roegen, *Entropy* . . . , 318–19, 339.

32. *Ibid.*, 340.

33. Robert L. Heilbroner, *Marxism: For and Against* (New York: W. W. Norton, 1980), 42.

3

"Economic Man" in Micro- and Macro-economics

Microeconomics and the Behavior of the Individual: The Retreat from Explanation to Formalism

In one of his more important articles, Veblen argued that marginal utility economics embraces a world-view and a methodology that force it to focus exclusively on *causa formalis*, pull of the future, rationalistic calculation, to the obvious exclusion of historical or environmental influences upon behavior.[1] *Sufficient reason* is the philosophical basis of explanation in such an approach, not *efficient cause*, as philosophers have debated these concepts for several centuries.

Arthur Koestler, in his book entitled *The Sleepwalkers*, asserted that throughout historical time until the seventeenth century the basic human view or conception of the universe was Aristotelian.[2] Isaac Newton published his monumental work of science and philosophy in 1687. This was the seventeenth century turning point, and man's ideas about the universe have been Newtonian since that time. No doubt this is taken by most readers to refer to the physical universe, certainly the planets, suns, stars, galaxies, but also atoms, molecules, and other microphenomena when that question might arise. Surely the statement by Koestler was not meant to apply to human behavior.

Even a cursory examination of the definition used for economics strips away that exclusion possibility. Economics is the study of the allocation of given, scarce resources to given, unlimited wants. At times the wording is "limited means to unlimited ends," which means the same thing. Economics is defined as rationing, or the study of the behavior called rationing. It is not the study of the process of the rise and fall, coming and going, of either means or ends. Thus for the main part, history is excluded, and the subject of study and the findings are timeless. Truth can be ever more closely approximated and ultimately the foundations would be axiomatized. Euclidian methods and solutions would be found. Analytical functions would be contrived, making it possible to calculate magnitudes of variables in a consistent way on the basis of information applicable at any interval no matter how small. A book of data of economic relationships would be feasible, analogously to such publications concerning chemical processes or engineering data.

This definition of economics rests upon an implicit conception of science, that of Classical mechanism. As Koestler stated, Newton was the central figure. It is reasonable to apply his name to the system of thought that comprises this doctrine even though there have been many other important contributors to the doctrine both before and since.

The accomplishments of mechanistic economic science may be many if viewed in a certain sympathetic light, and its fault only one. It cannot confront the behavior of its subject matter, human beings. The truth is that the only sense in which it solidly confronts behavior is that of its child, christened economic man, *homo economicus*. But imaginary creatures do not behave, a term that scientifically speaking is applicable only to real beings. Real persons—the object of study in economics—have emotions, habits, neuroses, whims, and behavioral traits that take their form only through the experience of events through time. That is why economic man had to be invented; only he is purely rational and devoid of influence from historical circumstances. Thus, economics as a theoretical science, on the Classical mechanism conception of science, can never be fully relevant to the world of real humans. In this sense irrelevant, economics should not be considered a full-fledged science at all. It cannot give reliable answers to basic questions such as what is progress or welfare or fairness. Worse yet, the price and income predictions it enables cannot be reliable, for the subject matter is human behavior, a changing and evolving phenomenon that is nonmechanistic and hence cannot be axiomatized. There is only small comfort in taking the view that orthodox, Classical, mechanistic economics is good enough because whatever its faults, it is all we have.

The starting place for improvement is to admit that we do not and cannot have a theoretical economics that is highly relevant to the behavior of its subject matter as long as it is anchored or based upon mechanism as the conception of reality and thus of science. What is to be substituted? Since virtually all aspects of the universe have evolved and continue to evolve, in the frame of reference Koestler addressed, the answer begins with tentative substitution of Darwin and Clausius, in biology and physics respectively, in the place of Newton as the means of making cultural evolution the central world view for economics as a realistic social science. Neither materialism nor spiritualism-idealism alone can serve as a suitable ontology or perception of reality. Change must be a key concept, and would replace the orthodox preoccupation with equilibrium and the static position of *being*.

A great number of sharp critiques of orthodox economics and its methodology have been made through the years, and most of them have both succeeded and failed. They have shown that economics, being Newtonian, does not confront evolutionary reality very well, and therefore has a poor record for either explaining or predicting events. But the critiques have largely failed in efforts to formulate adequate alternatives, and in their frequent implication that if shortcomings and failures are pointed out, that constitutes falsification, which will mandate change. Critique, however, has been rather like "water on a duck's back"; it merely runs off.

It is certain that the mechanistic model is impervious, and this is because it is correct on its own highly rationalistic terms. The mechanistic conception of science in application to human conduct is what is illicit, since it attempts axiomatization in a domain that is dominated by change. Economists will continue to hone the logic of the models, beyond doubt, and will continue to believe that proper and valid criticism would consist of showing either, or both, different facts or demonstration of errors of logic. Our chosen task will be to show that orthodox economics has always meant microeconomics at core; that its practitioners meant it as an empirically valid procedure that would be confirmed by data when problems of unit identification and measurement could be overcome; and that this research program has failed entirely. Furthermore, we will suggest that the profession has backed off from attempting explanation of behavior because of this failure and has turned instead to *causa formalis* purely formal modeling that is said to be "predictive." In some fundamentals the models are tautological or nonfalsifiable, and hence not scientific in their own alleged framework of science. In addition we will assert that a few of the fundamental ideas underlying the orthodox structure are valid and useful, but in a different context and for a different purpose.

To accomplish our stated tasks, we must present a sketch of the history of economic thought, showing that there has been a preoccupation with microphenomena that has been almost definitional of the science. Where does economics for this purpose begin? Adam Smith is said to be the first economist, and he did, in fact, make the first great leap into application of Newtonian mechanism into social and economic affairs with the laissez-faire, self-adjusting mechanism. Universal gravitation rests its meaning on discrete units of mass, and such a world-view clearly enthrones the individual person in the realm of economics.

Not long thereafter, David Ricardo moved far ahead with efforts at constructing purely abstract logical or rational models. Then Karl Marx made a devastating criticism of the purely formal nature of the models and the exploitation of labor implicit in the labor theory of value of the Classical models themselves. Jevons in England and Menger on the European continent shifted the focus from objective costs as the basis of value to subjective utility. At this stage of development, economics was truly the science of "felicific calculus," as Jeremy Bentham had labeled it a little earlier.

Economic man performs felicific calculus, the maximization of utility or pleasure. In so doing, he makes his decisions at the margin—a bit more of this, a bit less of that. The measure would be called utils of utility, which was envisioned as a cardinal phenomenon (that would be additive). For several decades economic theorists believed or hoped that psychophysics would come up with a means of detecting and measuring states of mental or physiological being and their change to reflect the state of pleasure or utility. As is universally acknowledged, such measurement procedures never came into being. An additional problem was the complementary nature of utilities (bacon goes with eggs in the choices of many humans, overcoats are paired with hats, and such considerations). Incidentally, principles of economics textbooks continue almost invariably to discuss microbehavior with cardinal utility examples: the subject person buys more, or less, of beer, burgers, and Cadillacs until his marginal utility weighted by price is equated for all the considered possible purchases. The idea is intuitively appealing as a means of demonstrating how to reach equilibrium with utility maximization. Stating these ideas is one thing, but to present them as science without strong qualification is quite a misleading act. At any rate, the research efforts failed, and will not be summarized here.

We economists take ourselves and our theories quite seriously, and apparently do not expect to be challenged when we commit lapses of logic, or the like. An example, from an excellent book by a well-respected economist: "This assumption or hypothesis is often called the law of diminishing marginal utility. This law states that. . . ."[3] In one sentence an assumption became an hypothesis, and then a law. The next sentence proceeds to the explication of the assumption that has thus been established as a law! Apparently neither the author, Edwin Mansfield, nor the editor checked that part of the manuscript with great care, which is understandable in view of the consideration that parts of almost any presentation of microeconomic ideas, including this one, are little more than a paraphrasing gleaned from the multitudinous published statements of it. Perhaps truth once attained never changes, but who would care to deny the fact and relevance of evolution in human affairs?

Economists during the 1930s transcended cardinal utility with ordinal utility, which means ranking preferences and claims to bypass any need for cardinal measurement. Utils is an embarrassing term that can be dropped. A primary purpose of cardinal measures had been to show that demand curves slope down to the right in Cartesian quadrant diagrams, which would demonstrate the validity of the Law of Demand: quantity demanded is an inverse function of price. Once established, an analytical function could be contrived or alleged, and we would be off and running. The quantity that would be demanded at any price would be precisely calculable in terms of the assumptions. Later the ranking or ordinal comparison was seen as a weaker argument but still adequate to yield the negatively sloped demand curve. Indifference curve analysis was the diagramatic methodology employed, and it likewise is appealing or convincing as being quite logical. But certain of the ghosts from cardinality lingered in the arguments.

Let us start from the beginning and state some major considerations concerning consumer theory and its more generalized form, rational choice theory. For more than one hundred years this theory has undergone little real change. We must observe that there have been shifts of concepts, and discuss why, because we think that the important changes have been ad hoc, intended to preserve the theory from failures to be empirically confirmed. What has emerged is not an empirically well-substantiated nomological (law-based) account of economic action or behavior.

Early and late, marginal theory has been based shakily on three specific general claims: first, complete information by the subject person, meaning true beliefs about all facts relevant to the given situation; second, that the individual subject can rank the alternatives his circumstances provide, in order of preferability by considering the cardinal utility each possible course of action would bring; and third, the subject individual has at all times the desire to maximize cardinal utility, and hence will do so. We choose not to emphasize the implicit claim that the individual is the appropriate unit of study for decision-making theory.

Complete information, everyone would agree today, would be a boundary or limiting condition to simplify theorizing. The early marginalists did not treat this idea as a simplification, however; they treated it as an approximation of reality that was adequate for maximization calculations. Action as utility maximization was taken as a specific instance of a general principle that underlies all human behavior. Jeremy Bentham made this abundantly clear in his 1789 *Principles of Morals and Legislation* and elsewhere in his writings, as did P. H. Wicksteed in his 1910 book, *The Common Sense of Political Economy*.[4] Utility maximization made one goal or desire paramount, and treated actions and other desires as the means to this dominant end. The field of economics, with appropriate modesty, was limited to the application of these ideas to goods and services only. And here a further psychological general claim was made: the utility or want-satisfying capacity of a commodity is a marginally decreasing function of its quantity (available to the subject person). Still further, by assuming limited purchasing power of an individual, it was logically deduced that the quantity an agent person chooses is, therefore, a marginally decreasing function of the price of that good. Certain highly limiting *ceteris paribus* assumptions were required, such as the price of all other commodities, income, tastes, terms of availability of money and credit, expectations of change of any of these or other variables, etc. If this type of procedure is to be performed, the limitations must be regarded as necessary and feasible.

The utility principle would require adequate generalization to provide independent confirmation. It is all too easy to say that whatever item or action is chosen must maximize utility or else something else would have been chosen, but such clearly is a circular or nonfalsifiable argument. Economists would need to identify some attribute that is measurable and changes as quantities of goods change. Blood pressure, heartbeat characteristics, pulse rate, body temperature, breathing rate, etc., might do. Some physical or psychic characteristic might be closely correlated to quantities of commodities possessed since utility is supposed to bear a relation to felt pleasures or satisfactions.

Utility is defined as want-satisfying power of commodities. Desires as mental states are presumed to change if they have a strong effect on actions such as consumption (utility) or work (disutility). Reciprocally, actions have a strong effect on desires. The action of consuming bread lessens the desire involved *in*, thus diminishing the marginal utility *of*, bread consumption. The mental or physiological state is postulated to change with consumptive action. During the early decades of development of utility theory, the proponents of it appeared to have little doubt that psychology or psychophysics, or some such field of study, would solve these problems. The work of the economists can be acknowledged to have been imaginative and important in a limited sense. The fact that neither Freudian, Gestalt, cognitive, introspective, behavioral, nor neurophysiological psychology—how many subsets are there that might be relevant?—has provided a theory, specification of unit, and mode for measurement that sustain the principle of such quantitative differences between differing states of desire is the real reason cardinal utility had to be downgraded.

Accordingly, the failure of cardinal utility was empirical, not conceptual. Therefore it is not surprising that it still plays a very important role in consumer theory in economics textbooks. Moreover, utility is not merely not measurable and additive, but studies through time made it appear that it was a function of the availability of other commodities, as complements or as substitutes. Also there emerged the idea of "normal" versus "inferior" goods as income changes, either from change of size of paycheck or change of prices of commodities being bought.

Various dissatisfactions occasioned a search for alternate explanation, which led to the discovery by economists of the already known concept of ordinality and how to apply the concept to utility. Edgeworth and Pareto were pioneers. Procedurally, the subject person must rank for preferability each available alternative, in a fashion that enables identifying when he is indifferent between specified amounts of any two commodities or commodity groups. Indifference curves and the entire resultant indifference map involves no direct use of price or money. Therefore, perhaps the cardinality or unit-measurability and hence mathematical manipulability of the same could be avoided or bypassed. The argument was rather technical, but one need not understand all of the details to grasp the nature of the flaws.

The assumption of maximizing behavior was kept by the stipulation that the subject person always chooses to be on the indifference curve that is furthest from the point of origin in the diagram, involving the greatest possible quantity pairings. But how much further out is one indifference curve than another? This is a valid consideration because the methodology yields a determinate quantity of the commodity represented on each axis. The cardinal aspects have not been scrubbed out of the theory, nor has it proved possible to do so. Objective mathematical considerations dictate that budget lines, essential to the diagrams, necessarily are linear. Therefore indifference curves must be curvilinear and convex to the origin or the model would run into serious problems. A linear indifference curve, for example, might be identical to the linear budget line. However, the reasonable-looking curvilinear indifference curve necessarily displays diminishing marginal rates of susbstitution between the commodities under analysis, a splendid idea that is comparable to the Law of Diminishing Marginal Utility from cardinal methodology. But since the indifference diagram can have, and must have because of the nature of budget lines, objective quantification of the axes, the rates of substitution are objective and quantified. This looks highly desirable and useful until one recalls that these strengths of desires are supposed to be ordinal, not cardinal. Units and methods of measurement simply do not exist. So again, it has proved impossible to eliminate the residues of cardinality, a procedure that itself has proved impossible to sustain empirically.

Since indifference curves rest on purely subjective phenomena, if it should appear that a person is doing something that transgresses his indifference map, which perhaps was derived from a questionnaire, then the theorist falls back on the argument that there has occurred an "exogenous change in tastes" on the part of the subject person. Who could prove this wrong? Unfortunately, such a procedure involves unfalsifiable tautological argument, and no one will accept it as fully scientific.

For a useful indifference theory, what is required, again, would be a law-as-nomological-regularity that connects preference order with some other variable that can be measured independently of actual choices made as a causal consequence of the preference ordering. This would put consumer choice in some degree on a "push of the past and environment," *causa materialis* basis, rather than the continuing actual theoretical basis of *causa formalis* "pull of the future." The shift would not be from idealism-spiritualism as ontological perception to wholehearted materialism, but rather to a dualistic Realism ontology. As stated in relation to cardinal utility theory, the kind of measurable phenomenon that varies as a direct or inverse function could be heartbeat rate, blood pressure, body temperature, breathing rate, or something else. By way of comparison, we can administer measured increments of alcohol to a person, and measure the resultant changes in some of these listed physiological attributes and others. Utility theory, whether cardinal or ordinal, requires such an empirical basis as a foundation. Since we have little reason to believe such a measurable and independent basis for the theory will be found, we continue to regard the theory as formal only, a spiritual-idealist-rationalist means of rationalizing the socioeconomic status quo. Whatever is going on *must be* maximization or nearly so.

The modern operationalist-empiricist basis for scientific theory to which we allude as essential is not to be cast aside lightly, nor is there reason that it should be. The presumed necessity of grounding theory in empirical facts renders ordinal as well as cardinal utility approaches to consumer behavior quite unscientific and thus unsatisfactory. They both may appear plausible at first glance, but there is little scientific plausibility in asserting that they are scientific because they imply that economic affairs are satisfactory if and when left to the vagaries of market forces and the resultant choices. That is the policy direction in which such theories point, necessarily so if consistency of theorizing is to be sustained. Thus the foundations of economics are micro, focusing as they do on assumed maximization by rational, atomistic individuals. In the absence of such a regularity, as previously discussed, to make legitimate the preference order as the unit of the causal variable of desire, ordinal utility sinks into as much of a swamp as does cardinal utility.

Since indifference curves have determinate spatial differentiation, which is cardinality, and each of them yields cardinally measurable and precise numbers for rates of substitution, it is not possible to argue that the ordinalist revolution merely was progress in the form of a shift to Behaviorist psychology. Ordinal preference theory failed in part because cardinality could not be eliminated, and measurement was not possible. Like marginal utility theory, the indifference approach could do little other than assert that people choose their preferred alternatives, which is tantamount to stating that people do what they like to do. So we do. What is desired is desired, but this does not establish that it is desirable, or that it maximizes.

The next substitute of note that economists patched together to salvage what they could of the overall method and world-view of orthodox, neo-Classical theory is called "revealed preference." It frequently is interpreted as the use of Behaviorist, black-box psychological theory to explain consumer and other "rational" choice. Such a view rests on the belief that economists probably cannot but fortunately need not know why choosers do what they do. Presumably stimuli feed into the mind—which is a black-box sort of apparatus—and response, as choice of action, comes out. This is a tautology or truism, because it certainly is nonfalsifiable. We regard the methodological changes as not so much a shift to Behavioral psychology and thus one form of accepted scientific treatment of choice behavior, as the surrender of any genuine attempt to explain behavior. Our interpretation of revealed preference as not straight-forward Behavioralism (which itself we do not claim to endorse) relates to the economists' self-serving mode of application of Behaviorist principles. Recall that the economist has reasons, which may become ulterior motives, for trying to salvage orthodox theory, for example, as both self-adjusting behavioral modes and as maximization of several variables. The model requires negatively sloped demand curves (which we agree is a feasible view), but revealed preference theory is distorted Behaviorism designed to achieve the downward-sloping demand curve by the minimal assumption of choice among alternatives as always transitive, however determined (since concern for determination or explanation has been dropped). Transitivity means consistency of choice: if one chooses A over B, and B over C, then he must never choose C over A. Since consumers and other choosers in fact make choices of the "C over A" type, the theory is saved by the ruse that, as before with cardinal and ordinal approaches, "exogenous change in tastes" has occurred.

Since the possibility of such a shift cannot be denied, we continue with the tautology that people do what they choose to do, or choose whatever they like, and we have made no progress. However, the problem is not merely that the theory is nonfalsifiable tautology, but that it involves the fault that in giving up the attempts to find objective measures concerning desires, independent of change in choosing apples over oranges or the like, the revealed preference approach gives up entirely on efforts at explanation. Because revealed preference theory begins with actual behavior, it is unconcerned with any theory or competing theories about the causal determinants of that behavior, and it is not concerned with explanation of it. Economists turned to prediction as the possible basis for a claim to scientific standing because the efforts at explanation failed. The various methodological statements by Milton Friedman have been particularly glaring examples of this ruse. One can read almost anything desired into his *Essays in Positive Economics*.[5]

One of the most pointed statements of the rejection of efforts to explain the behavior of the consumer was provided by Sir John Hicks in his 1939 classic work, *Value and Capital*. He wrote that "economics is not in the end much interested in the behavior of single individuals. Its concern is with the behavior of groups. A study of individual demand is only a means to the study of market demand. . . . [Because] our study of the individual consumer is only a step towards the study of a group of consumers . . . falsifications may be trusted to disappear when the individual account is aggregated."[6] If such a view is taken as valid, we ask if there is such a thing as microeconomics?

Neither economists nor psychologists have ever made much progress toward the solution of problems of measurement of strength of desire independently of behavior. However, the need to measure the extent and content of beliefs (or information, as this more commonly is labeled) has been recognized. Study of this problem has eventuated in an entire field of study, that of decision-making with imperfect information. The assumption of perfect information, whether explicit or implicit, was set aside, and the focus became decision making under conditions of risk and uncertainty. The latter term applies to situations concerning which the knowledge of availability and content of alternatives is perceived as too limited for even the assignment of probabilities. Risk, quite consistently, means situations or cases in which beliefs about alternatives theoretically can be assigned probabilistic measures reflecting the degree of confidence that these alternatives will be available or will result.

As far back as 1944, the work was published that remains the benchmark, seminal statement on decisions under risk, von Neumann and Morgenstern's *Theory of Games and Economic Behavior*.[7] Notably, they kept the assumption of maximization of utility, and showed that one can construct a utility measure that determines actions of the subject in confrontation with alternatives to which risk probabilities can be assigned. An explanation of action accomplished outside the bounds of certainty was a great theoretical step forward, but the problem of specification of preferences remains, and the new problem of specification of probabilities clearly became crucial. We have no objective way to measure probabilities assigned by the subject to perceived alternative action courses. We might apply the reasoning used in the revealed preference models, and infer probability assignment after the fact of actual choice, and argue that the subject maximized the "expected" utility. Such procedure does not provide the objective and independent probability specification that genuinely is needed. Moreover, the von Neumann–Morgenstern axioms, five in number, have difficulty with the apparent fact that some subject persons derive pleasure from the opportunity to take risks (for example, those of casino gambling, even with the knowledge that the odds are against winning); while other people go to almost extreme pathological or irrational measures to avoid risks. Risk avoidance and risk attraction are possible attitudes, but we know little in any given case, and we certainly have no means of measurement.

It is a fair statement concerning the problems of economic theorists that to make a nomological or lawlike assertion or stipulation to the effect that behavioral actions reveal or reflect maximization of preferences subject to beliefs about alternatives requires specification of the beliefs and desires or preferences under consideration. No specification or measurement has proved to be possible. This is true not only of the categories of efforts to wrestle with these problems that we have detailed above, but of what is called general equilibrium theory as well. Gerard Debreu received the Nobel Prize in economics for work done in this field, and to acknowledge that the work is important and impressive should not detract from the central consideration that a long list of specifications of conditions and assumptions is necessary to the model, including perfect information for a time span that essentially reaches to infinity.[8] The theory is impressive, but real markets do not all clear, quantity supplied equal to quantity demanded at the relevant price, most notably that for labor. It is not adequate merely to imply that such is the fault of the real world, not the fault of the theory. If the theory is to be evaluated solely on the basis of its predictive power, setting aside unreality of assumptions, the nonclearing of important markets calls it into question. As true Newtonians, however, we economists are able to avoid falsification of our general equilibrium theory via ruses, for example, by alleging that something government does, or does not do, is the cause of the failure. All societies, in fact, have more government than Newton or Smith envisioned, so such evasion can be interminable.

We have identified and commented on several theories of the behavior of the individual: cardinal utility, ordinal utility, revealed preference, game theory, and general equilibrium theory. Books have been written about each, but for our purposes there is no need to go into greater detail. There remains the theory that seems most fruitful and that came later than the others. The place in the time sequence is not purely accidental, nor was the theory made possible because of necessary earlier development of other ideas as preconditions to this remaining approach. It was the clear failure of research programs to confirm and empirically substantiate the prior doctrines or theories that led to efforts at development of our next topic of discussion.

The body of theory or ideas we refer to was developed during the 1950s and 1960s by Herbert A. Simon, and is called the theory of "satisficing."[9] The label itself may be a bit problematic because few dictionaries of the English language contain this term, but the meaning is clear enough, that is, following a course of action that one thinks will be likely to yield results that seem satisfactory is called satisficing.

Perhaps it is helpful to observe at the outset that such a formulation is thoroughly unsatisfactory to devotees of standard doctrine. It yields results that are not deterministic. It is not at all clear that it is a nomological or law-based operation or that it yields lawlike results. The concept of equilibrium takes on a different meaning in this way of thinking, most pointedly perhaps in the example that considerable "disequilibrium" unemployment of resources might be acknowledged to exist but judged "satisfactory." And, crucially, while maximization actions and results *might be* subsets of satisficing behavior, there is no argument, necessity, or even likelihood that "best possible" results will be secured.

Simon became involved in efforts that led to his development of the theory through study of actual decision making processes and his recognition of the necessity for the assumption of full, perfect, and free information by the agent within the confines of the orthodox models. Clearly all of these are limiting or boundary cases, perhaps suitable for the world of *homo economicus* but not subject to empirical confirmation. Faced with both risk and uncertainty, what does the real person do? Likely he or she undergoes expenditure of time, energy, and money to acquire information to lessen both of those great problems, which exist, by the way, in unmeasured magnitudes. Information, hardly to be assumed "free of cost" since there is no free lunch, is rarely if ever "full"—and how would we know whether and when it was?—so we make expenditures to obtain a degree of it that is perceived as adequate in the circumstances, which is to say, satisfactory. Then we make decisions, with the course of action thus reached being worthy of that same label, satisfactory. We have no way of knowing whether or not the action is maximizing of utility or any other variable or goal.

Multitudes of examples come to mind. Characteristically we look around a bit at cars before buying one, and we draw upon information from our personal experiences when it is available, and from experiences of friends and acquaintances. Perhaps we read some trade journal materials if the expenditure is not too great. We road test or drive a few models or specimens that seem of interest to us, and then make a decision to buy a particular car. Presumably it seems satisfactory, but theorists have little or no warrant to assert that the choice "maximizes." Satisficing is a condition more readily attainable than maximizing.

Who doubts that all or certainly most of us choose commodities, choose careers, choose jobs, and even choose mates, by something approximating this satisficing procedure? For work of this type, Herbert A. Simon received the Nobel Prize for economics in 1978, even though it was true that he had done his first university degree in political science, the Ph.D. in psychology, and had spent his professional career doing things that were not specifically economics. Not surprisingly, this challenger to maximization and orthodoxy has never been given much attention by the economics profession.

The satisficing individual is not irrational, but it is apparent that his behavior may depend heavily upon habit, emotion, whim, casual impulse or the like, as well as calculation concerning choice among alternatives. Satisficing obviously involves deliberate, purposive behavior and decisions. How else would one find courses of action that could be considered satisfactory? But the procedures involved are not limited to calculation alone, of the marginalist variety that Veblen protested against. Habit, conditioning or experience, concern for ostentation, emulation, emotionalism, push-of-the-past or *causa materialis* all have their place. Social structure and the resultant income distribution patterns bear heavily upon economic decisions of many more types than merely consumption behavior, but certainly are crucial here.

To be sure, anticipated pleasure or utility must be taken into account in any workable microbehavior theory, allowing for the *causa formalis*, sufficient reason, pull-of-the-future calculations as influences upon behavior. Veblen's famous concept of conspicuous consumption can have full rein. The patterns and peculiarities resultant from the Leisure or Privileged Class nature of our society are conformable with the theory known as satisficing. Orthodox economics postulates that individuals maximize (or minimize or optimize, depending upon the issue), and hence society, perceived as the summation of individuals, necessarily maximizes benefits or utilities. Accordingly, laissez-faire is the appropriate social policy, since it is requisite to efforts at maximization. Business firms, large and small, also are merely legal individuals or persons who also maximize, and to the same purpose. We reach the conclusion that was immanent in our assumptions: laissez-faire is the appropriate policy.

The concept from marginal utility economics that we wish to single out here as valid and useful in a different context is that of diminishing marginal utility, an idea blessed with the standing of "economic law." Increments of purchasing power, via the commodities it enables us to purchase, apparently diminish, at the margin, the satisfactions to be derived from them. This enormously important principle might well be applied the world around in conjunction with efforts to overcome abysmal poverty by way of much more even distribution of commodities.

An effort to use microeconomic ideas to gain understanding of how a capitalist economy functions will turn to use of laissez-faire, maximization, equilibrium Newtonian mechanism as a theory of business firms, as well as in application to consumer behavior. When this parallel application is made, it is immediately perceivable that a theory of resource use is implicit in the mechanistic model. How do business firms know what to produce? They get signals from the wide, generalized, impersonal, atomistic or individualized market as to what the public not merely wants but is willing and able to pay for. Then, on the peculiar assumption that whatever is desired is desirable, firms buy and use resources to produce what will sell at the highest rates of profit.

On occasion economists indicate awareness that profitability will center on those commodities desired by people with relatively high incomes. The poor have little purchasing power with which to transmit "signals," and they, of necessity, spend most of their limited funds on commodities of such low quality and low price as not to be very profitable to produce. For the most part, firms can ignore the poor when making product design decisions; they basically will buy whatever is offered that is cheapest.

How equal or unequal is income distribution the world around? For the United States, the four-tenths of families with highest incomes each year get almost exactly two-thirds of total disposable income. By way of contrast, in Brazil two-thirds of disposable income goes to just two-tenths of families (and/or persons; we should not impute absolute precision to the statistics). For most countries the skewedness is pronounced, and lies within the limits given for the United States and Brazil. A crucial consideration is that the economics profession almost of necessity, given the prevailing neo-Classical philosophy, does not protest the highly skewed distribution of income (money and commodities). Furthermore, standard methodology involves insistence that there is no scientific basis for interfering to change the patterns. Persons and firms get paid amounts equivalent to their marginal revenue product, and this outcome results from the working of inexorable laws that are not casually to be transgressed.

A diagram of the orthodox type may be useful for clarification. As shown in diagram 1, at prevailing prices this hypothetical economy could produce amount L, on the vertical axis, if all available resources were devoted to production of commodity L, which is luxury and military goods. Alternately, if all resources were devoted to production of necessities, the amount that could be produced is designated as point N on the horizontal axis. Studies by economists identify these two points, and also trace out the possibilities for combinations of the two commodity groups. The trade-off curve is called the production possibilities frontier, and it certainly is correct in a certain frame of reference or logic. The economist as scientist refuses to argue that any point on this curve is more desirable than production of the combination involved at any other point. He will agree, of course, that given the fact of highly skewed or uneven income distribution, production likely will be in some combination dictated by the wishes or preferences of the relatively affluent, perhaps at point X'. For very complex reasons, there ordinarily results a substantial rate of unemployment of resources, and actual output is near point X.

Are there no arguments that can be labeled scientific for preferring operation at point A instead of one of the Xs? Observe first that point A is inside the production possibilities curve, acknowledging the likelihood of some continued unemployment, although at a much reduced rate. In language lacking the tight logical precision of proper general equilibrium theorizing, we argue that production at or near point A is preferable or "better" because:

1. Greater production of necessity goods would tend to lower their price and thereby raise the real income of most people because necessity goods are bought in large quantities by the vast majority of persons.

2. The consumption of greater quantities of necessity goods would improve the health, nutrition, and general well-being of the masses of people, and such improvements would measurably or importantly raise their productivity levels.

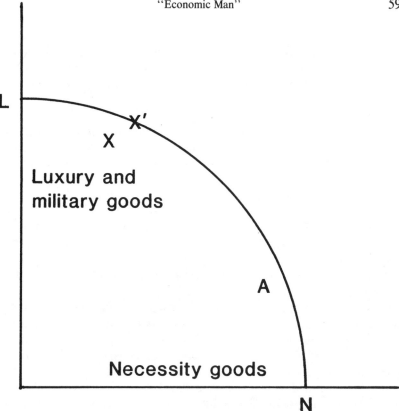

Diagram 1.

3. The skewedness of income distribution would be lessened by this procedure, and since the poor and relatively poor have higher than average propensities to spend on consumption items, the markets for many such commodities would be enlarged to the benefit of producers as well as the consumers.

4. The broader markets involve greater employment for most resources, labor as well as capital and raw materials. The ubiquity of productive operation inside the production possibility curve is a compelling demonstration of unemployment of resources.

5. As a generalization, the production of necessity goods is more labor intensive than is the production of luxuries or military goods, and the unemployment of persons is a more compelling

problem than is true for other resources. Labor power not currently used is lost forever since it cannot be stored. Lives blighted by poverty living standards from unemployment and its dreary psychological impacts can never be fully overcome or compensated.

6. Military goods generally speaking are not consumable, and on balance detract from levels of human well-being. Nearly all countries would benefit more from the production of other things. A full argument against military programs is too long and complex to be detailed here, but it does exist.

Programs would have to be set forth to shift production from point X to point A. Later in the book we will offer suggestions. For the moment it is our purpose to demonstrate that there exists an objective basis for preferring A over X, which fact cannot be granted by orthodox economics.

Closing this section presents an opportunity for further clarification of methodology employed in orthodox economics. The staunch commitment to the laissez-faire, self-adjusting, maximizing model derives straightforwardly from Newton, as do the emphasis on individualized decision making and individualized, decentralized property forms. Supply and demand, pain and pleasure, are the two functional relationship patterns in human affairs that are methodological equivalents of mass and motion in Newtonian science. All modern science seeks reliance upon facts or data, which necessarily derive from employment of the senses. The empiricism of science derives from Newton-the-scientist and as well the epistemology of John Locke-the-philosopher. Economists still rest our case for private property firmly on Lockeian ground, even if we are not openly aware of this.

Economists are both aware and proud of the fact that data or facts abound for our science, and in macroeconomics we use data extensively. As we noted earlier, economists almost desperately have sought to construct our micro models on bases of data as well, but such research efforts have failed. We think this failure is because micro-behavior is heavily influenced by human propensities, habits, emotions, quests for status, and the like—which are group or macro in nature and scope. There is little that strikes terror into the heart of economists so much as a suggestion that we really are mere sociologists! Classical mechanism can never succeed as an empirically based study of any biological species where behavior is neither fully deterministic nor individualistic, and continually evolves or changes. Economists long have sought refuge in Cartesian forms of mechanism because of Descartes's epistemological insistence that knowledge both derives from and rests solely upon functions within the mind. Mind versus matter is a complete dualism for Descartes, and knowledge relates exclusively to mind. Only one way is this operationally possible, and that is by use of mathematics, which requires no data. Economists also seek to be Newtonian and Lockeian, meaning empiricist, in our epistemology (theory of knowledge and its sources), but firm commitment to the Newtonian self-adjusting model mandates that a full set of microdata is quite impossible—hence, the resort to purely abstract mathematical modeling of the Cartesian *genre*. Because of our awareness that a great deal of data is potentially available in the sphere of economics, we economists are not full-fledged Cartesians.

Macroeconomics as Rationalism

Microeconomics, taken either as theory of consumer behavior or as theory of the business firm, simultaneously has the blessing and the curse of the inability to secure information detailed and reliable enough to allay apprehension and misgivings concerning its validity and the motivations of constituent decision makers. We do not know whether persons or firms maximize, or satisfice, or something else. Realization that information must not be assumed to be free, full, or accurate increases the uneasiness that pervades the field, and numerous scholars of sound reputation long have been expressing concern and doubt as to the scientific validity of many of our most cherished concepts in economics. We need not make a list of complaints or complainants, but a summary comment by 1978 Nobel laureate Herbert Simon carries a sharp rebuke: "I don't know of any other science that purports to be talking about real world phenomena, where statements are regularly made that are blatantly contrary to fact."[10]

How well substantiated empirically is our macrotheory, a domain where data and pseudo-data abound? It appears to us that the Herbert Simon statement is equally relevant for micro and macro. Problems with data enable the continuation of theories in the microsphere with quite poor empirical grounding. Hence highly Rationalist methodology abounds in a specifically teleological, pull-of-the-future, *causa formalis*, how things ought to be, mode. Rationalizations of the status quo necessarily are normative in character. Consumers and firms alike are said merely to seek to maximize utilities or short-run profits, and historical or data-based considerations that contradict preconceptions are set aside. "We know that rationally they would seek to maximize; therefore they do so," so to speak. In the macrosphere maximization is downgraded or not always heavily emphasized, and data have been assembled for many time series reaching back considerable time periods. How then could macrotheory be a highly Rationalist, teleological, ignore-the-past affair? Are "statements . . . regularly made that are blatantly contrary to facts" in macroeconomics? The answer is yes, and we must substantiate this assertion.

Prior to the Great Depression of the 1930s there was little that could validly have been called macrotheory or macroeconomics per se. Say's Law of Markets, the idea that supply creates its own demand, assured that there could be no genuine gluts in the markets because of inadequate effective demand. Thus there would be a quite strong tendency toward full employment equilibrium in the use of resources. But the Great Depression was wide, deep, and long—a three-dimensional disaster, so to speak. John Maynard Keynes led the field of experts who attempted theoretical explanation and policy recommendations for solution of the business cycle problem of depression in a modern capitalist economy. Say's Law was not valid in all circumstances, he concluded, which involved the fact of inadequacy of demand at times in a laissez-faire economy. Government spending would need to be enlarged when stagnation appeared, and underconsumption, meaning consumption spending at disserviceably low levels, was a constant threat. Likewise, businessmen could not be expected to spend much on investment when there was substantial idle productive capacity. When effective demand falls, clearly total production will follow suit, and accordingly Keynes concluded that the new equilibrium with unemployed resources might well tend to persist.

If government, investment, net exports, and consumption are treated as the subset categories of spending or demand, then it is arguable that consumption spending is functionally related to income, even if the latter is modified, whereas the other three spending categories are not functions of the same or any other income specification. The "consumption function" correctly is regarded as one of Keynes's major inventions.[11] He perceived that at moderately low current incomes most families would find it necessary to spend as much on consumption as they received in income. At lower incomes they would draw upon prior savings, or go into debt, or some of both, and spend more than current income in attempts to maintain the accustomed level of living as nearly as possible. In a condition of moderate or high prosperity, households would spend less than current income, the difference being saving. Thus, as either separate or aggregated household income changed, consumption spending also changed, in the same direction but by a lesser amount. The "marginal propensity to consume" could be treated as constant in the short run, giving a consumption function that was linear but had a positive Y-axis intercept in a Cartesian quadrant diagram.

Within some three years after Keynes's death, however, Simon Kuznets published convincing data showing that as aggregate income had changed in the United States during a lengthy period of years, consumption spending had continued at an amazingly constant percentage relationship to it.[12] This strongly implied a linear consumption function, but as a ray through the point of origin rather than with an intercept value. Nearly simultaneously with the publication of the Kuznets data series, in 1949 James Duesenberry published his *Income, Saving, and the Theory of Consumer Behavior*,[13] which coped well with the problem Kuznets had raised but of course did not address it directly. The Duesenberry solution was simple and straightforward. The proportion of income spent on consumption is a nonlinearly decreasing function of family disposable income by rank order, commonly referred to in the statistical series as size distribution. Families with relatively high income spend a smaller proportion of their income on consumption than do low-income families. The idea is called the relative income hypothesis. It has been tested numerous times and has not been falsified. Since the size distribution pattern has changed little—except in the 1980s—as real incomes have risen greatly, if the spending proportion done by each decile or quintile stays about the same through time, then it is quite understandable that national income would rise without a corresponding decrease in the overall consumption spending rate. The Keynesian consumption function, with its positive intercept stipulation, would be explained, with the additional information that although the slope stayed approximately constant, the curve shifts up as incomes rise through time. The problem of distinguishing a shift of a function from movement along a function is commonplace in economics. It is important to note that consumption spending accounts for approximately two-thirds of total United States demand and is much less volatile than are the other subsets. Moreover, it is the only component of demand that is treated as a function of income. Accordingly, the theoretical explanation employed for this function is of paramount importance as a foundation of macroeconomics.

Concern for relative position or socioeconomic status was a matter of great importance with Veblen, for example, in his first book, the 1899 *Theory of the Leisure Class*, which work Duesenberry cited.[14] In 1950, the year following the Duesenberry publication, Harvey Liebenstein published an article entitled "Bandwagon, Snob and Veblen Effects in the Theory of Consumer's Demand," which made a similar case.[15]

These studies did not satisfy the economics profession as providing a satisfactory theory of the consumption function. There were at least two major reasons. First, economic behavior that seemed to be determined by or correlated with rank or status was perceived as too nearly sociological to suffice, especially since such theory contradicts the basic methodological view that consumers, like all other properly economic entities, must be interpreted as individualistic maximizers, not status seekers. The latter is intrinsically a form of group behavior instead. It is possible that economics as a field of would-be science missed a notable opportunity for improvement of its oft-expressed concern to achieve empirical realism by refusing the Duesenberry hypothesis.

Second, the Keynesian concern with inadequate demand as the basic cause underlying the capitalist tendency toward stagnation or recession was still a major influence in academic social science fields and in governmental policymaking circles as well, in relation to such concerns as tax programs and government spending and welfare programs. At that time proposals were commonplace to make taxes progressive (or more progressive, if that were applicable) because the poor spend their money at a higher rate than do the rich, and hence progressive taxation would strengthen consumer demand more than would regressive taxes. Moreover, some hardy souls were advocating high rates of taxation of wealth, for example, via high inheritance taxes for the same reasons. A quite different theory of the consumption function was certain to be well-received in circles of wealth and power.

Whatever their motivations, Franco Modigliani and Milton Friedman rose to the occasion, separately. They both have been acknowledged via grant of the Nobel Prize in economics, with specific recognition of their consumption function work. Modigliani's explanation is called the Life Cycle Theory, whereas Friedman called his idea the Permanent Income Hypothesis. In fact the theories are similar enough for joint treatment for most purposes. Consumers are perceived to spend with a view to maximization of utility, not because of sociological status or ranking. On average, families are assumed to spend virtually all of their income over their entire lifetime, blurring over bequests. During the long span of working years and on through the golden years of retirement, they spend at a rate that is approximately a constant proportion of their anticipated life-cycle income rate. When relatively young, for example during the early years of married life, families spend more than their actual current income, thinking and planning in terms of what their permanent or lifetime annual income rate will be. They incur debt obligations as requisite. During peak income years, typically a matter of two or three decades, they continue to spend annual amounts equal to earlier spending, which is to say at that same percentage of the permanent or life-cycle income rate. This involves considerable saving during the highest income years. Serious analysis would have to ask what do data reveal as the actual rates of saving in these highest year situations, high-income families versus those with low income, and whether the rich do not usually die rich whereas the poor of necessity die poor? If so, the proportion of income spent is not equal, and the issue cannot be buried away in the quicksand of bequests.

Theorists finesse such questions, focusing instead on the self-assigned purpose of individualistic explanations of why the macroconsumption spending proportion of income has not fallen as incomes have risen. Clearly they have an explanation of that phenomenon. In 1957 Friedman published his *A Theory of the Consumption Function*,[16] and standard presentations of the model in macroeconomics texts to this day closely paraphrase his statements. We quote the 1988 *Macroeconomics: Theory and Policy* by Steven Sheffrin et al.:

> According to the life-cycle hypothesis, it is the variability in income *over time* that gives rise to the positive relationship between income and the saving ratio *within a cross section*. If each individual's income was always equal to his expected lifetime average, everyone would save the same proportion of his income, regardless of age and income. For such a group, the aggregate cross-section consumption function would pass through the origin.[17]

The authors continue:

> Essentially, the high saving ratio of the high-income group within a cross section reflects the relatively large transitory incomes. Since tran-

sitory income is saved, the high-income group has a high saving ratio. Similarly the low-income group has a large number of individuals who have negative transitory income and who therefore have low savings ratios.[18]

Hopefully it is necessary only to point out that all of the assertions in the theoretical formulations are merely assumed, and in no sense rest on fact. If people behaved in the particular ways specified, they would behave that way. But they do not, and the theory makes no contact with reality. Could we walk into a slum and point out to the residents that they are merely suffering from negative transitory income, which condition soon will be righted, so that over their lifetime they will save as big a percent of lifetime income as do the rich and high-income near-neighbors living a few blocks away? Then we enter the affluent districts, and observe that their savings rates are high only temporarily, because their incomes are merely temporarily high, and they are saving the transitory income. Over their lifetimes, the affluent will suffer negative transitory incomes, such that their lifetime saving rate will be no greater than that of the denizens of the slums. Everybody has periods of positive and of negative transitory incomes during their lifetime, and it all equals out. Let them all eat cake, rich and poor alike!

The a priori commitment to neo-Classical mechanism in the face of overwhelming facts is both impressive and depressive. The self-imposed necessity of formulating a theoretical model that enables the conclusion that the rich and the poor spend the same proportion of their incomes is either tragic or amusing, or both, for the stipulations are "blatantly contrary to fact," utilizing again the felicific phraseology of Nobel laureate Herbert A. Simon. We cite additional critics.

In his 1985 book entitled *Choosing the Right Pond*, Robert H. Frank commented that Duesenberry's solution proposed in 1949 was much the same as his own suggestion, which was that demonstration effects tend to weigh more heavily on lower income people, causing them to consume larger fractions of their incomes. He wrote:

> This sense of relative deprivation is not diminished by across-the-board changes in absolute income, and Duesenberry thus saw no reason for aggregate income growth to alter the share of income consumed over time.[19]

Frank cited careful studies by Thomas Mayer, by H. W. Watts, and by P. A. Diamond and J. A. Hausman, all of which showed consumption falling as a proportion of income. Diamond and Hausman summarized their findings as follows:

> our most important finding is the extent to which the savings to permanent income ratio rises with permanent income. Not only does the level of savings (wealth) rise with permanent income, but it does so in a sharply nonlinear fashion . . . [for permanent incomes below $4770 per year, the savings-permanent income ratio rises by 3.3% for each extra $1000 of permanent income;] beyond $4700 it rises by 5.7% for each extra $1000 and beyond $12,076 it rises by 14.2%. These results strongly confirm . . . that a simple linear relationship between savings and permanent income is not supported in our data.[20]

We have quoted from Frank, to include his added comments; we continue with his quoted summary of Mayer's paper with reference to various tests of these income-consumption hypotheses: "not a single one supports it. . . . I therefore conclude that the . . . hypothesis is definitely invalidated."[21]

It remains to include Frank's own summary conclusion:

> in view of the empirical evidence, the extent to which these theories have supplanted Duesenberry's relative income hypothsis must be seen as yet another testament to the power of economists' *a priori* beliefs. This outcome is both unfortunate and ironic, for, as we have repeatedly seen, concerns about relative standing are perfectly compatible with the economists' view that people pursue their own interests in a rational way.[22]

Moreover, it is not merely theory of consumption that calls macrotheory into question for clinging to mechanistic formalism, even in the face of data. Keynes had specifically rejected laissez-faire as early as 1926, with rejection of mechanism and automaticity as fundamental aspects of the overall critique.[23] The thrust toward a belief in general equilibrium was challenged by the Keynesian idea of markets not clearing, especially for labor. More workers sought jobs at prevailing wage rates than could find them, but wage rates did not fall as mechanism required. Also, Keynes argued that falling wage rates likely would have lessened the amount of employment, not increased it, by reducing effective demand. Keynes was a heretic. J. R. Hicks in England, then Alvin Hansen in the United States, set about fitting the most useful of Keynesian ideas, such as the consumption function and the related multiplier, into a framework of Classicism.

Neither Keynes nor anyone before or since has ever come up with an adequate theory of the interest rate. Does it result from wishes and actions of banks and the central bank, or perhaps from stated wishes of the government? Does it result purely from the working of forces of supply and demand? If so, what is the specification of money, or it is also credit, that is being supplied? Keynes had assigned a role, even if not preponderant or determinative, to interest rates as an influence on both investment and saving, and post hoc (after income was determined), there could be seen an equality of saving and investment, properly specified. Saving plus taxes plus imports equals investment plus government spending plus exports. But what is involved in tax collections and governmental disbursals is sharply different from private sector voluntary saving and investing.

If one abstracts enough, a function incorporating saving and investing can be contrived, and called the IS schedule. Another function can be fitted into the same quadrant, with aggregate income on the horizontal axis, interest rate on the vertical, to show liquidity- or money-preference as dependent on income and interest rate. The IS-LM model reestablished the macro approach as neo-Classical mechanism, and whatever its weaknesses it seemingly will be kept unless and until a superior mechanistic substitute emerges.

Hicks originally had sought in part to explain Keynes's model, not destroy it. But a series of developments transpired, including the idea of wealth as an effect on consumption via the "real balance effect" and the assumption of highly flexible prices. If a depression hit an economy, for example, after a year or two prices would have dropped greatly and millions of workers would stream back into the stores to spend part of their now excess money balances. This is gallows humor, to be sure; many workers are unemployed and virtually without income after an extended period of depression, and others are barely getting by. None have savings accounts of any significant size, but some sort of theory of self-adjustment to new full employment prosperity, without governmental intervention, can be alleged, necessarily so if the laissez-faire mechanistic model is to be preserved. Hicks, we note, backed away from this counterrevolution against Keynes, most pointedly in *The Crisis in Keynesian Economics.*[24]

We want to comment on one peculiarity of the anti-Keynesian counterrevolution that was developed in the 1980s. The sizable tax cuts engineered by the Reagan administration, combined with simultaneous large increases in government spending, resulted in massive deficits. As deficits grew to approximate the size of household saving, the argument was made that the government was outbidding the business sector for the supply of savings, and hence investment spending was "crowded out." Interest rates predictably would be bid up to rates prohibitive in relation to profit expectations. Hence the business sector was being rather cynically crowded out of its proper role. The government deficit should be greatly reduced to make private savings available to business at lowered interest rates.

All this has an air of plausibility about it. But is it true? What if investment spending hinges more closely upon the strength of demand in relation to present productive capacity than on interest rates, as Keynes had believed? A careful study by Robert Eisner, president of the American Economic Association in 1988, revealed that:

> As generally expected, deficits were associated with increases in consumption spending, 0.642 percentage point of consumption for each percentage point of deficit. . . . But each percentage point of deficit was associated with even larger increases in private investment, 1.383 percentage points. . . . Far from being crowded out, investment was crowded in.[25]

Neither nonavailability of personal saving funds nor the fact of high interest rates has "crowded out" investment, and the governmental deficit has been having an effect quite the opposite of that envisioned in the orthodox models. Economists continue to believe what the mechanistic, self-regulating model requires; but according to Eisner's data and "model chiseling," Simon was correct in his assertion that "statements are regularly made that are blatantly contrary to fact."

Macroeconomics is on ground fully as infirm as that on which orthodox mechanistic microeconomics has been erected, with empirically unsound degrees of insistence on Rationalist interpretations. In neither microeconomics nor macroeconomics would there appear to be any realistic chance of coping with actual qualitative or evolutionary change to combine concern for qualitative change with powerful modern analytic techniques.

Notes

1. Thorstein Veblen, "The Limitations of Marginal Utility." Reprinted in *Place of Science* . . . , 231–51.

2. Arthur Koestler, *The Sleepwalkers* (New York: Grosset & Dunlap, 1959), 497. He wrote, "If one had to sum up the history of scientific ideas about the universe in a single sentence, one could only say that up to the

seventeenth century our vision was Aristotelian, after that Newtonian. Copernicus and Tycho, Kepler and Galileo, Gilbert and Descartes lived in the no-man's-land between the two—on a kind of table-land between two wide plains; they remind one of the stormy mountain streams, whose confluence finally gave rise to the broad, majestic river of Newtonian thought.''

3. Edwin Mansfield, *Microeconomics: Theory and Applications*. Shorter Third ed. (New York: W. W. Norton and Company, 1979), 49.

4. Jeremy Bentham, *An Introduction to the Principles of Morals and Legislation* (London: T. Payne and Sons, 1789); Philip H. Wicksteed, *The Common Sense of Political Economy* (London: George Routledge and Sons, 1933).

5. Milton Friedman, *Essays in Positive Economics* (Chicago: University of Chicago Press, 1953).

6. John R. Hicks, *Value and Capital* (Oxford: Oxford University Press, 1939).

7. John von Neumann and Oskar Morgenstern, *The Theory of Games and Economic Behavior*. 3rd ed. (New York: Wiley, 1964).

8. Gerard Debreu, *Theory of Value; An Axiomatic Analysis of Economic Equilibrium* (New York: Wiley, 1959).

9. Herbert A. Simon, *Models of Bounded Rationality* (Cambridge: MIT Press, 1982); and "Rational Decision Making in Business Organizations." *American Economic Review* 69 (September 1979), among others of his writings.

10. Herbert Simon, *Challenge* (November-December 1986), 23.

11. Keynes, *General Theory* . . .

12. Simon Kuznets, *National Income, a Summary of Findings* (New York: National Bureau of Economic Research, Inc., 1946); *Shares of Upper Income Groups in Income and Savings* (New York: National Bureau of Economic Research, Inc., 1953); and *Selected Essays in Business Cycles, National Income, and Economic Growth* (New York: W. W. Norton, 1953).

13. James Duesenberry, *Income, Saving, and the Theory of Consumer Behavior* (Cambridge: Harvard University Press, 1949).

14. Thorstein Veblen, *The Theory of the Leisure Class* (New York: MacMillan, 1899).

15. Harvey Liebenstein, "Bandwagon, Snob and Veblen Effects in the Theory of Consumer's Demand." *Quarterly Journal of Economics* 64, 1950, 183–207.

16. Milton Friedman, *A Theory of the Consumption Function* (Washington: National Bureau of Economic Research, 1957).

17. Steven Sheffrin, et al., *Macroeconomics: Theory and Policy* (Cincinnati: Southwestern, 1988), 617.

18. Sheffrin, et al., *Macroeconomics* . . . , 626, n. 26.

19. Robert H. Frank, *Choosing the Right Pond* (Oxford: Oxford University Press, 1985), 157.

20. Frank, *Choosing* . . . , 158–59.

21. *Ibid.*, 160.

22. *Ibid.*

23. John Maynard Keynes, *The End of Laissez-Faire* (London: Woolf, 1926). Reprinted in *Laissez-faire and Communism* (New York: New Republic, Inc., 1926).

24. John R. Hicks, *The Crisis in Keynesian Economics* (New York: Basic Books, 1974).

25. Robert Eisner, "The Federal Deficit: How Does It Matter?" *Science*, vol. 237, 25 September 1987, 1581.

4

Evolution and Economics

In a series of articles written near the end of the nineteenth century, Thorstein Veblen worked out a philosophy that recognized the peculiar characteristics and inadequacies of the received Classical mechanism, and replaced it with a theory of society as an evolving phenomenon.[1] We will present a sketch of major ideas basic to evolutionary philosophy, followed by concern with specific ideas of Veblen.

Evolutionary Social Theory and Policy

If one considers that economic and political affairs in the world of today center upon one or the other of two systems, that of socialized planning or individualized markets, then we can assert that there is a high degree of determinism involved in the models appropriate to either case. Socialism involves Marxist determinism derivative from Hegelian dialectics. Capitalism utilizes neo-Classical determinism from what is called Classical mechanism, in the form of market equilibria, which envisions quantitative growth but not qualitative change, that is, there would always be market-force determination of socioeconomic affairs. Therein the conclusion inevitably is that history has brought us to capitalism, but qualitative change to transcend such a stage has ended since we have learned to think in terms of the mechanistic model. There is no leeway to think of transcending capitalism. It is the final stage of logical human socioeconomic organization.

An evolutionary view differs from this. "Humans take control" is a concept that emerges once one sets aside Classical, Marxist Hegelian, and all other highly deterministic systems or theories of systems.

Control is a matter of limited degree, and possibly that term should be avoided. "Humans acknowledge and exert their own influence" would be more accurate, if less awe-inspiring. To exert influence requires judgment and concurrence as to how we want things to be. Hence moral decisions are requisite throughout all branches of human social affairs. The conception of science as necessarily only the rationalization of what is—the status quo—is set aside. It is stunning, in fact, that such an ideology continues to be so rampant. Capitalist ideologues can never conclude that socialist-communist societies are achieving social optimums, of resource use and allocations, because individual choice is impaired, private property is critically restrained, and the like. Marxist or socialist-communist theorists will necessarily have parallel misgivings concerning market-oriented societies. Power and income distribution are seen to relate to family position, wealth, predation via market rigging, scandalously fraudulent and misleading advertising, political intrigues, deals, etc. What is desired, as evidenced in the markets, cannot be said to be therefore socially or culturally desirable. Since the truth value of this complaint is irrefutable—being desired cannot logically prove being desirable—capitalist theorists are capitalist rationalizers. The argument then becomes "but capitalism comes closer than socialism-communism to rational results because of its flexibility and reliance on relatively high degrees of individual choice." This we-are-better-than-you argument is not demonstrably irrefutable and is not highly constructive as a basis for social policy. A more basic consideration is that what is desired in Marxist-type societies likewise cannot be taken as definitively what is desirable.

At this point the evolutionist has an opening. We argue that science and technology continually undergo revolutionary or evolutionary qualitative change, not merely quantitative growth. The increasing know-how and technical capability will always create or constitute pressure and opportunity for socioeconomic change of qualitative type. The Marxist distinction between dynamic forces of production and static relations of production is substantially valid. It is not whimsical nor accidental that human societies have changed from primitive tribalism, slavery, feudalism, mercantilism, market capitalism, colonial imperialism, and other forms. These types are not wholly distinct from each other in every particular, but they are meaningful distinctions. They illustrate what is meant by qualitative change, even if Marxist insistence on historical inner necessity of a precisely certain historical sequence of societal forms is unwarranted.

The evolutionist proposes and seeks change in a manner only partly paralleling what is done in various fields of biology, but what is involved in animal and plant breeding and improvement programs is a useful analogy. Scientists have a conception of what would be desirable types of change for wheat, rice, beef or dairy cows, and the like. They know that the species have all evolved or changed through time into the forms now in evidence, and that further evolutionary change is certain to come. They seek to influence the direction of genetic change, and as well the relevant environment. Are the human impacts revolutionary or evolutionary? That is a point we need not debate here. It is clear that some of the changes evidenced in the Green Revolution, as an example, have been rapid and pronounced. The phrase is well-established. Throughout science and technology the same principle of deliberate human choice is involved, and identification of deliberate direction of change sought is commonplace. Human purpose and progress are not purely whimsical. We could develop wheat varieties that have small, weak plants, cannot stand drought, produce few kernels of grain, are susceptible to insect ravages, and tend to fall over at maturity, but we have a working conception of what is progress in wheat breeding, which we call improvement. To a lesser degree the same thing is true concerning socioeconomic affairs, even without pushing for dominance over change so pervasive as what is called "social engineering." Hopefully we will be able to transcend sloganeering such as "the free play of market forces brings the best possible results," or the obverse view that "socialism provides the answers; just state the problem."

Scientists try to improve horses, dogs, wheat, etc., and the surroundings in which they live, and almost everyone concurs in the general view of what constitutes progress. Accordingly, anyone describing herself or himself as a scientist is free within broad limits to conduct experiments as may be desired. But neither economists nor other social scientists have equal freedom, nor should they. Social scientists try to influence the evolution of customs, beliefs, know-how, environment, means of supply, the nature and dimensions of demand—but not genetic characteristics of humans. Thus, we deal with Lamarckian acquired traits, not Darwinian biological evolution or "Social Darwinism."

Why does anyone think it is suitable for bankers and businessmen, via control of advertising and investment decisions, to be in charge of societal change? There is confusion as to what constitutes progress in social affairs beyond such generalities as raising GNP, lowering the rate of inflation, or lessening instability of various types. Many people concur in our view, however, that part of the appropriate role of social scientists is that of proposing tentative goals for society. Numerous commissions have been established in recent decades with the charge of presenting appropriate goals for America, goals for this decade, for each state or city, and the like. Since everyone seems to agree that change is inevitable, surely it is desirable to try to shape it in some degree. Stated the other way around, we humans influence change, whether deliberately or not and whether wisely or not.

It is reasonable to refer to long-term social change as societal evolution. But what is it that evolves? An eminent social scientist offered an amusing comment on an event that pushed him to clarify his views on evolution. Kenneth Boulding related the following experience:

> My Oxford philosophy tutor, who had the curious habit of crawling under the table while giving his tutorials, commented in a high British voice coming from underneath the table on a paper I had given on evolution, "It is all very well to talk about evolution, Mr. Boulding, but what evolves, what evolves, what evolves?" After forty years I have at least a glimmering of the answer. What evolves is something very much like knowledge.[2]

He was concerned with general evolution of the entire universe and all of its subsets, however. We are concerned with social and economic evolution specifically, and therefore must be on guard against a tendency to take a "survival of the fittest" perspective and regard everything that has happened and the society that has resulted as proven to be feasible, enduring, and right. We social scientists are advisers, seeking to critique the status quo and offer suggestions for directions of both inevitable and induced change that we argue would constitute progress or improvement.

However, Boulding did not clarify certain issues concerning evolution in the way we need to do, and a few simple points must be made. Late in the eighteenth century—much before publication of Darwin's *Origin of Species* in 1859—a French naturalist named Jean Baptiste Pierre Antoine de Monet, chevalier de Lamarck, fortunately known simply as Lamarck, published several books and pamphlets that presented Lamarck's theory of evolution. The idea was that characteristics that appear in an organism as a consequence of a need created by its environment are genetically transmitted to its offspring. The concept is known as the inheritance of acquired characteristics. The biological attributes of the human species were set many millennia ago, however, and have evolved little since. The principle of inheritance of acquired characteristics *as a genetic phenomenon* hence is no more valid for humans than it has long since proved to be for other species. Since Darwin's theories of transmission of innate traits, which themselves were adapted via mutations and "natural selection" or survival of individuals with environmentally fittest traits centers entirely upon (evolving, changing) innate or genetic traits, how does evolution relate to economics? Here Boulding's comment focuses on the issue: "What evolves is something very much like knowledge." Thus we take non-transmission of acquired *biological or genetic* traits from Darwin, and combine this principle with the (altered) Lamarckian concept of (cultural) transmission of acquired traits of know-how, custom, beliefs, values, institutions, and other *cultural* phenomena. This sentence summarizes our conception of evolution.

Man's influence on his own evolution is of paramount importance. As what is desired is not necessarily desirable, in parallel what evolves is not necessarily desirable. So long as Classical mechanism is taken as the appropriate form of science, then individualistic, private property, equilibrium economics is the outcome, by assumption rather than demonstration of long-term efficiency, relevance to the real world, or any other criterion of suitability. The conclusion is immanent in the nature of the Classical/neo-Classical model, beyond logical argument or empirical proof. Pure competition or a close approximation always must be assumed as the norm, with no market transcending power in evidence in anyone's hands, and externalities as mere details to be dealt with by way of market tactics. In fact the evolutionary tendency presumably always will be strongly toward increasing concentration of power, wealth, income, influence, and whatever else might be considered worth concentrating.

Therefore, in some respects Marxism is correct in recognizing the need for qualitative change in socioeconomic relations as a consequence of qualitative change in forces of production or science-technology. Marxist thought has been useful in identifying a capitalist tendency toward concentration of power (with poverty at the opposite pole), existence of business cycles of some kind, socioeconomic stagnation, and seemingly irresistible pressures for a drift toward militarism as a means of containing crises and maintaining the system. That class struggle emerges as a historical necessity, forcing revolution and the establishment of socialism, seems as nearly disproved as sustained. However, since wealth, income, and power are much more concentrated than are talent and effort as their justification, dialectical struggle is a possibility as a developmental trend. Veblen's argument that Leisure Class emulation and concern for status are endemic seems a more accurate assessment of what transpires in our modern societies. Status struggle is not class struggle.

If the evolutionist is going to influence the direction of social change, he or she needs some tentative goals or ends-in-view. Societal habits, customs, and history will be heavily determinative of possible change. The push of the past interacts with specification of what is rationally possible as a pull from a teleological perception of the future. In the case of the contemporary United States, we list our perception of some feasible values and directions.

First, the freedom guarantees embodied in our Declaration of Independence and constitutional Bill of Rights are highly serviceable and have fortunately become firmly institutionalized. Similar philosophy has prevailed at the international level with acceptance of the principle known as the "right of self-determination of peoples." Generalized beyond its narrowest possible interpretation, it is a strong statement against imperialism, seen as substantial domination of one people by another.

Second, with their history based emphasis on individualism, some of which cannot be continued forever, Americans not surprisingly are a work-ethic society. Welfarism seems to most Americans to be a form of something-for-nothing, free lunch drag or burden on the majority of society, who are assumed to get their goods via the sweat of their brow. Corporate stock coupon clipping is not widely recognized as something-for-nothing. There is no free lunch is a slogan not lightly to be dismissed in the United States during this century. Consequently it is important to confront the issue of what activities and situations are worthy of their pay. If self-determination of persons and ethnic groups is to be realized in practice within the scope of work ethic values, it seems certain that good employment opportunities have to be available. Racism, sexism, and other such discriminatory practices interfere with genuine self-determination. In a positive vein, health services and educational opportunities must be available to all aspirants to self-determination seen as development of potentials. Whereas education is costly, ignorance is catastrophic.

There apparently is no way by which *economic man*, hedonic individualism, and the mechanistic model would provide equal opportunities because it is of the nature of a "Law of the Jungle" philosophy. Few people take seriously such proposals as the use of vouchers for all students to pay their tuition to any school of parental choice, or the so-called negative income tax as the means of providing a guarantee of adequate welfare. The school voucher proposal would amount to putting the public schools on the auction block for sale to private school companies, which might be appealing to voters in a short-run time frame while they enjoyed the sales proceeds. Concern for status is a major factor preventing the haves from supporting the have-nots at a level or standard that is significantly above a mere sociological subsistence, whether via a negative income tax or by some other procedure.

With the advent of cybernetics, robotry, and what is called high tech methods of production, it is uncertain that full employment at tasks and positions that afford real opportunity for personal development, contrasted to dead-end drudgery and hamburger frying, is possible. In the second half of this century, particularly, there is a trend toward securing foreign sources of supply on the part of many U.S. companies via the multinational forms of business arrangements. Numerous traditional American industries have totally or substantially cut back domestic production, including such basic industries as steel, shipbuilding, operation of ships, some heavy chemicals, other metals and machinery, and also such high tech fields as a wide range of electronic and optical gear. The enormous trade deficits apparently must be turned around some time soon, because of the risk of major collapse.

We will not pursue an effort to list all particular details concerning our vision of *a good society*, but we confess to being somewhat utopian, and insist social science involves effort to influence continuing change so that broad vision is desirable. Social science requires a touch of utopianism. In a sense, the greatest institutional change we urge is that of a curtailment of the amount of debt outstanding in this country and the entire capitalist world, with an adequate demand for final goods and services to derive from a much more equal distribution of income than has been the case in this entire century of industrialism. Conspicuous consumption as the route to status should be curtailed, and pecuniary values and practices should be sharply deemphasized.

Perhaps what we envision can be explained by pointing out that it would comprise almost a deliberate effort to make Say's Law workable. We assume as part of our values that considerable features of capitalism will be continued in the United States for a long time. A basic problem of our economy continues to be that of a tendency to underconsumption, which seriously restricts markets and has led to rapid rates of increase of debt to secure high levels of demand. Debt increase has to be at a rate at least equal to that of the applicable interest rates to permit long term expansion of purchasing power to be reliably effective, however, because interest as well as principal have to be repaid, and only the principal constitutes original increase of purchasing power. Interest payment goes mostly to the rich, who have low marginal rates of consumption spending. If income distribution in the United States had altered toward *equality* as much as it has moved toward further *inequality* during the past decade, higher consumption would now occur without rapid expansion of debt. Governmental spending should have been held nearly constant during this time, with no increase in military spending and a surge of infrastructure projects instead. The tax system should have been simplified and the rate structure made substantially progressive instead of becoming regressive in some ranges. If we then permitted expansion of the money supply at six or eight percent per annum (instead of the actual ten or twelve percent), severely limited other forms of debt increase, approximately balanced the federal government budget, and gave up our self-assigned role of being the "Demand Creator of Last Resort for all of World Capitalism," we could now have the economy in at least moderately workable condition.

Common sense, experimentation, and utilization of various quantitative measurement techniques would be necessary to achieve an approximation of our goals. We will not attempt number-crunching here, but the enunciated principles are sound. Vested interest groups would be opposed to these proposals, but that is not surprising.

A Matrix Model of the Zero-Sum Nature of Status Behavior in Interaction with Consumer Borrowing

In the shortsighted ways of thinking that constitute what Veblen called "the conventional wisdom," it is taken as axiomatic that consumer debt occasions or causes expansion of consumer spending. Unless the debt expansion rate exceeds the interest rate, however, after a few time periods this will be generally untrue. For example, if borrowing were at an annual rate of any constant amount with repayment of principal and simple interest at ten percent, with four-year terms of loans, repayment would exceed new borrowing during the fifth and all succeeding years. (See table 1.) Over their lifetime, householders ordinarily can consume much less if they utilize credit than if they do not because they must repay both principal and interest,

Table 1: Hypothetical Effects of Lending Process on Purchasing Power

Assume: 1. $100 loan each year at start of year
2. Repayment in 4 equal payments at end of year
3. Interest rate of 10% on outstanding balances.

REPAYMENT

1	2	3	4	5	6	7	8	Net Contribution to Purchasing Power 9
Year	Loan ($100)	1 yr debt	2 yr debt	3 yr debt	4 yr debt	5 yr debt	Total Payment	
1	100	0	0	0	0	0	0	100.00
2	100	35.00	0	0	0	0	35.00	65.00
3	100	32.50	35.00	0	0	0	67.50	32.50
4	100	30.00	32.50	35.00	0	0	97.50	2.50
5	100	27.50	30.00	32.50	35.00	0	125.00	−25.00
6	100	0	27.50	30.00	32.50	35.00	125.00	−25.00

assuming no resort to default. For this same reason of interest payment, after only a few years of carrying a load of debt it ceases to be true that use of credit enables householders to get goods now instead of later—a common rationalization for use of consumer debt—because of the curtailment of purchasing power occasioned by interest payment. Most households have been heavily in debt for extended periods, and therefore pay back more each year than the amount of funds obtained from new borrowing. And income growth is too low to save the day.

What, then, is the reason that households have turned to widespread use of large sums of consumer debt? Concern for status apparently is a big part of the answer.

The use of game theory matrix analysis will aid our explanation. This simple matrix introduces game theory technique. (See table 2.) *Hea* (top) and *Heb* (side) are *Homo Evolutionario* persons, A and B, concerned with status. They must choose whether to accept jobs with pleasant working conditions but pay not as high as that of alternative jobs available to them where working conditions are hectic. By assumption, both would prefer the more pleasant jobs, but we also assume concern for status.

If *Heb* took the hectic job, he would thereby be enabled to out-

Table 2: Game Theory Technique

HEA

	Hectic job, higher pay	Pleasant job, lower pay
Hectic job, higher pay *HEB*	Third Best for each (resulting from status race)	Best for Heb, worst for Hea (assuming status race)
Pleasant job, lower pay	Best for Hea, worst for Heb (assuming status race)	Second Best for each (possible by avoiding status race)

consume rival *Hea* and gain status if *Hea* relaxed and took the pleasant job. But if *Hea* has a stronger aversion to losing status than a concern for working conditions, he would fend off *Heb's* threat by also taking the more hectic job. The upper right and lower left sectors in the diagram show the first choice alternative for each, but such a situation requires loss of status by the other person, a worst-possible choice for him. If a status race persists, both will move into the upper left quadrant, accepting hectic working conditions to get higher pay.

Not only is this not first choice outcome for either, it is in fact the third best result, because a second best possibility exists. This would consist of their recognition that neither can win a status race so they achieve continued equal status via acceptance of the more pleasant working conditions for their jobs. Clearly we are assuming that the primary reason for seeking higher pay is quest for gain in status, rather than intrinsic utility of commodities. We do not insist that this assumption is always valid.

Next we introduce a complicating factor in the form of the additional consideration of different outcomes depending on the time span employed in the decision making, short run (perhaps two or three years) versus long run. (See table 3.)

In terms of our matrix diagram, *Hea* continues to be a person known as *homo evolutionario "A,"* and *Heb* is *homo evolutionario "B."* They are not *homo economicus*, economic man, purely individualistic felicific calculators. They have a cultural history and are influenced by customs and emotions. They are highly motivated by or concerned with social rank or status. They are assumed to be very conscious of

Table 3: *Game Theory Matrix Approach to the Theory of the Second Best*
(Short Run vs. Long Run Maximization)

	HEA	
	High debt (low consumption and saving, long run)	Low debt (high consumption and saving, long run)
High debt, (low cons. & sav. long run) *HEB*	3rd best for each, long (2nd best short)	Best for *Heb*, worst *Hea* short (best *Hea* worst *Heb*, long)
Low debt, (high cons. & sav. long run)	Best for *Hea*, worst for *Heb* short (best *Heb*, worst *Hea*, long)	2nd Best for each, long (3rd best short)

their ranking within their peer group. They perceive status, social position, and prestige to be matters of appearance. Therefore, a high level of conspicuous consumption is important in their scale of values and gauge of success in life.

In a short run setting, a high rate of debt expansion would permit more consumption purchases than would be possible by paying cash. In the long run, however, repayment of principal plus interest would necessitate reduced consumption and/or saving. This means that in the long run, high debt correlates with lowered consumption and possible deterioration of status position.

To use a lot of debt or a little is the question. Our status-conscious person must turn to game theory to reach a rational decision because status is social rather than purely individual. A zero-sum situation is involved in the sense that a winner is possible only if there is a loser. If one person moves up in rank or status, the rank of someone else necessarily is lowered. As in chess, checkers, or stud poker, the player rationally must observe the opponent's situation and anticipate moves and countermoves.

Our matrix formalizes the game situation. *Heb* must take into account the likely course of action of *Hea* and *vice versa*. If *Hea* would content himself with a low use of debt, *Heb* could turn to a high use of debt or credit purchases and out-consume his rival in the short run.

This is shown in the upper right-hand sector. If *Hea* opts for high debt use also, to avoid letting *Heb* surpass him in consumption spending, they end up in the third best sector (upper left), viewed in a long run perspective in which interest payment infringes amount of consumption of commodities. In a short run view, however, this sector is the second best since both are achieving high consumption levels and hence high gratification of wants, needs, utilities, or whatever orthodox considerations might be appropriate in this context.

Continuing, if *Heb* should opt for low use of debt, *Hea* could surge ahead via high debt, which is the lower left sector, best for *Hea*, worst for *Heb* short term (reverse names for long term impact). Thus we see that what is "short run best" for *Heb* is worst for *Hea*—and would therefore be forestalled, and what *Hea* would like most would be the worst situation for *Heb* and hence would be thwarted. However, if they cooperate, even if totally impersonally and without collusion, they can secure what is second best for each, which is high debt use by both if they are planning merely for the short run, but low debt use by both in the long run.

If long-term logic is applied, short-term, status-race consumption is restrained. Restricted use of debt increases fund availability for higher consumption in the longer run. Note that the lower right sector is the second best outcome for both parties in the long run, but only on assumption of long-term rationality. Keep in mind that the "First Choice" option for each is an inaccessible option because they have a clear motivation to block each other.

In the earlier example relating to jobs, it was necessary only to achieve the coordination made possible by realization that gain in relative position or status was impossible—it would be thwarted—in order to reach the second best solution for each participant. Hectic working conditions on the job are undesirable, short run as well as long run, but contracting a large amount of debt is undesirable only long run. In the more complex model, coordination yields a second best solution that is the opposite for the long run from that of the short run. The time span must be considered, as well as recognition that a status race is futile since each would block the efforts of the other.

Observe the following complication or indeterminacy: both participants would achieve their first choice outcome if *Hea* would turn to high debt use, but think only of the short run, while simultaneously *Heb* used little debt but thought in terms of the long run. Alternately, they would achieve first choice results if the situation were reversed:

Heb being the high debt user who thinks short term, while *Hea* uses little debt but thinks in terms of the long run.

The quest for status via consumption clearly leads to third best behavior patterns so long as short run individualized felicific calculus maximization is the decision algorithm, which is the standard procedure assumed in orthodox mechanistic economics. Our perception of maximum rationality in this situation obviously depends upon the assumptions made, which is true of all modeling that is primarily mechanistic as is the case with this model. On average humans have lives long enough that high use of debt reduces the lifetime consumption total of individuals because lenders obviously require interest obligations and total repayment rather than default.

The most rational social maximizing behavior requires giving up both pronounced concern for status via consumption, and the tendency to think and plan in terms of the short run. Consequently, debt rationally should be used rather little for consumption spending, for example, in emergencies since it does not ordinarily directly enhance income. Unfortunately, the actual evolution of American society has placed emphasis on both of these somewhat irrational behavioral patterns or tendencies. Hence, what is desired is not necessarily what is desirable. Speaking metaphorically, whereas Adam Smith said that people are led by the unseen hand of market forces to promote an end that is no part of their intent and the end is benevolent, Veblen said that people are led by the unseen hand of concern for social status to promote an end that is no part of their intent, but the end is not benevolent. This principle was recurrent in Veblen's writing, but was given special emphasis in *The Theory of the Leisure Class*.

This matrix model analyzes possible behavioral responses in one part of society, households, in relation to others, rather than individual maximization, and highlights the logic of collective action. Being within one sector, it is not truly macro in scope. From the perspective of the rich, one sees that expanded use of debt means additional interest income to them, and for a time adequate effective demand can be contrived without downward redistribution of income. In fact the rich, being lenders to the not-so-rich (the four-fifths of society with lowest incomes, let us say) much more than borrowers from them, collect much more interest than they pay. The debt-and-interest process alters the income distribution pattern toward more for the rich. Lessening the use of consumer debt as one part of programs to make income distribution more equal may be fully as important as reduction of concern for status.

Notes

1. Thorstein Veblen, "The Preconceptions of Economic Science." *Place of Science* . . . , 3 parts, 82–179.

2. Kenneth Boulding, *Ecodynamics* (Beverly Hills: Sage Publications, 1981), 33.

5

Basic Veblen

Among American academic economists, sociologists, historians, philosophers, and anthropologists, the name Thorstein Veblen is widely known. He was the strange person who wrote about the Leisure Class, describing how its members like to show off their wealth and social position with displays of superficiality. True enough, but so what? Did Veblen merely carp about the foolish behavior of the rich, or is there a foundation of theory on which we might build?

It would be easy to list a dozen or more books that summarize and dissect Veblen's work, but although familiar with much of this material, we refrain from such listing because summary of institutionalist-type commentary is not our purpose. Also, one might copy the dozen book titles listed under his name. Four of these books are collections of materials he previously published elsewhere, in two cases with substantial rearrangement. One book is a translation of an Icelandic saga, the lengthy introduction being the only part that is Veblen's. Our purpose is not to reinterpret Veblen, nor write a biography, nor contribute to the history of economic thought by developing arguments as to what Veblen must have meant in certain contexts. Further, we choose not to argue that he has been misunderstood straight through, not to try to correct any interpretations of Veblen per se, and certainly not to portray him as the one great writer whose ideas are capable of saving us all.

Perhaps our purpose can be indicated as follows. In 1934 Joseph Dorfman published a lengthy biography of Veblen, under the title *Thorstein Veblen and His America*.[1] We have changed the focus to *Our America* to present ideas that either come from Veblen or seem congruent with his ideas and that have relevance as the twentieth century closes. In addition, he was the first theorist to make full application of the principles of evolution into social science.

There are a few considerations concerning Veblen that need to be recognized, or he cannot be understood or his work appreciated. He was of a decided philosophical turn of mind or disposition all of his life, and he possessed an extraordinarily great intellectual curiosity as well as innate ability. He had what is called a photographic memory. His college and university study was largely of a contemplative, theoretical, speculative, philosophical *genre*, as contrasted to business or pragmatic matters. Apparently he studied mathematics to the usual level of the day, and he once taught a course on quantitative methods for economics. His first degree was awarded in economics, although the fields studied were broad. His Ph.D. was in philosophy. The concern with philosophy sets the tone and constitutes the background or preconceptions of Veblen throughout almost all of his writing, but at no time did he spell out in detail, systematically and affirmatively, his philosophical views or preferences. One can put together the most important aspects of his philosophy, however, with considerable certainty.

He was much influenced by his family background, which was that of Norwegian immigrants of upper peasant stock who came to the New World for land, freedom, and opportunity. The community was isolated, by design and circumstance, from the "Yankee traders" of other cultural traditions. The immigrant group was disposed toward the development of strong family bonds, group self-sufficiency with its consequent reliance on craftsmanship, production for community use rather than prime concern for vendibility, and emphasis on enduring quality rather than salesmanship. Many of these characteristics were quite foreign to the coming Age of Robber Barons, that is, the "force and fraud" pecuniary values of American life in the post-Civil War era. Veblen can never be understood without bearing in mind that he was an exceptionally gifted intellect who had, both in school and after, been thrown into contact with some of the great American minds of the day such as John Bates Clark in economics at Carleton College, William Graham Sumner and Noah Porter at Yale, and John Dewey and Jacques Loeb at the University of Chicago. Right along the values of the society in which he lived were far removed from his own enduring values, those of the community of honesty and craftsmanship.

His first book was an essay in cultural anthropology, not at all narrow-scope "rationing" economics. Nearly all of the most important ideas from Veblen's eleven books have their origin and foundations in this first book. Can we then enumerate the ideas and discuss them one by one? The concepts overlap and are not at all discretely distinct. In a sense there is just one idea: the Leisure Class and all its ramifications. Or, one can have a list of a dozen moderately separate concepts. Let us compromise and specify five: the Leisure Class, conspicuous consumption, pecuniary emulation, status, and institution. These categories will capture the peculiarly Veblenian interpretations. In proceeding this way, however, we must note that one crucial institution, private property, is not listed but is not ignored. It is treated as having derived historically from the cultural evolutionary process that involved the leisure class. Private property evolved rather than suddenly being imposed, and in a sense we are treating it as part of the cultural milieu or background. There could be no more important institution in a capitalist society than private property.

The Leisure Class is a group or subset of people, part of the total population. Leisure class *behavior* is something we all do, and consists of patterning our actions after those of persons of higher social rank than our own. There is one primary criterion for leisure class membership, and that is stated negatively by Veblen: exemption from industrial employment, which means working in any form of physical production or materials handling, distinguishable from deal making or forms of salesmanship. Veblen never thought a sharp line of distinction could be drawn, but the main idea was separability of making things from making money. The industrial classes primarily manipulate or use material things, whereas the Leisure Class manipulates tangible property, ownership claims, laws and regulations, people, debt, money, credit, salesmanship imagery, and the like. For the most part, the Leisure Class works or does deals with the head, whereas the industrial class works with its hands as well.

At all points in history, industrial employment has been requisite to life, whereas the Leisure Class pursuits were not so necessary. Drawing the line this way means that some functions of planning, experimenting, managing, and the like are industrial. Rises in productivity, mainly from scientific and technological developments, brought about surplus production or the making of more than bare subsistence minimums, as the necessary condition for the emergence of a Leisure Class. Thus the beginning of the Veblenian Leisure Class approximates the beginning of capitalism for Marx if one does not inquire about details.

The Leisure Class, perhaps better understood as the Privileged

Class, is that group of people who have claims on production done by others. In the functioning economy these claims take the form of property. Efforts at theoretical explanation of modern economies have led to recognition that such forms of property as deposits with financial organizations, corporate stock, mortgages, and much else, are intangible, abstract claims. It is certain that production could proceed in their absence, and therefore in the absence of the claim holders. The Russians, the Chinese, the Cubans, and a few other Communist groups have attempted the abolition of such property-as-claims, but they have replaced the old forms with the trappings of their new bureaucratic classes. The degree of efficiency they have achieved—or failed to achieve—is a related question.

At any rate, the Leisure Class is composed preponderantly of owners of large property claims. They are not an idle group, or lazy, or indolent, foolish, stupid, incompetent, or the like. Leisure does not mean that they necessarily take long vacations, retire early (at night or in life), have much free time around the house, etc. Veblen had his own meaning for the term, possibly unwisely so with respect to the chance of being understood. Communication of his meaning might have been enhanced had he used the term "privileged class" instead. It is clear that the Leisure Class typically is quite "harried," as one writer noted in choosing the title for his book on the subject.[2] The quest for on-going status is an on-going effort.

Centuries ago priests and warriors were examples of the Leisure Class. The warriors used overt force, fraud, and seizure, while the priests might be said to have produced ritual, ceremony, devout observances, incantations, and the like as the basis of their claims on the production of items authentically related to human necessity and well-being. Human slavery, also involving force and fraud, was likewise a major form of early property, a means for the owner to get something for nothing, benefits far exceeding costs. Women have been held in slavery by men in varying degree for unnumbered centuries, and Veblen was fully aware of what he called "The Barbarian Status of Women" as a major example of Leisure Class, exploitative, property-type relationships continuing into the present.[3]

Much wealth or property is transmitted by inheritance, the method by which Leisure Class membership is achieved and continued. Social affiliations also serve to put favored persons into Leisure Class status, and hence very nearly are property. Being brought up in classy neighborhoods in classy cities means getting to know the right people and going to the good schools. Positions, contrasted with jobs, are arranged for the nice people, and Leisure Class participation is passed along. Property certainly knows no sharp boundaries and involves more than just legally actionable claims. Does the person who is "booted upstairs" because of repeatedly displayed incompetence, to serve as an executive something or other, derive the pay and perquisites from ownership of the position conferred? The standard conception is that people get paid an amount equal to their marginal revenue productivity, and if a better executive officer were available, he or she certainly would be given the job. There is no free lunch, so the worker is worthy of his pay. One believes this, or one does not.

Manipulations involved in business enterprise are the most common route to Leisure Class membership, even if inheritance is a common mode of transmission. Financial deals and salesmanship, including advertising and promotional activities, are the Veblenian labels for the major subsets. His second book, *The Theory of Business Enterprise*, 1904, and the final book, *Absentee Ownership*, 1923, treat the pecuniary manipulations at length, and we will not explore the details at this juncture.[4]

"Conspicuous consumption" is second on our list of institutions for comment, and the idea is quite well-known. Indeed, it has come into the literature of standard macroeconomics as "the Duesenberry effect."[5] James Duesenberry, but not most of the succeeding practitioners, credited Veblen as a source. The idea is that people do their consumption spending with attention to appearances of affluence, success, and status for themselves, not just to meet creature comfort needs. Therefore, it is much easier to expand consumer spending when purchasing power expands, at or near the established ratio (C/Yd in common notation) than it is to achieve a contraction of such spending when purchasing power falls. Hence, a functional relationship between changed consumption and changed net income would have to have a shift, an offset, a discontinuity, a kink, or some other mathematical anomaly to accommodate this so-called ratchet effect. Such terms as income, disposable income, purchasing power, permanent income, life-cycle income, and so on, have specific meanings in macroeconomic theory. But consumer spending is not a reliable analytical function of anything; not disposable income, or such a measure lagged, or such a measure adjusted for changes in age or sex distribution in the population, or anything else. Regarding consumption spending, Veblen noted that

The standard is flexible, and especially it is indefinitely extensible, if only time is allowed for habituation to any increase in pecuniary ability

and for acquiring facility in the new and larger scale of expenditure that
follows such an increase. It is much more difficult to recede from a scale
of expenditure once adopted than it is to extend the accustomed scale in
response to an accession of wealth.[6]

To clarify the meaning and the importance of conspicuous consumption, let us distinguish *level* of living as the pattern acually being
achieved from *standard* of living as the pattern being sought, say for a
family. Veblen elaborated the view, now widely accepted, that such a
distinction is factual, and second, from such a relationship we infer the
specifics of consumption behavior that is called "keeping up with the
Joneses." The family—hardly an atom—not the individual, for most
purposes is the most useful unit for study of consumption, and the
"Veblen effect" (easier to expand than to reduce consumption) aids
our understanding of the impact of sales promotion and advertising.
Television, slick paper magazines, mailed materials, and other promotion means all tend to present or display images of the life-style of
well-to-do people, and present forcefully the message that large and
new cars, sumptuous homes with swimming pools, elegant clothing,
attendance at horse races and gambling casinos, patronization of costly
hotels and restaurants, etc., are the very essence of success in life. All
Americans are told every day just what is "the good life." Only those
people who are failures, with regard to everything that really counts,
do not make it into "life in the fast lane." The simple life is failure.
However, the race to match the next-higher pattern obviously cannot
be won by most players. Strictly speaking, those who most earnestly
seek to succeed are those who are most shattered when they fail.

But could one not just move up a few easy notches, and then stop
clamoring and enjoy life? Of course some few persons and families do
just this; they find a comfortable niche and relax. Most do not. No one
can determine with precision whether finding a comfortable niche and
staying there constitutes rational behavior, or whether pursuance of
the rat-race goals is more nearly rational, since individual differences
may be substantial. Nearly all observers agree that we confront here a
cultural malaise. This year's new car is old next year, three cars are
better than two, big boats are better than small boats or no boat, a
vacation house is nice, eating out is fun, but it is *embarrassing* to tell
friends that you are taking the family to a fast-food restaurant. Obviously we can "live beyond our means"—what else are credit cards
for?

Not everybody can get ahead of everybody else, so there will be multitudes of losers in the consumption rat-race. That fact itself certainly provides a basis for honoring those who can and do win. In the short run, the answer to the question of how to afford it comes as readily as the question itself: debt. *Buy now, pay later* is a far better slogan for American society than *E Pluribus Unum* because one hundred percent of us understand it and almost the same percentage practices it. In recent decades household debt has been the most rapidly growing category of debt in the American economy. This is lamentable, for consumer debt must fail as a means of raising the amount of purchases. Such debt does not enlarge the income of the person or family contracting it. Since one must repay principal plus interest, one necessarily can do less consuming during his lifetime by the use of debt than by the avoidance of it. Of course, a few people beat the system by expanding debt and then declaring bankruptcy, but such action is considered revulsive and not the sort of thing decent persons should contemplate. It is only slightly less indecent than suicide.

Pecuniary emulation is a term that could send us to the dictionary if we needed the precise meaning. Veblen intended a broad meaning, however, and pecuniary as "relating to money," along with emulation as "copying and comparing" will serve nicely. People at any point on the scale of social strata tend to compare their standing with that of others, and exhibit a bit of snootiness or disdain for lower-ranked persons, and obsequiousness, affected respect, and even sycophancy toward persons of higher standing. We ape or emulate our betters.

Of course the ranking is a matter of appearance, so everybody spends and behaves with attention to being observed. High consumption patterns are visible, while large bank accounts are not necessarily so. Accordingly, who would anticipate high rates of saving by Americans, the home of leisure class pecuniary emulation *par excellence*? For the majority of income recipients, not only spending the entire take-home pay check but using credit card and installment debt supports consumption for today, never mind tomorrow. Why do Americans, who have notably high family incomes, not also have high saving rates? There is a high degree of pecuniary emulation, probably more than in most other high-income countries. Nearly all Americans agree that it would be nice to be rich, and some have done rough calculations, which show that if Americans would hold their consumption spending to amounts equalling that of European or Japanese families, a lifetime of working and saving would result in considerable wealth. Accumulation of wealth is a favored custom, but Americans do not take their consumption cues from far away cultures and countries. They pattern after high-spending American neighbors, and live from paycheck to paycheck.

There are additional contexts in which the concept of emulation has relevance, but we need not try to be exhaustive. However, let us pose a question. Marx believed that workers would see themselves as standing in opposition to capitalists in the sense that what one class gets, the other cannot have—high wages, low profits; low wages, high profits. Workers at all times would be engaged in a struggle against capitalists, and the struggle would become harsh and bloody during depressions. Because class consciousness and stratification would be pronounced, children of workers would grow up with a distinct feeling of solidarity with their class. Is such a view realistic? No doubt in parts of the world on rare occasions this scenario has prevailed, but presuppose a distinct or pronounced pattern of Veblenian Leisure Class pecuniary emulation, quite different from Marxist theory. Capitalists are the peak of the Leisure Class, having the greatest wealth and largest incomes. What is the predictable attitude of workers towards capitalists? Emulative is the appropriate concept. The capitalists run society, in pronounced degrees: they have power; they hire and fire; they promote people or do not; they give or withhold important support in politics and elections. They build or invest, or they do not. They have position, class, and status in the community. They are respected. Therefore, they must be respectable. The old Utilitarian adage that "what is desired is desirable" becomes "what is respected is what is respectable." In both cases, what *is* begs the issue of *what ought to be*. The old-fashioned positivism is readily seen as little more than a rationalization of the status quo.

Not surprisingly, workers want their children to grow up to be capitalists, not workers. The latter case is a disappointment, a failure. A white collar job with a big corporation is a common aspiration by working class parents for their offspring. Even where the contrary situation arises, in which one or both parents urge the offspring to "take a job here in the mill, and don't think for a minute that you are any better than your old dad," the youths involved in the majority of cases rebel against such hackneyed provincialism. Workers in the United States do not so much hate or resent the capitalists as emulate them, and seek to join their ranks. Is anyone surprised that a full-fledged Labor Party has never emerged on the American political scene? Whereas Marx was certain that laborers would rise up during a depression to make a socialist revolution, Veblen was almost as certain that they never will. Talk, complain, demand higher wages, drive cars as big as those of the capitalists, send their sons to colleges where the capitalists' sons are if possible—but make a revolution? They never have, and when it might look as if they will, the chiefs merely wave the flag, and virulent nationalism takes over. How does one get American workers even to vote into being a progressive tax system, or seriously modify the inheritance customs?

What is to be said concerning "status"? The word means state or position, and accordingly we could have in social theory such relative standing or state as high position, middle position, low position. But the word status has a positive connotation. One has status, or one does not. The negative usage, low status, is avoided. That is what status is all about: high, higher, or highest standing. The concept is closely related to self-respect in meaning a self-perceived state of success and thus acceptability, with regard to socioeconomic position and the general affairs of life. But there is more to it than this, in that a person's perception of adequate status, rank, or position must be validated by the expressed or implied opinion of others. The possession of considerable wealth implies a sense of both self-respect and status, but the nouveau riche find that a given amount of newly acquired wealth yields less status than a smaller sum of wealth that has its roots suitably anchored in the distant past. The *Mayflower* must have been the world's longest ship to have brought to the United States enough people to sustain all the lineage claims since traced back to it.

What situation reliably establishes status in America? Demonstrated skill of certain types, as sportsman, entertainer, politician, physician, scholar, or the like might yield status, if notoriety does not interfere. Nothing can absolutely guarantee status, but large amounts of wealth, especially long held and used wisely in the quest, is the most reliable route and in fact rarely fails. If Al Capone did not make it, there is at least no clear reason that his children or grandchildren would not.

In communist countries where private wealth is considered to be impossible or strongly out of favor, the quest for prestige and status, position and standing, continues unabated. How is status conferred if not via pecuniary means? Perquisites, such as state-paid vacations, preferential housing, preferential educational facilities for offspring, access to special stores, tickets to artistic, cultural, or sporting events, or medals and citations—lots of medals and citations—are the means of conferring status. Pecuniary considerations thus are merely shunted aside, not rigorously denied.

Was Veblen opposed to the fact of status or status-seeking behavior?

It is a matter of degree and kind. Reasonable bases for status for Veblen would have been craftsmanship, industrial skills in the sense of production for serviceability instead of pecuniary considerations, scholarship as a subset of craftsmanship or industrial skills, and other practical skills and expertise . It was status of the pecuniary type that he saw as socially unserviceable. A true statesman, in the noble meaning of the word, would merit status. But whom can we cite? The flag-waving jingoists of recent decades apparently like to be referred to as statesmen, but this is a mistake. As historian and anthropologist, Veblen was aware that all societies, in all ages or times, have witnessed a clamor by people for status, and in all settings status has been conferred, one way or another. It would be superficial and thus a mistake to dream that status and status seeking can be eliminated. Can anyone fail to believe that whatever the basis for status, a group phenomenon at essence, some people will be able to distort or pervert the system to their benefit?

Is it love of money that is the root of all evil? The strongly pecuniary basis of honor and status is what we follow Veblen in cautioning against. To put into place a system of progressive taxes on the inheritance transmission of wealth would have a desirable fiscal impact, and of equal importance would demonstrate our awareness of the follies intrinsic to our status-laden customs. Willingness to make major corrective measures would constitute social evolution of near revolutionary scope. Forces of motivation could be constructively employed by letting each generation work for its own place in the sun, under such slogans as "there is no giant-scale free lunch," and "you can't take it with you." Because the quest for status is highly important and ties together several Veblenian principles, and because it is largely a zero-sum game, in the previous chapter we presented a formal game theory model.

There remains for discussion the concept of "institution." The word has long been overloaded with meanings, from which it follows that perhaps it should be dropped from usage as a cause of confusion. However, it is so firmly entrenched that it cannot readily be dropped. Indeed, Institutionalism is the label one of Veblen's students, Walton Hamilton, applied to Veblen's thought and methodology. We will enumerate several shades of meaning for institution, but let us note that the Leisure Class is a prime example, so these two concepts are closely intertwined and lie at the heart of Veblen's analysis: the implications of the Leisure Class institution.

Here are some near synonyms of institution: custom, social habits of thought and action, procedures, traditions, conventions, arrangements, beliefs, and occasionally ceremonies. One must bear in mind that the common usage of institution as an organization is not central to Veblen's usage. A university is an institution, each one separable from the others. But it is university as the organizational manifestation of "seat of higher learning" that accords with Veblen's conception. Likewise, the Federal Reserve System is an example of the institution commonly called the central bank. We need to observe that Veblen was trying to cope with the methodological problems of *causa materialis* versus *causa formalis*, which he studied as a graduate student of philosophy, when he came to his particular usage of institution to mean habits of thought and action. Habit connects with *causa materialis* or push of the past and present surroundings, while thought ties into rational processes, calculation, and the pull of the future, *causa formalis*. Since it is habit as a social phenomenon or the acquired traits of a society in the context of Darwinism that we are studying, we might choose tradition or custom as our closest synonym. We prefer the latter. As well as "habits of thought," institution usually means custom.

It is interesting to distinguish two classes of customs as ideal types, tool customs versus pecuniary customs, and then avoid the superficial conclusion that one of these is desirable or serviceable, while the other is undesirable or unserviceable. Veblen seemed to do this at times, but all dichotomized thinking runs the risks called in logic "the fallacy of the undistributed middle." This fallacy is well known in science as a pitfall of statistical technique. Examples would be the quite logical possibility of dividing society into two classes via several criteria: the rich and the poor, the rural and the urban, the young and the old, the agricultural and the industrial, and so on. More often than not, however, the prospects for gaining understanding are improved if we think of the appropriate range of universe as being a scale or continuum, with varying degree of whatever is involved. Tool customs would refer to patterns of behavior that focused primarily on tools and cause-and-effect procedures for getting things done or made, but in the context of economics would necessarily shade off into planning, hauling, storing, selling, financing, and the like. Pure production is a phenomenon unknown to human activities, but tool customs, tool activities, tool functions have meanings distinguishable from what we find at the other end of our continuum, pecuniary customs. Here is the range of thought and action concerned with selling, financing, promoting, and other actions that emphasize making money or profits, far more than concern with making things. Humans require things and services as a condition for life and what we call prosperity. They do not directly require financing, sales, profits, or other pecuniary categories. "The wealth of the nation is its annual product," said Adam Smith, and his purpose for such a delineation was about the same as ours. Pecuniary employments come to a place of dominance over industrial employments, Veblen argued in an important article, and his general meaning is clear.[7]

Acquired traits are what evolve in human civilization, not innate characteristics. Thus there exists only in an indirect sense a Darwinian struggle in which the fittest survive. Both tool customs and pecuniary-power customs survive and evolve in ways that are not appropriate for long-term survival and the well-being of either a society or its subset classes. In Veblen's model the pecuniary-power customs have come to center upon the Leisure Class, whose attributes are notably ill-suited to the full use of tool skills or productive know-how.

The social serviceability of all customs is to be perceived in terms of position on a continuum, serviceable at one end, disserviceable at the other. The position must be held to be subject to change. What is quite socially serviceable in one setting is not so in another, such that we are not dealing with something so simple as a dichotomy (meaning "division into two parts or into twos," in the *American College Dictionary*). If this were the case, we could simply conclude with the slogan, "up with all tools and down with everything pecuniary."

Customs, institutions, habits of thought and action, are traits that humans have acquired through time. They vary in pronounced degree from place to place, society to society. Are there no innate human biological traits of a genetic type such as would be inherited in a fully Darwinian schema? Dogs, deer, geese, salmon, and all other animal species genetically transmit not only structural and appearance characteristics, but also some behavioral traits. Disagreements among scholars who emphasize nature and those who emphasize nurture, as the distinction commonly is expressed, go on without end. The geese and the salmon seem to know how to behave or what to do as a matter of heredity. The common view may be summarized with the idea that historically, acquired or cultural traits evolved much faster and in a much more forceful way with humans than with other species because of the early development of a relatively very large brain, so that acquired traits have greatly overshadowed innate traits in their bearing on day-to-day behavior. Nurture overwhelms nature in this specific sense. Learning and education are highly regarded traits of humans, and they consist of learned or acquired rather than innate traits. What remains of innate, biologically inheritable traits for humans may well be referred to as "instinct remnants," the useful and appropriately vague language of the late psychologist Abraham Maslow.[8] His overall view was compatible with Veblen's emphasis on acquired traits, customs, or institutions.

Both environment and inheritable traits lie firmly in place in the background of decision making, such that *causa materialis* cannot be shunted aside for either a cosmology-ontology or an epistemology rooted only in rationalism or *causa formalis*. Some quotations are required:

> A genetic inquiry into institutions will address itself to the growth of habits and conventions, as conditioned by the material environment and by the innate and persistent propensities of human nature; and for these propensities, as they take effect in the give and take of cultural growth, no better designation than the time-worn "instinct" is available.[9]
>
> The distinctive feature by the mark of which any given instinct is identified is to be found in the particular character of the purpose to which it drives. "Instinct," as contradistinguished from tropismatic action, involves consciousness and adaptation to an end aimed at.[10]

Institution or custom likewise "involves consciousness and adaptation to an end," so that there is little necessity of trying to sort out acquired habits from inherited "drives" as these bear on behavior. Rational, pull-of-the-future considerations also influence behavior. Except for the instinct of self-preservation, the strongest of the specifically economic motives is the propensity for emulation. Almost always this drive expresses itself in pecuniary form, Veblen stated, which "is virtually equivalent to saying that it expresses itself in some form of conspicuous waste."[11]

In addition to this instinct of self-preservation, Veblen chose to talk in terms of what he called the "parental bent," the "instinct of workmanship," and unadorned "idle curiosity," also as inheritable traits. These are all closely related and are constructive in their bearing on actions that are serviceable for the survival and well-being of *homo sapiens*. Learning, producing, and a spirit of cooperation and group solidarity derive from these instinct-remnants.

On the other end of a continuum would be the drive for emulation, the individualistic tendency of predation as a means to power and glory, the sharply competitive viciousness exhibited in situations that can be construed as "it's me against you," and the like.

Instinct meant to Veblen much of what is conveyed in the everyday expression, human nature, and the habit-custom-institution complex is synonymous to "second nature" in common jargon. Both institutions and instincts include in their number and range constructive and beneficial items, and counterproductive, life endangering, welfare retarding, progress inhibiting tendencies or categories. Institutions are subject to change, adjustment, and improvement. A fact both encouraging and at the same time discouraging concerning these deep-rooted propensities is that the constructive and the destructive are both seated too deeply to permit easy change. To the extent that they cancel the impact of each other, instincts or propensities from both ends of the continuum can be set aside or treated only lightly for many purposes.

The parental bent is "an ever resilient solicitude for the welfare of the young and the prospective fortunes of the group," while "the instinct of workmanship is in the main a propensity to work out the ends which the parental bent makes worth while."[12]

As always, Veblen thought in terms of what we may label "comparative institutions." On frequent occasion he has been misinterpreted on this important point because he sometimes referred to "imbecile" institutions, and it is true that he considered many, or even most, institutions to be imbecilic or worse. But all cultures necessarily have habits of thought and action, customs, and tradition, so that what is involved in the evolving setting is a matter of relativity. In what ways were which institutions better in late nineteenth century Britain as compared to those in Germany, for example? His "merits of borrowing and penalty of taking the lead" argument very much hinges upon the issue of comparative institutional structures. As he wrote on the eve of World War I, in cases wherein elements of science and technology are given adequate rein,

> or where the institutional elements at variance with the continued life-interests of the community or the civilization in question have been in a sufficiently infirm state, there the bonds of customs, prescription, principles, precedent, have been broken—or loosened or shifted so as to let the current of life and cultural growth go on, with or without substantial retardation.[13]

Veblen saw inherited traits that had been standardized many milennia in the past as still playing "drive" or purpose-defining roles, some of which are constructive, others inhibitory of progress and well-being. But the biologically inheritable, standardized traits had long been overshadowed by institutions or acquired traits, which are what evolve and are transmitted in human culture. Here, too, we find both constructive and destructive customs, whether we consider tool customs or pecuniary-power customs.

More Veblenian Ideas and Some Applications

While he was finishing his Ph.D. work at Yale in 1884, Veblen published his first article, "Kant's Critique of Judgment," in which he perceived Kant's book as a linkage between earlier works by Kant, *The Critique of Pure Reason* and *The Critique of Practical Reason*.[14] Veblen observed that the former employs the "notion of strict determinism, according to natural laws," whereas the latter rests on the principle of "freedom in the person." The determinism intrinsic to pure science theoretical models, the appeal to formal mathematization, the fact that given the premises the results of such models are never wrong, and the mechanistic perceptions involved that avoid issues of qualitative change all have great appeal to theoretical researchers. On the other hand, the freewill aspects of the *Critique of Practical Reason* continue to be useful to humanistic philosophies, interpretations or theories of history, and such approaches in psychology.

It is necessary to dig deeper into this issue, for Veblen wrestled with it for some three decades, 1884–1914. He built a bridge between the views, in avoiding the dilemmas posed by accepting one view over the other, but he at no time published a clear statement of just what he did. Here is the issue: are events of the present controlled by the past, or by the future? Is human behavior to be understood and theorized as being "pulled" by anticipations from the future as all "rational" economic models since the advent of the concept of utility have urged? Such is a teleological conception, resting on the centuries-old concept in philosophy of causation as *causa formalis* or the perception of "sufficient reason" for behavior. From this approach has arisen what is called Rational or Rationalist social science, and much of the approach carries over into what is called Humanism, emphasizing human choice and values. A large number of decision models have been developed, and new ones appear frequently. What we ordinarily mean by history and social structure are shunted aside or ignored, simply by taking crucial considerations as given. Any science, or any thought for that matter, requires a degree of abstraction, so a framework or paradigm is necessary. A crucial question in any study is that

of what issues, facts, questions, and relationships will receive attention, and what will be taken as the structure of the model. When facts
or structures are chosen primarily because they fit a preconceived
model, one is committing what Alfred N. Whitehead called "the fallacy
of misplaced concreteness," which is one of the most important
insights and cautions ever offered to scholars.[15]

If we turn to the alternate view, that of the "push" of the past, is
the case any stronger, and is there better assurance of proper abstract-
ing, to avoid misplaced concreteness? Lest the questions be bypassed
or forgotten, we note that Newtonian mechanics deals with, as well it
should, an equilibrium of forces of mass and motion, and his calculus
is appropriately able *to calculate, not predict*, locations and locomotion on through time. The calculus functions are totally appropriate to
this world of mechanics, but there is zero of either real qualitative
change or of behavior. Universal gravitation has no bearing on the
issue of whether current phenomena in the sphere of human events are
controlled by push from the past or by pull of the future because
gravitation is timeless or history-less. Darwin–Clausius, to the contrary, support the push of the past view, being nonteleological, materialist, and not Spiritualist-Idealist, but support is less than endorsement as being adequate, or a claim that Idealism is irrelevant in this
matter. Of course the issue of misplaced concreteness, or appropriate
degree and nature of abstraction, is still wide open. Methods such as
analysis using functions could be wrongly employed in a push or pull
model, and bits of apparent evidence could be wrongly chosen, alleged,
or used. In the witty language of critics of econometrics, "torture the
data enough and they will confess." But what econometrician has ever
had occasion to hear of Whitehead?

To proceed with our question, however, we must ask, is behavior
caused, determined, or resultant from the push of considerations that
have come out of the past, such as habit or custom, know-how,
environment, and social structure considerations such as the distribution of wealth, income, and political power? This push from the past
and surroundings approach in large part is materialist, and can be just
as deterministic as can purely rationalist models. "Efficient cause" is
a standard label for the doctrine, as is *causa materialis*.

Historically, it is certain that religion, theology, philosophy, and the
pre-Darwinian forms of science long had clung to the doctrine that
mankind is a special form of creation. Humans, apart from all other
phenomena or life forms, possess advanced rational capacity, and
exercise their freewill potentials to shape their behavior in accord with

the pulls of calculated and anticipated benefits and pleasures. Such behavior accordingly is individualistic. A major part of Veblen's interpretations, analyses, and implied recommendations, however, rest upon materialist, determinist, Behaviorist, "efficient cause" grounds. This is stated explicitly and at length in the Darwin-inspired 1898 essay, "Why Is Economics Not an Evolutionary Science?" But his 1909 essay, "The Limitations of Marginal Utility," is perplexing and self-contradictory, in that he states approvingly both the push and the pull views:[16]

> The two methods of inference—from sufficient reason and from efficient cause—are out of touch with one another and there is no transition from one to the other: no method of converting the procedure or the results of the one into those of the other. . . . Current phenomena are dealt with as conditioned by their future consequences; and in strict marginal-utility theory they can be dealt with only in respect of their control of the present by consideration of the future.[17]

However, human behavior differs from that of other species in being determined by *anticipated* sensations of pleasure and pain, rather than *actual* sensations. Because of the rational faculty of man, the relationship between stimulus and response is more teleological than causal.

Veblen refused to make a clear choice between the two horns of the dilemma. He emphasized this teleological facet of human conduct, but sharply rebuked the hedonistic economists because their mechanistic postulates and methodology forced them to confine their attention solely to the teleological influence on conduct. In fact, economic behavior is subject to heavy influence from habitual and conventional requirements, which brings in the sequence of cause-effect, not *causa formalis*, sufficient reason alone.

Hence, biological make-up, habits, know-how, social structure, and total physical environment set the stage, so to speak, and determine or shape the desires. Then the person takes thought or does calculations in efforts to fulfill the drives, habits, pushes. Apparently Veblen considered the influences from the past as ordinarily the more important of the two.

When Veblen spoke of the human organism with "a habit of life" in the above quotation, he was writing in terms of his perception of the meaning and significance of institutions. Defined and construed as habits of thought and action, institutions were his connecting link between efficient cause and sufficient reason, Behaviorism and Rationalism. "Habit" tied into the efficient cause, materialist past, while "thought" connected with the sufficient reason, Rationalist future. Such a position may or may not seem to be satisfactory, but the immediate point is that it is clear what the issues were. Veblen refused to be fully Materialist or totally Idealist. Such an ontological position regularly is labeled Realism. By the time of his *Instinct of Workmanship* (1914), Veblen was utilizing "idle curiosity" as a major connector. Ontology is the

> branch of metaphysics which studies and theorizes on the ultimate nature of being. . . . In general, the ontological position of a school of philosophy may be appraised in terms of materialism, idealism, or realism. Materialism holds that all being is ultimately matter; idealism maintains that mind and spirit are all-important; and realism asserts that no monistic formulation explains the ultimate nature of being.[18]

Thus Veblen came up with both a definition and a role for institutions that are somewhat unique and must be elaborated. The push of the past versus pull of the future conception has been around for many centuries, tracing back at least to the Greek concern with why or cause, and the distinction between *causa materialis* and *causa formalis*. However, the details of that history need not concern us.

How did the Newtonian mechanism formulation relate to these polar opposite push-pull conceptions of cause? Since mechanism takes time and space as given, in what Whitehead called the doctrine of simple location, "God hurled the planets" and the functional relationships of mass and motion are the only focus of concern. "Ether" is a quaintly postulated medium, a necessary but inert nuisance of theory, to be taken for granted, such as came to be the case with pure competition in standard economics. Mass and motion necessarily are in an equilibrium or balance, or heavenly bodies would not maintain their orbits. There is no real change or development from mankind's perspective, and hence no beginning, no end, no causes, no effects in any sense other than locomotion. Human behavior is not caused or controlled by either past or present because there simply is no such thing as human or any other behavior in the model or outlook. Planets or moons, atoms or molecules, do not behave because this term implies decision making, thinking, choosing, or the like. Such actions as make up behaving necessarily involve freedom of choice, and such a thing does not and cannot exist or be a part of or arise as an issue in the doctrine of mechanism. Clearly there is, however, a god in Newton's system—

or rather, located outside the mechanism, the First Cause. Newton perceived nature as a vast mechanism created in a form so perfect that God then stepped back a bit, presumably watching the show but not interfering. Some scholars insist that God later died.

How has standard economics handled the causation question, push or pull? Ignoring it is the first impulse for an answer, and that is a major part of what is involved. A search through textbooks used in conjunction with the economics curriculum of United States' universities, particularly in reference to the micro- and macro-core courses, disclosed no concern with the issue. Even history of economic thought courses, where they still exist, put no emphasis on the topic, even in the section on Marx.

Let us ponder a bit more. Newton had at hand data, which he used fully in his publications. But the laws are stated totally without data, quite properly, and his format has indeed served as the very paradigm of science, and almost a part of the definition. Identification of laws as abstract functional relationships is crucial to the development of mechanics, and is both the strength and the weakness of the standard method of economics. Monopoly would prevent the maximized social efficiency results, and oligopoly would throw the whole apparatus into uncertainty and indeterminacy. So our foundation model assumes the conditions of pure competition. We then calculate that utilities are maximized, and beyond doubt such is the case. As Descartes saw quite clearly, keep it all in our minds and ignore the senses, and in terms of the reach of mathematics, we will never be wrong.

But what have we done to the issue of past versus future as controller of our behavior? Of necessity, we must abstract so we take from the past the ideas of conditions of pure competition, we postulate utility and cost functions of mathematically well-behaved characteristics. Therefore, our conclusions emerge time and again as mere restatements of our assumptions. This is "the analytic method, which supposes a problem solved, and examines the consequences of the supposition."[19] As long as we are not overly concerned with either measurement or evolutionary change, what difference can it make? In their own terms, our models and their findings are certainly correct. If the "real" world is characterized by unemployment, inflation, debt, poverty, alienation, pollution, war, protests against the system, and the like, so what? We have numerous subset fields of economics, such as international, labor, monetary policy, development, and many others, that are perceived to be free from strict adherence to theoretical purity. Mainline theoretical formulation remains a matter of "zeroing in on the truth," bigger and better logical constructions. Hence, finesses of utility-disutility, demand-supply, substituted for mass and motion, are handled as logical, mathematical exercises in calculation of how the future pulls us. We may not be able to handle the past and questions of what happened and why very satisfactorily by totally ignoring sense experience, but with a few postulates or assumptions we can talk about the future and the logical way we individuals will maximize. The future cannot have been sensed, but the mind certainly can rationalize about it. Utility in the past is dead, so let us maximize for the future as we calculate, even if it is all by assumption. Economics is a rational, pull-of-the-future apparatus.

In view of this, Professor Georgescu-Roegen posed an intriguing question when he asked, "Why Is Economics Not a Theoretical Science?"[20] How could his statement possibly be valid or correct? Perhaps there is some trick or at least some clue in the way he defined science: "logically ordered description." He envisioned two distinct parts, having the form of an inverted pyramid. The small base consists of postulates and axioms. The large mass of the theoretical structure consists of theorems, corollaries, and whatever that rest upon, or logically derive from, the postulates of the base. This is a totally unexceptional, standard definition or structural perception of science, and one thinks that surely economics conforms to the form, model, or definition. Perhaps Georgescu-Roegen was irritated that the base is not properly axiomatic or tightly drawn in the postulations. Such was the case, but that is not an adequate statement of his complaint. Perhaps testing of the propositions has not properly or sufficiently been done, with an eye on throwing out falsified propositions. This also was true; note his statement that the pretended "terrific gantlet of statistical analysis" may have been "a mere farce," partly because "if one formula does not pass the test, we can always add another variable, deflate by another, and so on."[21] It was the stubborn fact that both means and ends change, qualitatively or at their very essence, in a fashion that must be admitted to be evolutionary, and with a degree of rapidity that undercuts the postulates-theorems methodology of theoretical science that makes it impossible for economics to be such a science. Here we must clarify his mode of complaint, for the quotations come from his *opus magnum*, a central purpose of which is to protest and lament the fact that standard economics purports to be a theoretical science. That is both its strength and its weakness. Economic science has *rigor*, but it also has *mortis*, in a familiar statement. Does a proper definition of economic science include relevance to human actions? "The import of the conclusion that economics cannot be a theoretical and at the same time a relevant science may seem purely academic."[22] He saw the need to focus on the question of relevance.

Had it not been for the firm hold on minds by the mechanistic dogma that grew out of the Newtonian successes, possibly the Darwin–Clausius qualitative change perspective could have enabled social theorists to see that economic and social theory cannot be fully axiomatized because the base of human behavior, know-how, and customs keeps changing. A cause of the change is science-technology for better or worse. Hence there clearly is an inverse relationship, not capable of formalization into a function, between the rate of scientific change and the success of efforts to make economics a theoretical, axiomatic, nomological science that at the same time copes with the real world of human actions. Why, one may ask, does economics not cope with qualitative or evolutionary change by breaking from the mechanistic dogma and becoming an evolutionary science, presumably modeling itself after one of the other branches of biology?

First, because in the mechanistic dogma, science means axiomatization, which has to be based on mechanistic, nonqualitative change at the very base. Science-technology has subsets of physics and engineering that permit axiomatization, and this has been achieved with glittering success. Other, more penumbric or vaguely defined fields such as parts of chemistry, move forward rapidly in many respects without axiomatization. We leave until later the Veblen-derived idea that an evolutionary perception of economics would raise the question of the likelihood of some further stage of economic organization superceding capitalism, in the sense that capitalism replaced mercantilism, which replaced feudalism, etc. Either self-interest or ideology may hinder or prevent the development of economic systems that transcend capitalism. The denial of the presence of power in the hands of any agency, by postulating atomization and pure competition, and the denial-by-ignoring of qualitative change in social affairs clearly are prerequisites to rationalization of the *status quo*. Economics in summary cannot be a relevant and a theoretical science because the very subject matter base changes rapidly. It is not an evolutionary science because that would entail a different conception of science, perhaps one that biologists use. Such a change is replete with dangers to the social and economic status quo, and, tragic though it is, we economists, as self-proclaimed servants of science, lack either the insight or the courage to break out of the comfortable patterns of the mechanistic doctrines that we are taught in graduate school as well as earlier, to make shocking and revolutionary new departures. Our behavior is highly institutionalized.

Confronting Mechanism: Veblen, Marx, and Einstein

Because Veblen tried to build an emphasis on qualitative change into his theory, he turned to Darwin and evolution instead of attempting to use orthodox models for his purposes. As we have seen, Lamarckian, rather than strictly Darwinian, concepts have been required. His concern for change made him critical of the American society of his day, and the critical attitude led to his being branded, correctly, a radical.

His differences from Marx are important to attempts to understand Veblen. So we ask, how does the system of this other change-oriented theorist, Karl Marx, relate to the *causa materialis* push versus the *causa formalis* pull? Little discussion may be required because it is self-evident what the main lines of such association would be for dialectical materialism or "the materialist interpretation of history." Marxism is complex because one foot rests on the (inverted) Hegelian philosophy, while the other is implanted in the equally slippery mixture of British natural rights, hedonism, and the Newtonian conception of science as properly a nomological or law-based edifice. The Newtonian mechanism yields laws as strictly abstract mathematical relationships, in large part Euclidian geometry and Newton's own functions of calculus. The Hegel-derived dialectic puts process, history, change, and progress into the model, which clearly was an enormous step forward.

Is the Hegelian base the desirable or satisfactory form of dialectic and change? At either the hands of Hegel, or in the materialist shift of base by Feuerbach and then Marx, this dialectic incorporates strong elements of teleology that could not be wiped off by the materialists. Hegel had Spirit dialectically struggling toward a resolution of oneness of man with God and Spirit, or something of the sort. Marx saw history working through materialist, not spiritual, factors that were resolved by him into materialist labor in a class struggle against capitalism in our epoch. Materialism per se should not have a predetermined outcome or final stage of its development. The Hegelian source of teleological pull of something in the future raises questions concerning the melding of any form of Hegelianism with any strict form of materialism. Light is shed by the long-standing question, what are the forces, influences, or factors that cause or control the coalescing of workers into a strongly structured class that makes "The Revolution"? Do hunger and privation, in the event of absolute immiseration if that is the outcome of laws at work in capitalism, really bring worker class cohesion? Or is it largely a matter of calculated interest, a taking account of what the future could be controlled to become? Is it a mixture? Here we are skating close to the Rationalist, even spiritualist calculation of benefits or interests, and hence the pull of the future or *causa formalis* position.

Is the matter to be cleared up by appeal to Marx's famous and helpful summary of his own position, "It is not the consciousness of men that determines their existence, but, on the contrary, their social existence determines their consciousness"?[23] This states a clear direction of determinism, thoroughly materialist as Marx uses the terms. If this determinism were, in fact, the case, perhaps the distinctions would fade and there would be absolutely no difference between matter and mind. The latter would be purely an outgrowth or mirroring of the former. The rational calculating of the mind hence would not at all be a matter of formalism or spiritualism or pull; everything would come directly out of the materialist past and the present surroundings. This is the general line taken by many Marxists, and it leads further into the swamp, not out. More than two-thirds of a century has passed since the successful Bolshevik revolution, and so far the communist man, with the communist mind, simply has not emerged. How close the approximation has been only bold souls would say. Like Veblen, we choose to steer clear of such a form and degree of determinism.

What is involved perhaps is best exemplified by the great Lysenko excitement in the USSR some years back over the official party line and pronouncements that their scientific studies indicated that acquired traits, of humans in this immediate context, were transmitted by way of strict heredity. It may be obvious that such meaning or method for evolution is critical to the presumed advent of communist man, but Marxists, or Russian communist functionaries, wanted too much. Cultural evolution is not like that.

What relationship or similarity, if any, does the Veblenian schema bear to the Marxian categories of forces of production, relations of production, and cultural superstructure? Are tool customs about the same thing as forces, and pecuniary-power customs similar to relations plus superstructure? There are similarities, but overall they may be superficial, more apparent than real. Notably, the Marxian forces and Veblenian tool customs are each seen as the most basic elements of what are called science and technology, and thus in the respective models play the role of essential dynamic, the factor that intrudes qualitative change into human affairs more than do other influences. At the hands of Veblen there lingers the phenomenon of instinct-remnants or inheritable propensities, a few of which, such as the urge for self-preservation, some kind of familial concern or parental bent, and even an urge or drive for fulfillment or utilization of talents or abilities, in fact, are difficult to deny. Few psychologists nowadays use the expression instinct, but Maslow and Freud are not the only psychologists ever to use such concepts.

To observe that pecuniary-power customs is a much broader category than relations of production, a Marxist economics term, and then throw cultural superstructure in with relations, is not a very satisfactory procedure. The matter requires that we differentiate Veblen's use of Darwinian concepts from Marx's use of neo-Hegelianism. The dialectic at work means that there is a struggle between economic classes, forced by the dynamism of the productive forces in confrontation with class interests bound up with the (static) relations extant at a point in time. The struggle supposedly reaches revolutionary proportions and intensity, and the eventual synthesis is a new epoch of human history, for example, a shift from feudalism to some form of capitalism. In Veblen's handling of the evolution of acquired traits, the pecuniary power customs or institutions are always out of date and ill-suited in one degree or another. Revolutionary or rapid change does occur on occasion, for example, the cases of the rise and fall of Imperial Germany and of Imperial Japan, and likewise the changes constituting the "economic miracle" of each of these countries much later, subsequent to World War II. A further example is the change wrought in the first few decades of the Bolshevik Revolution, but definite class struggle and hence revolution is not the common case in Veblen's view. Status struggle is more central. His proposal for some form of "Soviet of Technicians" for the United States in the 1920s was perhaps a lament that such a mode of change was needed but would not be at all likely to occur. Veblen saw change as being as desirable for purposes of furtherance of human well-being as did Marx, but the needed change may simply not come.

As he argued so pessimistically in the closing chapter of the 1904 *Theory of Business Enterprise*, what follows the peak development of industrial and commercial capitalism is more likely to be a form of military state than socialism. His evolutionary system drifts, with qualitative or cultural change coming sporadically and rather unpredictably as to time or type, instead of inexorably at a steady pace and unilinearly. Veblen would have agreed with Georgescu-Roegen's statement that

> the intricate issues surrounding the ideas of Change have divided philosophers into opposing schools of thought, one holding that there is only Being, the other that there is only Becoming. Science, however, can follow neither of these teachings. Nor can it follow the dialectical synthesis of the two into Hegel's tenet that "Being is Becoming." Science can embrace only the so-called vulgar philosophy according to which there is both Being and Becoming, for by its very nature it must distinguish between object and event. In other words, science must try to remain analytical throughout, even though . . . it cannot succeed in this forever.[24]

Several ideas converge upon the Marx-Veblen distinction. Let us ask, what is the nature of capital for each of these two theorists? For Marx the answer is simply two words: congealed labor. The concept is entertwined with his version of the ancient labor theory of value, and it leads into his use of the dialectic, the break-down of capitalism, the inexorable arrival of socialism, and the core of Marx's mature years' reliance on analysis. His model consists of two productive departments, one for producers' goods, the other turning out consumer goods, plus two consumption sectors, the capitalists and the workers. Labor power and the products, from labor power, sell for what they are worth, what they (now) cost. Competition assures that quantities of equal value in fact sell for money of equal amount. The rate of exploitation of labor is brought to equality for each department by the forces of competition. However, there is no reason to believe that a requisite condition for the analysis, that of equality of "organic composition of capital"—that is, of variable and constant capital—in fact prevails. Then prices will not accurately reflect values. Marx sought a way out of his analytical impasse by asserting that total surplus value could be redistributed between the two departments in a way that would equalize the rate of profit. Such redistribution seems totally implausible, and neither he nor anyone since has been able to explain how and why this happens. The capitalists involved are not going to pool profits and then split the pool in a fashion that will yield equal rates. Analysis is sacrificed to a preconceived outcome. When a question is asked repeatedly for many decades and the answer is not found, there is reason to suspect there is something wrong with the question. Such is the case with the transformation problem. Marx's analysis breaks down because if the organic composition of capital is unequal, pure competition does not prevail, and under conditions of partial monopoly nobody should expect profit rates to be equalized. Productive processes with unequal organic composition of capital are qualitatively different. Hence qualitative change is at work in a much shorter time frame than Marx had assumed and the dialectic involved is not strictly Hegelian. Different industries will be at different stages of development at any point in time, which is not the same thing as society itself moving from one stage to another. There is less than pure competition prevailing at all historical time periods in certain industries and *à la* Veblen, the property-and-markets system has always staggered, never performed as per any of our analytical models, and change remains an open question.

The insolubility of Marx's problem derives from the fact that all of the important relationships are contained *within* the postulates of the model from the very beginning, and there is accordingly no flexibility concerning the conclusions. Grant the validity of the full set of postulates, assumptions, functional relationships, etc., and capitalism fails. But Georgescu-Roegen's work as a matter of careful analysis, and that of Veblen as a matter of intuition, conclude that no analytical, mechanistic model can adequately account for everything that is relevant to human behavior taken in large slices. The Marxian transformation problem is indeed a paradox. Production processes with unequal organic composition of capital are qualitatively different from each other. That, of course, can be granted as a truism. Then Marx's analytical model holds where only quantitative differences, of scale let us say, pertain. Neither his nor any other analytical model can properly deal with qualitative aspects of process-as-change.

Veblen stayed outside these traps of overreliance on analysis, and by his choice of the Realist ontology was able to avoid the determinism intrinsic in both totally materialist and in completely rationalist models. He left room for considerable freedom of choice by humans, both at the individual and the macro or large group level. Neither Marxism nor standard economics, that of "economic man," in fact permit freedom. Whatever one does, it *must be* that such a course of action was utility-maximizing, or in the case of Marxism, furthering the class struggle.

To return to the other half of our query, Veblen wrote an article, "On the Nature of Capital," in which he asserted that *in capitalism*, capital at root is nonmaterial, a matter of community skills, with customs that permit a business enterpriser to gain control of skills as property and raise money by selling equity claims and borrowing against apparent earning power.[25] In capitalism, capital is a purely pecuniary category relating to earning power, and it is neither saved into existence nor exploited from workers. Accumulation of know-how or skills is the crux of capital formation for Veblen.

How would Veblen answer the query, what is the amount of capital involved in a certain firm? He might well begin by asking, what is the value of your house? The answer in both cases is "whatever it would sell for." A firm is worth a figure derived by the equation, annual profit divided by appropriate interest rate. A firm with one hundred thousand dollars annual profitability is worth one million dollars, if the interest rate is ten percent. Note that putative earning power, and hence amount of capital, are entirely dissociated from issues of amount invested, savings, accumulation of surplus value, etc. Calculation of value reaches toward the future, not toward the past.

The dialectic is the mode of adjustment of static relations to dynamic forces in the Marxian schema, with class struggle and revolution taking society from one phase to another at a higher stage of development and mode of production. Veblen saw a time lag between qualitative changes in tool and know-how customs, and adjustment in other aspects of traditions or customs, those relating to power and pecuniary considerations. Tool customs or know-how are dynamic; power pecuniary customs are change resistant because the controlling Leisure Class holds wealth, status, and power at a point in time and thus has strong motivations for opposing change. The ruling capitalist class will permit expansion of society as presently structured if such growth does not constitute a threat to their control. Cultural development, meaning qualitative change in how things are done, for whom, and who is to be in control—the considerations that might take us from capitalism to some other form of society, just as feudalism was replaced by capitalism—is far beyond the pale of change that is legitimately to be contemplated. History has been "zeroing in on the truth" in bringing capitalism, and it is preposterous to think of transcending this trend.

With regard to the Leisure Class:

the characteristic attitude of the class may be summed up in the maxim: "Whatever is, is right"; whereas the law of natural selection, as applied to human institutions, gives the axiom: "Whatever is, is wrong." Not that the institutions of to-day are wholly wrong for the purposes of the life of to-day, but they are, always and in the nature of things, wrong to some extent. They are the result of a more or less inadequate adjustment of the methods of living to a situation which prevailed at some point in the past development; and they are therefore wrong by something more than the interval which separates the present situation from that of the past.[26]

Concerning the evolutionary change of acquired traits, it is easy enough to see which class stands to lose from change and opposes it. Because of its wealth, its power, and the respect accorded it by the community, the leisure or privileged class is to a high degree sheltered or protected from most stresses and strains of commonplace economic exigency—but not fully from major crisis or collapse. Members of the leisure class need not concern themselves with struggle for the means of life, but instead struggle for status. By definition at the top of the hierarchy of wealth, power, and privilege, the class and its members strongly oppose most forms of genuine social, political, and economic change. The function of the leisure class in cultural evolution is to retard change and conserve what is obsolescent.

In effect, to advocate social change is to renounce one's membership or identification with the Leisure Class because, in colloquial terms, the class at the top can only come down if there is change. Hence, conservatism is a characteristic of the upper classes and therefore is decorous. Social innovation or change, being a lower-class phenomenon, is vulgar and unseemly. Protest of the status quo is bad form.

If one summarizes Marx concerning the prospects for capitalism with the statement that it is the accumulation of capital itself that constitutes the essential barrier to uninterrupted accumulation of capital, then one might summarize Veblen by saying that it is the conservatism of the Leisure Class that constitutes the greatest hindrance to progress in a business dominated industrial society. Since structural change of a major qualitative sort theoretically is possible within the boundaries of what we would call capitalism, Veblen's view is not equivalent to that of Marx. Capitalism may keep moving along, likely tending towards a state of stagnation. Drift toward a military state is more likely than revolution leading into socialism. Any statement of either position requires elaboration to afford much understanding.

Veblen saw fit to set aside the usual application of Newtonian worldview and philosophy to the realm of geological and biological evolutionary phenomena, including the subset called economics. Biological heredity involves mutations, which interfere with or run alongside functional calculations of what traits an offspring will inherit from its biological lineage. When considering human culture, however, we might bear in mind the idea well expressed by Georgescu-Roegen, that there is

> a fundamental difference: the biological evolution is Darwinian; it does not transmit acquired characters. Tradition, on the contrary is definitely Lamarckian, that is, it transmits only acquired characters, especially those that have proved to be useful to the community. Needless to say, tradition, just like biological heredity, often transmits institutions that are indifferent or deleterious.[27]

This statement serves to clear up the matter of why human behavior does not develop the patterns appropriate for communist man, and at the same time leads us to a key issue concerning the philosophical significance of Darwin. What difference might it have made had Darwin's work been done a century or so before that of Newton? The direct impact could have been a profound separation of science from theology, religion, and the churches but on a nature-centered base of biology and its evolutionary processes of qualitative change rather than the doctrine of mechanism from Newton. The important evolutionary process in human affairs is this evolution of tradition or culture, consisting wholly of acquired characters.

There is immanent here a strong challenge to all forms of racism, but that is not the present topic. Cultural anthropology is the standard name for the branch of science concerned with the study of cultural evolution. Had cultural anthropology of this type originated long before Newton, the history of science and especially social science might well have taken a different course. Anthropologists have found a great diversity of human organizational and valuational patterns that seem to have got the job done. Rarely do anthropologists eulogize economic man. Following the previously quoted statement that "tradition . . . often transmits institutions that are indifferent or deleterious," we would obey the dictates of anthropological methodology and ask, what are the desirable but also the undesirable attributes of an economic man, mechanism-based economics, and the forms that capitalism in fact has taken in our day and age?

Economics is the study of man's efforts in turning the forces of his environment to account. In a cross-sectional or point of time frame of reference, this could be taken as similar to the allocation of given, limited means to given, limitless ends. One may take no exception to the pursuit of that line of thought by some scholars, but the greater issue is the question of how both the ends and means arise and evolve through time. Anthropology, history, and qualitative change are the greater concerns, not statics nor mechanism.

Likewise, another profound critic of Newtonian views and methodology chose to set aside much of the apparatus of Classical mechanism, an eminently famous figure in Newton's own fields of physics and cosmology. Albert Einstein also disregarded the laws of our orthodox economics:

> historic tradition is, so to speak, of yesterday; nowhere have we really overcome what Thorstein Veblen called "the predatory phase" of human development. The observable economic facts belong to that phase and even such laws as we can derive from them are not applicable to other phases.[28]

Who consciously would consider "Laws of Predation" satisfactory as the foundation of social science? The answer has two parts, both of which lead into evasions. All modern economists of orthodox persuasion would fail to see any validity in Einstein's assertion that we remain in a predatory phase of development. Second, economists simply cling to the mechanistic world-view without seriously questioning it. Descartes was correct when he held that if one keeps everything in the mind, and deals only with logic and mathematics, one can avoid ever being wrong. Economics thus has models that are correct forever. We are zeroing in on "The Truth." Facts or data will be embellishments, always supporting, beyond doubt and because thusly assumed, the maximization of utility and profits, etc. Einstein held a pessimistic view that our modern values and modes of thought are critically faulty:

> I have now reached the point where I may indicate briefly what to me constitutes the essence of the crisis of our time. It concerns the relationship of the individual to society. The individual has become more conscious than ever of his dependence upon society. But he does not experience this dependence as a positive asset, as an organic tie, as a protective force, but rather as a threat to his natural rights, or even to his economic existence. Moreover, his position in society is such that the egotistical drives of his make-up are constantly being accentuated, while his social drives, which are by nature weaker, progressively deteriorate. All human beings, whatever their position in society, are suffering from this process of deterioration. Unknowingly prisoners of their own egotism, they feel insecure, lonely, and deprived of the naive, simple, and unsophisticated enjoyment of life. Man can find meaning in life, short and perilous as it is, only through devoting himself to society.

The economic anarchy of capitalist society as it exists today is, in my opinion, the real source of the evil.[29]

Einstein went on to argue forcefully for the establishment of a socialist economy and an educational system focused on social goals, fully recognizing the crucial problem in socialism of protecting rights and freedoms of the individual as a "democratic counterweight" to the power of bureaucracy.

Does one merely ignore the shrugging of shoulders that likely would result from asking economists what they think of Einstein's statement? The simplistic response is to say that he should have stuck to physics since he probably never took a course in economics. But there is an important thought hidden away here: people who take economics courses are spoon-fed the mechanistic dogma, and once so inoculated generally do not ever break free of its hold. Einstein, of course, had struggled against that same mechanistic doctrine and had freed his mind and gone on to develop his own alternate system. The fact that he had transcended Newtonism is what makes his insights valuable, coupled with his innate genius, not whether he had studied what some professor and a few authors had believed concerning economics.

Einstein's conception of the importance of drives, threats, organic ties, insecurity, prisoners of their own egotism, and the like, definitely established his vision of psychology as somewhat akin to Veblen's view of humankind as an evolving biological species. There was a strong rejection of any basis for interpreting human behavior as a matter of natural order individualistic maximization of utilities, and there was powerful protest against institutionalization of attitudes and practices of "the economic anarchy" of capitalist society. Einstein asserted that man can only find meaning in life by devoting himself to society. Veblen sought the same goals when he laid emphasis upon the parental bent and the instinct of workmanship. A further point is that Einstein's views of psychology and his concern for democracy to constrain the power of bureaucracy establish an affinity with the thought of the young Marx, not the later Marxist effort to salvage Newtonian mechanism and the methods of analysis by dumping all aspects of qualitative change into the great quicksand of Hegelian dialectics.

But is there not a social phenomenon at work beyond the Leisure Class as a socioeconomic construct? Additional understanding of why social conservatism is so deep-rooted and effectively resistant to change may be gained by positing what we will call "careerism."

Differing forms of this idea have been around long enough so that it is unnecessary to try to establish legitimacy through precedent. Except for inherited wealth, the source of most incomes is employment. The categories of employer are limited in number, the important ones being self-employment, business companies, government, and organizations such as churches and labor unions. There are few categories. If success in life involves moving up a ladder of promotion and income, as it certainly does for nearly everyone, then the essential meaning of careerism comes into focus. Careerism means conducting one's life in terms of whatever actions are supportive of a successful career.

Is there an identifiable pattern to actions that support or enhance the chances of success in a career, particularly with reference to contemporary American society? First, one may observe that with the exception of self-employment, which accounts for one in ten employed Americans, we work for organizations. Nearly all organizations have a formal managerial structure that is of a hierarchical nature. We work for bosses, who work for bosses, who work for bosses. Promotion, status, pay increases—in short, success—comes by way of doing what is expected or well-regarded. It is the regard of superiors that is important to career success. This means in turn that one must recognize that pleasing an immediate superior means doing things that please *his* or *her* superiors, to support his-her careerism. It is a basic tenet of management that decisions must be taken in light of authority considerations, meaning at the top. Always the stipulation is added that "lines of communication" should be kept open, so that ideas and information flow or move both ways, up as well as down. People at the top either are owners or else are associated with owners if we are considering that largest category of employer, private business. Top people in government are not notably different, and frequently have been in business positions and aspire to return to business positions. Or if they are working in civil service posts with job security, career success is still facilitated by doing, thinking, speaking, voting—in a word, living—as the people above one's place in the hierarchy regard as proper. Those persons at the very top comprise the upper class, and conservation of the system at the pinnacle of which they are located is a deep-rooted tendency. We see that in the interests of careerism, power is fully acknowledged to reside with persons at the peak of the hierarchy, and it is incumbent upon all reputable people to follow their lead. One can hardly fail to see that incumbent is a term that carries great force. Whom might we follow other than the leaders?

With respect to scholarship and efforts at theoretical explanation of society, one might argue that the universities long have been the locale for "the leisure of the theory class." Does the practice called tenure provide protection from the pressures of careerism and encourage the scholar to "tell it like it is"? Tenure is indeed helpful, but more is to be said. The scholar was first a student, sitting at the feet of scholars who were students. One learns what is being taught, and it is a rare soul who jumps out of the methods and models laboriously mastered in graduate school. The aspirant for an academic career attends the proper schools as a career supporting act. The proper schools are so in the eyes of people who matter because the schools support the social status quo, receive private grants and governmental financial support, have personnel of demonstrated career success in government and business, have reputations for success of their graduates in the careerism track, etc. Conservatism accordingly permeates university campuses and has been sidetracked in the United States only briefly and somewhat superficially by such phenomena as wars of which draft-age male students did not approve. Academics of conservative and reactionary persuasions not uncommonly complain that their views do not get fair hearing in the academic world because of the liberalism that is asserted to dominate the campus scenes, but what is involved is more nearly the opposite. The conservatism that dominates the scene discourages expression of views that are far off the beaten path. Radicalism is not a road to academic employment except in the rare case of a school that may be seeking a "house" radical.

Once employed, all modes of scholarly behavior, such as materials used in teaching, scholarly publications and efforts at the same, membership and participation with the appropriate professional organizations, and so on, serve effectively to shape the career candidate into respectable pursuits as a condition of promotion, and of course into that cloak of protection, tenure. He is demonstratedly safe before he is tenured. It is naive to assume that once tenure is granted, the budding leopard will change his spots.

When one works for someone else, success in the climb up the career ladder depends upon receipt of a boost here and there from colleagues both higher and lower on the ladder. To be well regarded is to be conservative. "Innovation is bad form." With the self-employed the case differs only slightly. There is no formal organizational hierarchy, but the need to be well-regarded is equally great for the small-scale operator, and regard is bought with the coin of conformity and conservatism. Playwright Arthur Miller captured the meaning precisely in his *The Death of a Salesman*. Willy Loman was "well-liked."

We conclude with the thought that it is hardly surprising that there are no major political parties in the United States that are not staunchly conservative of the business system status quo, which is the crucial consideration bearing on the prospects for change. As long as no real change is proposed, it is quite acceptable to indulge in empty expressions of obvious types, such as "capitalism would work even better if we did something about poverty, racism, sexism, and environmental destruction." The effort of course is to conserve all too much of society as it is, for evolution moves along.

Notes

1. Joseph Dorfman, *Thorstein Veblen and His America* (New York: Augustus M. Kelley, 1961).

2. Steffan B. Linder, *The Harried Leisure Class* (New York: Columbia University Press, 1970).

3. Thorstein Veblen, "The Barbarian Status of Women." *Essays in Our Changing Order* (New York: Viking, 1954), 50–64.

4. Thorstein Veblen, *The Theory of Business Enterprise* (New York: Scribners, 1904); *Absentee Ownership* (New York: Viking Press, 1954).

5. James Duesenberry, *Income, Saving. . . .*

6. Veblen, *Theory of the Leisure Class*, 102.

7. Veblen, "Industrial and Pecuniary Employments." *Place of Science . . .* , 279–323.

8. Abraham Maslow, *Towards a Psychology of Being* (New York: Van Nostrand Reinhold, 1968); Abraham Maslow, *Motivation and Personality* (New York: Harper and Row, 1954).

9. Thorstein Veblen, *The Instinct of Workmanship* (New York: Huebsch, 1914), 2–3.

10. *Ibid.*, 4.

11. Veblen, *Leisure Class . . .* , 110.

12. Veblen, *Instinct . . .* , 48.

13. *Ibid.*, 25.

14. Thorstein Veblen, "Kant's Critique of Judgment." *Essays . . .* , 175–93, esp. 175.

15. Alfred N. Whitehead, *Science . . .* , 75ff.

16. Veblen, *"The Limitations . . . ,"* in *Place of Science. . . .*

17. Veblen, *Place of Science . . .* , 237; see also 238 and 235n.

18. *The Columbia Encyclopedia.* 2nd ed. (Morningside, N.Y.: Columbia University Press, 1956), 1443.

19. Russell, *A History . . .* , 560.

20. Georgescu-Roegen, *Entropy . . .* , 322–30.

21. *Ibid.*, 339–40.

22. *Ibid.*, 329.

23. Karl Marx, *A Contribution to the Critique of Political Economy* (Chicago: Charles H. Kerr & Company, 1904), 11–12.

24. Georgescu-Roegen, *Entropy* . . . , 211.

25. Veblen, "On the Nature of Capital." *Place of Science* . . . , 324–86.

26. Veblen, *Theory of the Leisure Class*, 207.

27. Georgescu-Roegen, *Entropy* . . . , 359.

28. Albert Einstein, "Why Socialism?" *Monthly Review*, vol. 1, no. 1 (May 1949): 9.

29. Einstein, "Why Socialism?," 12–14.

6

Evolution and History: Modern Germany and Russia

Industrial capitalism does not function any more smoothly over the long haul for Veblen than for Marx. The predatory system could be expected to follow its own deep-seated animus into nationalism and militarism, rather than, by some unlikely procedure, break the power of the ruling apex of the Leisure Class and establish an industrial democracy. He feared that nationalistic militarism was more likely than industrial democracy.

Veblen was opposed to the opportunistic forms in which the pragmatic action of his day usually was exhibited, and asserted that pragmatism usually leads merely to the creation of "maxims of expedient conduct." Science creates only theories, and knows nothing of programmatic policy or utility or better or worse, but work or wisdom of the pragmatic type does not contribute to the advance of knowledge of fact. Its bearing on scientific research is chiefly that of inhibition and misdirection.

> Wherever canons of expediency are intruded into or are attempted to be incorporated in the inquiry, the consequence is an unhappy one for science, however happy it may be for some other purpose extraneous to science. The mental attitude of worldly wisdom . . . [has as its] . . . intellectual output . . . a body of shrewd rules of conduct, in great part designed to take advantage of human infirmity. [1]

However—and fortunately, to be sure—there is no intrinsic antagonism or conflict between science and scholarship, comparable to that between pragmatic attitudes and scientific inquiry. Scientific pursuit of scholarship shares with science the quality of not being pragmatic in its purpose. But since Veblen acknowledged having been influenced in his philosophical views by both Charles S. Peirce, under whom he studied for a time at Johns Hopkins, and John Dewey, a colleague at the University of Chicago, his views on pragmatism must be dualistic. In later years Peirce expressed revolt against what was being thought and taught as pragmatism, and declared his inclination to label himself a "pragmaticist," instead. It was the tendency to treat pragmatism as expediency or the handmaiden to what we are calling "careerism" to which Peirce objected, and on this point Veblen seems to have followed suit. The authentic pragmatism was based in a foundation of what Veblen called "idle curiosity," or search for truth in cause-and-effect "cumulative causation." With both men, their opinion of pragmatism depends totally upon definition or specification.

Two perceptions or theories of history of great sweep but profoundly different content underlie what Veblen was attempting in this material concerning both pragmatism and the rise of modern Germany and the USSR.

First, the Marxist interpretation of history derives from Hegel and envisions a dialectical process that deterministically takes mankind through stages of society, feudalism to capitalism to socialism to communism.

Second is an alternate view, which is less clearly structured and is ill-defined in most manifestations, being of the nature of philosophical preconceptions. Prior to the Bolshevik Revolution in 1917, the world consisted of two parts: Western civilization, which had come through the Renaissance and the Industrial Revolution, c.1750–1850, and the backward areas that comprised the rest of the planet. Western Europe and its progeny were bringing progress to the world, via science, private property, representative government, and laissez-faire *homo economicus* policies. Social theory necessarily would comport with Newtonian atomistic individualism, with little need for concern with history since decision making resulted from Rationalist, Idealist-Spiritualist modes.

Anchoring of scholarly effort in constructions of dialectics has rendered Marxist and communist-world thought inflexible and deterministic. Societies are thought to be led through stages culminating in communism, but Western world social science orthodoxy is still bogged down in remnants of Classical mechanism, and holds to the idea of linear progress via the individualistic laissez-faire model as the last word in efficient organization. It is pragmatic or expedient to constrain social thought and interpretations within the bounds of the received model. Unfortunately, major departures in interpretation and recommendations are treated as bad form and are infrequent. For example, institutional lag and difficulty or inability to make changes in the way things are done, who has power, who gets the wealth and income and how it is used, are issues not readily raised. This is the case because they intrinsically constitute radical questioning of the status quo. Careerism is pragmatic, and we know by assumption or postulation that we are already in or near equilibrium of supply-demand, at or near maximum efficiency. As quite clever people, we would be unlikely to be doing things poorly or in a way that failed to maximize. Hence it is impossible to visualize our economy as genuinely out of equilibrium. After all, a balance of forces is as intrinsic to Newtonian-Smithian economics as to Newtonian cosmology and physics. The status quo thus is nearly perfect, and any conceivable faults are attributable to interference with natural forces.

On the Merits of Borrowing and the Penalties of Taking the Lead: The Case of Germany

Within the scope of Veblen's better known theoretical contributions, the 1915 *Imperial Germany* contains an example of institutional lag that is noteworthy in its own right, but frequently is cited with omission of an important lag phenomenon. During the late Middle Ages, England was culturally in arrears in comparison with several other countries, including Germany. England borrowed bits and pieces of know-how and put them into service in her own cultural milieu, which was different from anything on the continent. She surged ahead with an Industrial Revolution during the eighteenth and early nineteenth centuries. Late in the nineteenth century, the British thought they were doing nicely with their Victorian Era, but their empire apparently was more fundamental to their prosperity than was their own efficiency. They failed to modernize as well as they might have done for Germany "stole a march" on them. Britain then suffered the consequences Veblen called "the penalty of taking the lead." Productive and transportation apparatus in Britain were locked into patterns laid out during the earlier surge of improvements, and customs concerning what were the right and proper ways of doing things were firmly cemented into place so that change was out of the question. In the homeland of

Newtonian philosophy, progress could hardly have been viewed otherwise than as a matter of getting things straight, and then conserving what is right.

Germany, brought out of the quagmire or hodgepodge of princely feudal states into consolidation as a nation only by 1871 and the Franco-Prussian War, was comparatively quite backward. Her leaders, in turn, borrowed what they chose of British science and technology, and put it rapidly into service building the Fatherland as a relatively close-knit, planning society. Cartelization was taken for granted and used to effect economies of scale, sharing of research findings, and the layout of industry and the transportation network, particularly railroads, with a view to national-scope efficiency. Friedrich List had published his *A National System of Political Economy* in 1844, and Germany had long been the center of the Historical School of economics, which opposed nearly every tenet of British laissez-faire economics.[2] It is a fair statement that the doctrines of Adam Smith have never, to this day, been fully and widely accepted in Germany. Since Bismarck and the time of which we are speaking, a large and positive role for the state has been evolved and has come to be taken for granted in Germany. British institutions lagged badly in making adjustments appropriate for the efficient use of the never static state of technology or the industrial arts. Germany incorporated the know-how into a pattern of conventionalities that permitted far more efficient use.

The patchwork of states and principalities that comprised pre-Imperial Germany had involved the formation and use of a far-flung bureaucracy that necessitated training for its needs and provided experience in its running of the types useful in building a coordinated Fatherland. In some respects the educational standards in Germany were equal to those of any other European country of the time. Her backwardness was not that of stagnation and frustration, which might have been the case earlier, say in 1848. Subsequent to the Franco-Prussian War, Germany was characterized by multitudes of handicraftsmen and traders with good skills and experience. What was needed was modern large-scale technology, properly laid out and managed. Germany was fortunate enough to avoid the invisible hand of Adam Smith, and instead followed the "ancient cameralist aim" of using the nation's resources for dynastic purposes of the state. British or American economists, as true sons of Adam Smith, would have called the German system mercantilism and would have argued that the giant role assigned the state, the bureaucracy, and monopolistic cartels would insure that the entire scheme would be doomed to gross inefficiency and failure. But as Veblen saw the matter, and apparently this view was shared by the Germans and was borne out in historical fact, they avoided much of the waste, duplication, competitive back-biting, and overall poor planning—if indeed the word can even be used in this context—that would have accompanied business enterprise *à la* the competitive model.

There were clear enough reasons for coordinated planning for an industrial revolution:

> As is well-known, the Fatherland is not at all specially fortunate in natural resources of the class that count toward modern industry. As regards mineral resources Germany has a decided advantage in one item of potash alone. The iron and coal deposits are well enough, but can by no means be accounted as better than second best, in point of quality, location, or abundance.[3]

Forest and food producing resources could not be said to rank any better, and the location was problematical, with much of the industrial resources lying near the frontiers of traditional rivals and enemies. Agriculture, where both the latifundist Junker and the minifundist peasant were continued, was "kept" (subsidized) through the use of tariffs and other transgressions of market forces, as has long been the case with most countries. It goes almost without saying that banking, commerce, and industry were favored and sustained via cartels and the prevention of free market competition. Giant banks and cartels of business and industry were put into place where it counted most for both rapid and sustainable industrialization and modernization and what is called heavy industry. Chemicals, metals (especially steel), machinery, shipbuilding, locomotive and other railroad equipment, and mining and smelting to match were planned and put into place. The parts of the burgeoning puzzle fitted together nicely in that the arrogant but traditionally powerful Junker class spread their power via new business giants, including banks, with dominant influence in government. They dominated the military machine, as would have been expected and was unavoidable, and through measures that kept the peasantry going they had the support of that always reactionary group.

The British had their easy reliance on their gigantic overseas empire for supply of materials they wanted, and the demand for finished products. They were content with what was resulting from their practice of laissez-faire, pure competition, "each man for himself cried the fox in the henhouse." Indeed, the poet laureate Kipling coined or popularized the phrase "white man's burden" with reference to what they were doing overseas and what the Americans were doing to savage the Philippines. The British lag at home of not making the institutional adjustments necessary to modernize and rationalize their industrial potentials cost them dearly when the world war came in 1914. A matter of importance is the consideration that wars do not merely "come," as if without cause or provocation. The British, like everyone else, should have seen the likely outcome of the German armament that proceeded at a pronounced pace for two decades before the eruption of war in 1914.

Ironically, in 1890 Alfred Marshall published, at home in Britain, his *Principles of Economics*, regarded ever since as a benchmark of neo-Classical economics, a lullaby for the British. In 1890 the government of the United States passed the Sherman Anti-Trust Act, ostensibly intended to keep the remnants of the competitive system in place as the norm of the economy by opposing further monopoly.

Also in 1890, Germany explicitly endorsed monopoly and began preparation for war. She assumed leadership in the application of technological skills to what might be called industrial arts of war with as much zeal and effect as in their utilization in arts of peace. Preparation for war on a large scale went forward unremittingly, and at an accelerating rate, whether measured in terms of absolute magnitude or as expenditure per capita, or of percentages of real income or of accumulated wealth, and most emphatically in comparison with corresponding efforts of neighboring states. Each of the elder statesmen of European powers may have been hoping that the German expansionary thrust would devastate someone other than his nation.

The British were enjoying their empire and were reading Alfred Marshall, no doubt omitting those footnotes not supportive of the doctrine of mechanism. Britain was a heavenly body doing her "thing," including the logical practices ordinarily lumped together with the slogans "Free Trade and Comparative Advantage." The same was the only reasonable policy for Germany, seen through the lenses of economic orthodoxy. The latter country was being foolish by establishing monopoly instead of preventing it. Marshall, along with all others of the long line of British economic great men, showed unmistakably that inefficiency and international failure or collapse would be the outcome of the German foolishness. After all, they were deliberately reversing almost every economic doctrine that the British officially held dear. Surely economic collapse from monopolistic and cartel inefficiency would arrive before war.

Such was not to be the case, and "in Flanders fields the poppies blow." The British, the French, the Austro-Hungarians, the Turks, and even the Tsarist Russians scrambled to protect their trading patterns and empires, and set up quaint agreements, treaties, and pronouncements to show that they were just as tough as the German war machine. Veblen complained that German leadership and diplomacy appeared to work on the principle that it was not necessary formally to desire war in order to bring it about if care was taken to make the preparations so complete as to make war virtually unavoidable. His vision and German actions were closely parallel in some important respects.

It was readily to be seen that supercession of competition of the atomistic type via giant monopolies was a necessary precondition for realization of the productive potentials of modern industry, but that once Adam Smith's social control mechanism, competition, was thrust aside, business and bankers could be more predatory than ever. How was their power to be challenged? Several cultural factors made for political and cultural conservatism, so that the state was a creature of the vested interests. The financial trappings and institutions of the system would bring real, qualitative change, however ill-suited for the longer term, into the pecuniary or nontool conventions or customs. The use of loans, debt, and credit as the mode of financing industrially efficient expansions was at one and the same time the mode for grabbing "something for nothing" in the pecuniary arena. Fraud and chicanery were the order of the day, and asset valuations set during booms would necessarily collapse during bleak periods of forced retrenchment. This wild horse might be constrained from either the left, by a form of industrial democracy, or from the right in the form of "national integrity," state imposed order, and militarism.

The Germans took a shortcut. Junkerism had been powerful, especially in Prussia, for decades. The laboring classes had been permeated with Marxist ideology for decades, certainly since the revolutionary upheavals of 1848, and the Social Democrats (Marxists) had the largest membership of any political party in Germany on the eve of World War I. Veblen was more accurate as a forecaster than was Marx. Germany made her leap for a place in the sun based on central control and Prussianism, with jack-booted troopers and harsh social discipline right from the start. The workers yielded. They had talked of their power of making war impossible by simple refusal to produce war goods, refusal to give up their sons to the war machine, and so on, but once the flag was waved, they supported the dynastic state. The advanced, cartellized, and monopolized system of business enterprise had its period of glory but was overwhelmed by the war and its necessities.

Business enterprise comes under pressure to rationalize by consolidation in order to use modern technology, and the consolidated system will come under pressure to swing sharply either to the left or to the right. What can be said of the German experience in the context of our concern with mechanics-as-science, Newtonian philosophy, and Marx and Hegel, etc.? Imperial Germany had little in common with the laissez-faire advice of Adam Smith and orthodox economics, nor was its downfall an example of inefficiencies of either monopoly or statist mercantilism. Germany made war against too many countries. Adam Smith could not have a theory of the positive state since there was to be no such thing. Nineteenth-century Germany was saturated with Hegelian philosophy and various movements of roughly similar character, about to the degree that the English-speaking world was dominated by the Newtonian outlook. The Germans even had their own inventor of calculus, Leibnitz. Kant had laid the basis for the rise of German Idealism, far removed from contemporary British philosophy. Hegel was the epitome of the Idealism movement, having laid the basis for the inversion made by Feuerbach and Marx, and it is Hegel's dialectic and the state as its *modus operandi* that fills the gap between the earlier Idealism and Marxism. Hegel's philosophy, being dialectical, was as far from Newtonian ahistorical mechanics as the mind can imagine. Smith's individual (whether person or firm) mechanically made decisions to maximize his well-being, but he was a static, basically inert or nondevelopmental sort of creature, not part of a process of active change. Equilibrium, not process, is the final term of all that analysis. Likewise, the Hegelian vision is far removed from our concern with Darwinian evolution, shifted to focus on the evolution of acquired traits or habits of thought and action instead of biological gene inheritance and transmission.

We wish to note that neither Hegel nor Marx was responsible for the conception of the state that long has been held in Germany. Nor do our English language, British-derived cultures have a reasonable conception of a proper role for the positive state to this day. Be that as it may, Veblen could match the German proclivity for complexity:

> It is as difficult for the commonplace Englishman to understand what the German means by the "State" as it is for the German to comprehend

the English conception of a "Commonwealth," or very nearly so. . . .
The State is a matter not easily to be expounded in English. It is neither
the territorial area, nor the population, nor the body of citizens or
subjects, nor the aggregate wealth or traffic, nor the public administration,
nor the government, nor the crown, nor the sovereign; yet in some sense
it is all these matters, or rather all these are organs of the State. In some
potent sense, the State is a personal entity, with rights and duties superior
and anterior to those of the subjects. . . . The citizen is a subject of the
State. . . . Plainly, government by consent of the governed is not a State.
The sovereignty is not in the people, but it is in the State. Failure to
understand this conundrum is perhaps the most detestable trait of unrea-
son that taints the English-speaking peoples, in the apprehension of
intelligent Germans.[4]

What we need for our purposes is a model of social, political,
economic behavior and social organization that avoids the vision of
the state-as-sovereign, and likewise does not rest on the no-positive-
state vision of individualism that was derived from Newton. The
German view of history and of the place of the state cannot be called
Newtonian or mechanistic since it involves progressive change of a
type that is dialectical. But struggle writ large means war, and in the
nuclear age one more major war might well bring the graveyard of
humanity. Thus far, struggles that have brought "the dictatorship of
the proletariat" as the form of state dominance must be admitted to
have a poor record of withering away after theoretically establishing a
system of workers' control. Where is a "Workers' Council Society"?
There need have been no illusions that the treaties at the end of
World War I could bring permanent peace. The settlements and treaties
assured the coming of World War II, with such an intimate and certain
connection that we might call it one war: Phase I and Phase II. The
German state resurged as Hitler's fascism, substantially duplicated by
Italy and Japan, and less so by Spain. Militaristic nationalism was
strongly in evidence in France and in certain of the Balkan states
during all of the first half of the twentieth century, and recent examples
of military dictatorships abound. There is no merit in the argument
that these are only authoritarian regimes, not totalitarian like our
declared arch enemies the communist states because it is certain that
these labels do not distinguish two distinct types of society. No society
has ever succeeded in being totally totalitarian, and no authoritarian
regime has ever even tried to keep its hands off intellectual and cultural
affairs, the manipulation of which is totalitarian.
The leaders of Christendom made serious errors by letting greed and

suspicion dominate the patterns of settlement of World War I, instead of moving toward industrial democracy. The shooting was stopped but the war went on, in the sense of rampant nationalisms all through the 1920s and 1930s in which there was a clamor and struggle for colonies, differential production and trading advantages, and highly skewed income distributions. As predictably as night following day has been the turn to militarism as the means of trying to make the greed-based, Leisure Class, Privileged Class type of societies endure. A specific instance is well-known to our "conventional wisdom," as Veblen called it,[5] and consists of the fact that the League of Nations was never ratified and put into place. The ruling class of the most powerful nation, and the only industrial nation not severely damaged by the war, did not choose to give up any aspect of their advantages. Only the giant among nations could have made the League a success, and it was only this giant, the United States, who refused to ratify the document.

In Germany the empire was replaced, in form and short term, by a republic. This Weimar adventure merited more support than it received. It was the most leftist government in Western Europe, and after the economic disasters of 1923 (chaos, runaway inflation, unemployment, bankruptcies, etc.), it played an important role in a rebirth of science and culture in Germany. By the time of the stock market crash in the United States in the fall of 1929 and the subsequent slide of all Christendom into depression, Germany was a center of intellectual, artistic, and creative activity in the West, but control of the German economy was concentrated into even fewer hands after the war than before, and the emphasis on heavy industry was continued. Patriotism became more virulent and more antirational than even before the war, and in the chaotic world of 1920–30s capitalism, full productive potentials of the economic structure of heavy industry could not be used for peace and prosperity. Adequate markets simply did not exist in the laissez-faire world, and it is not surprising that leaders of the capitalist German republic would have to fail, or that they would be replaced by persons and programs that rejected laissez-faire, reinstated the concept of state as sovereign, and put the military machine back together, with this machine as the strong market for the product of the industrial structure. Militarists, Junkers, bankers, industrialists, avid nationalists, and workers seeking jobs all found what they needed most in the resurgent state.

It was international capitalism that failed, and badly so. The form of the German response to that failure was tragic but not surprising.

Other capitalist countries were turning pointedly to the forms of an earlier epoch in their history, understandably the pre-laissez-faire mercantilism. Beggar-thy-neighbor nationalism was the textbook terminology. Such an authority as Keynes, from within the heartland of capitalism, entitled a chapter of his *General Theory*, "Notes on Mercantilism," in which he recognized that planning and programs, not laissez-faire, were the requirements for solving the problems, and these could only be done on a national basis at that time.[6]

What *might* have been the case in post-World War I Germany? Argumentation can be lessened by looking at what was done after World War II. The Junker class had to be broken, and this was accomplished after World War II by the Russian occupation of Prussia and the establishment of East Germany as a separate nation. Possibly the severity of that solution could have been lessened by reasonable actions post-World War I, but reason had hardly a chance. The League of Nations might have been adopted, with a structure and purpose at least as functional as what was done post-World War II. The Marshall Plan aid, the actions of the International Monetary Fund and the World Bank, good and bad, the determined drive for international trade expansion rather than its stifling, the European and Russian insistence (against the United States wishes) that Germany not rearm—these have been much less than perfect programs, especially in the long run. But why not the European Economic Community in 1920? To state that "things just were not ready for such a program at that time" is not an answer.

Had some mixture of these programs been put into place during the first fifteen years after World War I in something near the scope and design as was done during the first fifteen years after World War II, the great collapse of capitalism of 1929 presumably would not have happened, or would have been notably less severe. Germany presumably would have stayed within the fold of semipeaceable capitalist nations, which at least would have been better than what actually took place.

Qualitative change in the means of production is brought by science, and since this change is the basis for wealth and power, few leaders would contemplate giving it up. Qualitative change in productive technique mandates qualitative change in other aspects of human behavior. Feudalistic social relationships are not appropriate for the factory age, and capitalist social relationships are not suitable for the nuclear age. All uses of nuclear technology, for example, are the concern of all of us, whether we consider the design, operation, disposal of waste, or whatever else. It is a misuse of language to speak of "private" nuclear technology because there simply cannot be any such thing.

Everybody can see that all nuclear machinery is community business. What about other things, for example, automobiles? In the modern era of concern for resource availability, pollution, environmental damage, and congestion of various types, everyone can see that externalities not only exist, but abound. The doctrine of mechanism is based on distinct separation of atomistic units. But the doctrines of evolution and entropy enable us to see that the truth is the opposite; everything impacts upon everything else. Mechanics is appropriate for building bridges and houses of varied forms, but it simply does not apply to behavior, which is a term properly reserved to the animal kingdom. "What is good for General Motors is good for the country" is a proper slogan to have emerged from such no-social-thought quarters, but recognition of power and process enables one to see the fallacy. What General Motors has always wanted is a growing automobile industry, with ever larger, fancier, and more profitable models. Thus looms the destruction of what public transport systems we already have (as per the infamous case of the Los Angeles electric trolley system), more efforts at public expense to pave larger portions of nature, cancellation of concern for prices and availability of petroleum products in the future, forgetting concern for safety, and so on. General Motors is not an atom, and does not live in splendid isolation. If we take into account the necessity of basing human behavioral science on evolution, specifically cultural evolution meaning acquired traits of know-how and beliefs, and on entropy, then we may see that economics is a group affair, and the relevant question on this point would be how much and what kind of private interference into public affairs is going to be permitted.

Since evolution is our watchword, not statics and the view that we are zeroing in on the truth, we do not leap ahead to argue for some sort of planned economy, with decisions taken at the top. The facts of evolution of our human cultures suggest the desirability of considerable personal and private initiatives, always subject to social control. Competition can accomplish this control function while permitting expression of personal wishes, urges, and talents, but only where giant scale does not effectively eliminate effective competition and where externality or community-effect considerations do not invalidate its functional character.

For example, farmers do not cause the price of bread to be unnecessarily high. They may, however, use antibiotics, growth hormones, pesticides, fertilizers, and a vast array of chemicals that are not socially feasible. Individual farmers do not require to be replaced by some system of intelligent social control that transcends competition, but companies that supply the sophisticated inputs to farmers absolutely require such market-forces-transcending controls. Obviously any farmer who put together an organization large enough to have an impact beyond pure competition, for example, producing his own antibiotics or growth hormones, would thereby have put himself into the category requiring social control beyond what competition can do. Such is a planning society, not a planned society. Corporations, including banks, *plan*, but for their own purposes, not reliably for the betterment of society, and the invisible hand reaches into many pockets, viciously assaults the environment, and turns readily to militarism to assist in predations the world around.

The human race could have done for itself at the end of World War I what it did after World War II. The United Nations and its specialized subdivisions such as the Food and Agricultural Organization (FAO), the World Health Organization (WHO), UNESCO, the banking organizations, and the semblance of world courts are overall much better than the rampant greed that followed World War I. The establishment of the European economic community could have been done after World War I. Why were these things done later, but not earlier? Part of the answer is to be found in the phenomenon called institutional lag. Institutional changes (habits of thought and action) having pecuniary bearing were abstractly possible when the know-how or technology came into place during early decades, certainly by the end of the nineteenth century. Tragically for most of humanity, even these most basic institutional adjustments were not made until after, and as a consequence of, two devastating surges of one war that ran at least from 1914 to 1945. Since the adjustments that have been made were tuned to fit the circumstances of the long War, they were archaic even at the time they were made. The United States as the banker of the capitalist world, which is the central provision of the 1944 International Monetary Fund (IMF), cannot be viewed as more than a stop-gap measure that could succeed for a couple of decades, 1945–65. There is general recognition that the IMF *as a payments system* failed by 1971.

The USSR: Failure of Dialectical Socialism

World War I ended without the forces of Junkerism and the military state being defeated in Germany, and all the so-called peace arrange-

ments were designed to accommodate a "return to normalcy" throughout the capitalist world. In part this refusal to learn is something more
than the dominant segment of the Leisure Classes merely riding the
usual crest of conservatism. There was a new menace on the scene, to
which Veblen devoted a lengthy article, "Bolshevism Is a Menace—to
Whom."[7] He wrote: "Bolshevism is revolutionary. It aims to carry
democracy and majority rule over to the domain of industry. Therefore
it is a menace to the established order and to those persons whose
fortunes are bound up with the established order."

A Bolshevik was a common man who had pondered the question of
what he might stand to lose, and not surprisingly had come up with the
answer: nothing. The elder statesmen were busy with treaty arrangements designed to disappoint even that trace of hope. How was an
"indifferent hope" that Bolshevism might bring something for the
common man of Christendom to be disappointed? How would the
vested interests and their elder statesmen proceed? Keynes had just
written the book that assured his fame, *The Economic Consequences
of the Peace*, in which he argued that viciousness and greed were
displayed by the Allied powers, especially France, in stomping on
prostrate Germany by imposing huge reparations payments and then
refusing to import German products, the only way she could possibly
make the payments.[8] Such an arrangement made German prospects
bleak and unworkable from which facts the seeds of further madness
grew.

What is called the Cold War had its beginnings with considerable
heat as the Great Powers sent troops and supplies to the assistance of
the White Armies in the cataclysmic Russian civil war of 1918, 1919,
and the first part of 1920 after the Bolsheviks seized power in the fall
of 1917. Winston Churchill pleaded for support of efforts to "strangle
the baby in its crib," and that is merely one of the more colorful
expressions of horror felt within the ruling classes of Christendom.
Veblen considered it likely that the strangulation efforts would succeed
if pressed hard enough. Ironically, it was the Russian backwardness
that might break the efforts to throttle the Bolsheviks because they
were able to fall back on earlier and less close-knit arrangements for
production.

Russians, not foreigners, emerged victorious and in control of the
vast region or empire, including the few bright spots of industrial and
cultural advancement, which for the most part had belonged to foreign
capitalists before the war. Both tool know-how (technology) and pecuniary customs (a subset of institutions) have been changed more or

less rapidly by the Bolsheviks and their successors. Technology has been "borrowed" from the more advanced countries, which means Christendom or the capitalist world, but conventions or ways of doing things, "relations of production" in Marxist terminology, have necessarily been mainly a mixture of Russian customs, projections of Marxist theory, and the wishes of the ruling Communist Party and its leaders. Veblen clearly would not endorse any of these three determining influences on how things were to be done. He was curious; he was interested; he wished them well, but it would have been naive in the extreme for him to have urged massive aid or trade with the one regime in the world of the 1920s that was a "threat" to the vested interests. As always, he made very little in the way of positive recommendations.

Adolf Hitler played a major role, if somewhat unknowingly, in the direction Stalinist policies were to take for two full decades, from the mid-1920s to the mid-1940s. He caught quite well the spirit of both the internal distress of capitalism and its tendency to do what humans have tended for millennia to do under pronounced stress, find foreign devils upon which to lay the blame for the home-grown failure and chaos. After his 1923 beer hall *putsch* attempt, he served a term in prison and wrote his *Mein Kampf* (*My Struggle*). It promised a *drang nacht osten*, a drive to the East, to take over the lands of the Slavs for the power and the glory of the Aryan master race, and to destroy communism. What could the elder statesmen of Christendom choose to do to oppose such a man? There were several specific treaty provisions forbidding German rearmament and the resurgence of the deep-rooted German militarism. But first things first. Both crude racism and resurgent militarism admittedly were dangerous, but Hitler's promise to serve as the bulwark against Bolshevism, in chaotic Germany as well as to the East, was simply too appealing not to outweigh all other considerations. Hardly a voice was raised, most importantly in Britain and France, as Hitler pieced the behemoth of the German military state back together, used and improved it— especially in Spain as early as 1936—and massively enlarged the entire military state. That Germany was going mad was certain, and most deplorable to the elder statesmen; but it was a madness of the far right against the far left, too good a deal to refuse.

The Bolsheviks also had read *Mein Kampf*, and knew what was coming. Never could a guess have been easier. Stalin's words to the Presidium of Ministers as early as 1931 are available for interested parties to read, and he bluntly told his subchieftains that Hitler was going to come to power, would move against communism and the

USSR, and that they had a decade to prepare for the German attack. He proved to be correct on all accounts. Stalin sought desperately, not at all nobly, to get the capitalist powers to intervene in accordance with their armaments limitations agreements concerning Germany, to enforce the accords, and stop German rearmament, but the lure of a bulwark against Bolshevism was too appealing. In 1939 Stalin signed a pact offered by Hitler, delaying a German invasion in exchange for German-Russian trade that brought highly desired war-machine raw materials to Germany from the USSR, and assured that the Russians were obliged or committed not to enter into an anti-Hitler pact or move. Hitler got what he wanted: raw materials from Russia, and a one-front war. The Russians got time to prepare for the German onslaught. Did the British and French leaders, and at a remove, the Americans, get other than what they deserved? How can we avoid the conclusion that the privileged class ruled the decision making and betrayed the nation and the common man, in Veblen's terminology?

Hitler took over most of what he wanted of continental West Europe before he hit the Russians in June 1941. The capitalist elder statesmen had been totally stunned by the announcement of Stalin's pact with him. They had adamantly refused to stop Hitler on their own account, which would have been easy at an early date because a clear majority of Germans themselves opposed Hitler at the early junctures. The elder statesmen had refused to enter into any pact with the Bolsheviks to stop Hitler. Hence Stalin's act called perfidy was, in fact, thoroughly understandable, if a *bit* perfidious. Was he supposed to twiddle his thumbs and wait for an earlier German attack against the USSR?[9]

We want to offer a necessarily brief and impressionistic appraisal of the success of the Russian Soviet system. To do so we must assume some philosophical position or ground from which to offer judgment, and not surprisingly, we operate from the preconceptions of Veblen's version—on our interpretation—of cultural evolution as our chosen paradigm. Consequently, our appraisal may agree in some particulars with what might be said from the point of view of an orthodox capitalist economic perspective, but likely will be sharply different in some other particulars. Hopefully it is clear that neither of such views would be correct, the other wholly incorrect.

Does the social system that emerged and now exists in the Soviet Union bear a close resemblance to what one reasonably could call industrial democracy? Perhaps reversing the words to democratic industrialism aids clarification, if making either word the adjective and the other the noun assists our understanding. The Soviets have accomplished much towards becoming adequately industrial, but their efficiency is poor by any of several possible measures. The same thing can be said of their attempts at democracy. They provide jobs for everyone to a degree uncommon in most of Christendom, and employment is critical to democracy, even if we posit the availability of welfare payments in lieu of jobs. Democracy must be participatory, not merely formal, which the Soviets seem to realize. However, their officialdom and bureaucratic apparatus seem clearly to prefer falling back on the standard Marxist idea that they are still working their way through a substage of development called the "dictatorship of the proletariat." In such a substage, "democratic centralism" is a basic principle, and means that the persons at the top of the hierarchy should seek at least some input of opinions and ideas from the masses, but once decisions are taken, little or no deviation is permitted. Admittedly, this is in no sense a form of democracy paralleling the models offered in the Western capitalist world.

Welfare payment to young and able-bodied people alone offers little means of expressing creative drives or urges, or anything that could be called a creative role in life. The Russian Communist state dislikes paying welfare, preferring to get the benefits of work effort by everyone. They have crippled efforts at improvement of productivity by pressuring enterprises to put too many supernumerary people on the payrolls. The Russian economy has become notably inefficient.

Unemployment long has been a scourge of capitalism, as Veblen and many other denizens of the underworld of social thought regularly have seen. The coming of robotry bids to make the problem worse, and Leisure Class societies find it difficult to take steps for sharing available work, for example, by greatly reducing the work week or providing early retirement on terms that most people can afford. Especially in the United States in the 1980s, massive deficits and debt expansion have been used as the means of insuring demand adequate to call forth high production and employment. In perverse fashion, this demand manipulation is called supply-side economics, but rapid expansion of debt cannot continue forever, the penalty being possibility of collapse.

In any event, democracy also means a real voice by the common man in determining social policies. Here again the Russians come through rather poorly. In theory Marxist socialism is perceived as involving workers' councils in a major way. That requires decentralization of decision making, not just a vast interconnected network of input-output units with centralized control of locales of production.

If efficiency in the input-output planning sense is what Veblen envisioned as necessary for efficiency in an overall economic sense, then worker council democracy is an idle dream, and a central plan is critically necessary. If our Leisure Class phenomenon were substantially overcome, we Americans could say enough is enough of consumption goods and thus of total expansion of their production. Methods of production could be evaluated and construed in terms of social efficiency, not exclusively productive efficiency. Assembly teams in lieu of assembly lines for automobile production and much else might well be our social choice, even if costs in some sense were higher. Obviously no trading partner country could be permitted to use lower cost methods and thereby undersell us. Trade would have to be infringed, which must not be regarded as a debased act. Likewise, safety features, pollution control, standards of quality, etc., would be matters of social choice. Once the mentality of endlessly rising consumption is broken, several possible routes to industrial democracy come into focus.

The USSR, on the other hand, is not in a position to give careful attention to considerations of pollution, worker safety, and alienation because of the on-going fact that is etched into Russian minds that production remains lower than clearly needed levels. They took note of both their own rapid growth during the first third of a century of Bolshevism, but they continued to lag behind production levels of the countries of Christendom and Japan. Hence they push for much more production. For the most part they have eliminated survival poverty and continue to provide employment, free medical, dental, and educational services, and some care for the aged. These are all giant achievements, some of which the United States manages poorly. The Russians are also saddled with a pervasive variation of Leisure Class antidemocratic attitude at the highest levels of society, in part fostered by the need for material incentives to encourage production. Production quotas construed in terms of physical output only, not considerations of quality, have abounded. In China the Maoists reacted violently against this phenomenon, at home and in the Soviet Union, and in contrast to their interpretations of Marxism-Leninism-Maoism.

At the apex of the Leisure Class is the ruling class. The Soviets have tried to avoid the worst of the logical consequences (which Veblen well described in 1899) by cancellation of the private property system. Such a move has made it possible to use highly uneven income distribution to achieve incentive goals without having power or income derive from wealth in the sense characteristic of capitalist societies. Dynasties based on wealth are avoided. All this is seen as necessary facts of socialism, with communism yet to come. Presumably they will change the name of the country if and when they reach that later stage, dropping *Socialist* and putting in *Communist*. But are they, in fact, moving past the "privileged (ruling) class socialism" stage on toward communism? Veblen, like the Maoists, would have his doubts. Invidious comparisons, pecuniary emulation, import-goods consumption far beyond what is possible for the "common herd," "social power" canons of taste—these and other attributes of Leisure Class society are evident in ruling circles in the USSR as elsewhere, even if sharply different in style. Communism will not be achieved until both high output and non-Leisure Class mentality are achieved. But what society has ever achieved high output without the trappings of a Leisure Class, itself an impediment to rational processes? "They pretend to pay us, so we pretend to work" is a slogan for a majority of socialist-communist countries. Is selfless "Communist Man" still as much a figment of the imagination as purely rational "Economic Man"?

Most of today's high production capitalist societies took centuries for the productivity achievements, and most have used colonies in either crude or sophisticated systems of predation. Today's communist countries are perhaps less predatory concerning their neighbors than have been the capitalist giants, but this does not cancel the fact of Soviet imperialism defined as domination of other countries or pronounced interference in their affairs.

The question remains: the Russians have emerged with a state-capitalist (the Chinese say), nonprivate property Leisure Class (Privileged Class), Big Brother-dominated society, and how is this phenomenon, which is choking off both growth and democracy, to be overcome? The Soviets also have wavered between relying on market incentives using something that looks like profits, and not doing so but depending on computerized central planning instead. The scale of enterprise and hence the prospects for competition as a mode of social control is a crucial consideration. Income disparity among workers would need to be reduced and kept small to permit undercutting Leisure Class emulation, invidious comparisons, and the like. In recent decades, a peculiarly Russian form of status race at the ruling-class top of society has soared to prominence, and they have not been successful in controlling its ravages. Competition, in parallel with cooperation, can be a crucially useful social mechanism, even though it must not be regarded as a magic solution to all problems.

To be sure, the Russians do not possess the only socialist system.

The Chinese certainly do not view matters the Soviet Russian way, and they are bringing qualitative change into social conventions by a zigzag course thus far. They have been employing a dialectical vacillation between demands for communism for a time, and use of capitalist "enrich yourselves" motivational techniques for a time. Social consciousness of workers should make it impossible for private managers who do not own much property or tools of production ever to establish either giants or dynasties, or become strongly predatory. In the 1980s at least, they are finding that private initiative can bring surges of investment and flexibility that the rigid and mechanistic central control models cannot even approach. Computers and mathematical modeling necessarily are mechanistic to the ultimate degree. Socialism, as a rigidly planned society, means socialism as mechanism, and such society would be no part of an evolutionary vision. Let us modify a popular slogan to read, "middle sized is beautiful." For giant countries such as the United States, China, and the USSR, concern for productive efficiency mandates near monopoly in fewer product lines than commonly has been assumed, as the Soviets are admitting.

Decentralization efforts may reasonably bring individual initiative into play, and as Gorbachev perceives, major change is required. In the capitalist world it is almost ubiquitously assumed that improved performance of Soviet-type economies requires reversion to capitalistic Classical mechanism. This is not clearly the case. To the extent that socialist systemic failures are failures of Stalinism, then change might be forward as cultural evolution, perhaps into democratic socialism of some sort after a few years. It is the phenomenon of the "privileged ruling class" that societies must wrestle with, even after revolutions have broken the worst features of Leisure Class capitalism. If the Soviet Russians, the Chinese, or anyone else can cut the knots of Leisure Class mentality, even as a postcapitalist phenomenon, we will all owe them a great debt of gratitude.

Notes

1. Veblen, *Place of Science* . . . , 19.
2. Friedrich List, *The National System of Political Economy*. Translated by Sampson S. Lloyd (London: Longmans, Green, 1928).
3. Veblen, *Imperial Germany* . . . , 180.
4. *Ibid.*, 160; also chap. 5.
5. Veblen, *Instinct* . . . , 39.

6. Keynes, *General Theory* . . . , chap. 23, "Notes on Mercantilism, the Usury Laws, Stamped Money and Theories of Under-Consumption," 333–71.

7. Thorstein Veblen, "Bolshevism Is a Menace—to Whom?" *Essays in Our Changing Order*. Edited by Leon Ardzrooni (New York: Viking Press, 1934), 399–414.

8. Veblen, "The Economic Consequences of the Peace." [Book review] *Essays* . . . , 462–70.

9. This interpretation is based in part on D. F. Fleming, *The Cold War and Its Origins*. 2 vols. (Garden City, N.J.: Doubleday & Company, Inc., 1961).

7

Three Thirds of the Twentieth Century

Late in the twentieth century United States, neither the economy nor the economics profession as a body of science is in good shape. The rate of measured unemployment plus known underemployment fluctuates around numbers that are more than twice as high as was thought feasible only a few years ago, and it has trended upward for twenty years. Economists confront the situation by writing of a natural rate of unemployment, and the discovery that many of these nonworking people are not unemployed but rather are engaged in job searches, which apparently may last a lifetime.

Inflation breaks into double digit rates on occasion and keeps everybody apprehensive even when it is down to four percent, double what was thought reasonable a few years ago. Stagflation is the term used to describe this malady of high unemployment and high inflation that nature or mismanagement has bestowed upon us. The cause of our malady must be interference with neo-Classical economic Laws of Nature at the hands of politicians and mistaken economic advisers. Sometime within recent years we must have fallen into the hands of fools.

Massive debt is problematic. A president of the country does not have to complete his permitted two terms anymore to accomplish a tripling of the federal debt, which means an increase much larger than that realized by his entire line of predecessors. But how can one fault a president if he insists the whole time upon enactment of a constitutional amendment requiring a balanced budget—albeit, to apply in the adequately distant future?

Business debt has been increasing just as rapidly, and household consumer debt has been increasing the most rapidly of all. Soothsayers express alarm that the rate of household saving has fallen (on a different interpretation it has not) and is lower than that of any other industrial country (it is not). Household purchases of houses now total a larger sum of money some years than net measured household savings. A sleight-of-hand is accomplished by calling the purchase of new houses investment spending instead of consumption, which might make sense if the concern were that houses last longer than either cars or clothes. Drawing the categories the way they are drawn and expressing alarm at the low rate of saving continues the myth that households provide net saving, by abstaining from consumption, as in the modeling of Jean B. Say. Conceptually, this saving is borrowed by businessmen at interest rates that must be just right to both entice the risk-taking businessman and reward the householder, who is thereby participating in American business. Juggling the figures to treat house purchases as consumption, it appears that households are not doing any net saving in the sense implied in the model, and hence businessmen including bankers are not paying any net interest. A related point is that the official procedure of putting an imputed price on rental value of owner-occupied residences raises the apparent consumption spending total, and thus increases the confusion as to just which figures are appropriate to what purpose. Homeowners do not, in fact, reduce their saving-to-income ratio by having a high total for consumption occasioned by the rental value of their home. Of course, they pay no such rent.

Is the international scene brighter? A few years ago the international price of crude oil, if we are permitted such a figure of speech, jumped or was raised from the absurdly low figure of three dollars per barrel, depending on the date chosen, to the absurdly high figure of thirty dollars. Petrodollars became a catchword for a time, and the issue was how to recycle them. Banks received giant deposits, and sent representatives around the world to find governments, dictators, con men, businessmen, or whoever else would pay interest at rates higher than the banks were paying to the petrodollar depositors. Multiple expansion of deposits would be pure cream resulting from the play of market forces. A vast surge of lending took place, and private investment was all set to develop the Third World, but loans to manipulators did not increase production at a snap of fingers, and the means of repayment simply have not materialized in many cases. Third World debt to foreigners has reached a magnitude that is easy to remember, as of this date about a trillion dollars.

A massive earthquake hit one of the worst-off debtors, Mexico, in September 1985, a few days before the president of that sad country was announcing to Washington, Wall Street, and his own *peones*, that Mexico "tiene que crecer para pagar" [must grow in order to pay]. One would have thought that instead the country needed to grow in order to feed its people. But how can Mexico borrow more unless the economy grows adequately to pay the foreigners? Debt in such a situation is clearly a trap and is perverse as a strategy for economic development. Oil price drops have changed the Mexican and certain other Third World oil countries' debt disaster into whatever is one step worse.

Meanwhile plans were going forward for U.S. taxpayers, charmingly referred to as "the government," to, in effect, pay interest to bankers on these uncollectible "investment loans," to a magnitude of more than twenty billion dollars. Perhaps we should tighten our belts and be generous because theoretically we are helping needy countries via new loans that do no more than pay the interest on old loans. The Nobel Prize for economics was announced that same month (October 1985), and the recipient, Franco Modigliani, promptly issued a statement that Third World countries certainly should pay these debts (whether such a thing is possible or not), and give no thought of reneging. There is a real need to avoid bringing stability into question. It would have been nice of him to have gone ahead and explained how they are to do the repaying. "Transfer of assets" is the slogan currently bandied about in international trade and development circles, but it has several major drawbacks. It is much less than certain that the majority of citizens in debtor Third World countries will quietly acquiesce in transfers of the profitable parts of their countries to Americans and a few other capitalists such as the IMF. Moreover, one must ponder the thought that the Japanese, to whom we owe some half-trillion dollars, might decide that since they are a very crowded, densely populated nation with 125 million people in a total area no larger than our state of California, they will take transfer of assets in the form of a couple of Pacific states. Perhaps Alaska and Oregon?

Also problematic, the United States continues to run balance of payments deficits of something like $150 billion a year, which is ten or twenty times the rate of just a few years ago. Must we not stop such enormous deficits? The value of the dollar is too high in relation to other currencies, limiting our exports and encouraging imports. Then why do we not let the dollar fall drastically enough to have the required result? The answer seems to be that we need a strong dollar, and

interest rates must be kept high to fight inflation, to cause the foreigners to maintain their deposits in the United States, and because bankers
would rather have high interest rates on money they lend than low
interest rates. The rich lend to the poor more than the poor lend to the
rich. If decline in the dollar adequate to the purpose is forestalled,
wage reductions to make our domestic production costs match foreign
costs is the appealing remedy. In a well-articulated system of international free trade, there is little reason that American steelworkers,
shipbuilders, automobile workers, and so on, should receive higher
real pay than their counterparts in Korea or Singapore, for example.
However, the several million American laborers involved find this
unappealing.

Protectionist trade restrictions might look inviting, except that our
biggest single trading partner is ourselves—our own companies' overseas production for shipment to the United States. Moreover, and
hardly a trifling matter, our import trade balance plays a crucial role in
the system by which foreigners get money with which to make payments on the enormous and growing debts. A further bit of unpleasan-
try is what likely would happen to our domestic rate of inflation if we
cut back on the importation of cheaper foreign goods. High levels of
imports have been restraining price increase for automobiles, household appliances, shoes and clothing, electronic gear, food items, and a
long list of other goods.

Several things are running out of control. Could Adam Smith's mode
of social control of the economy, competition, be put into place
adequately for the job? These problems do not exist in the mechanistic
model, but in our real world, economic activity goes along, doing
whatever conforms with businessmen's norms, while economists' activity goes along, doing whatever conforms with theorists' norms. In
many ways the two things seem disconnected and not interrelated.

As a further example of modern perplexity, ponder the question of
what would happen to interest rates if the money supply were increased more rapidly than formerly had been the case. The old knowledge was that the more abundant supply of money would be interacting
with unchanged short run demand for money, so interest rates would
fall. The assumptions and appropriate Cartesian quadrant diagrams
seem straightforward and convincing. But our latter-day knowledge is
that interest rates would rise, not fall, because the increased money
supply would cause prices to rise, as per the ancient quantity theory
of money. "Rational expectations"—literally the name of a body of
economic doctrine—would cause everyone to anticipate all changes

and not be mislead. Output should be rising because of a larger part of resources going to investment and modernization, even if the peculiar assumption of constant full employment were observed. Rising price averages is inflation, and both lenders and borrowers would see the necessity of higher nominal interest rates in order that the real purchasing power of the lender not suffer from the anticipated inflation. Obviously everything is to be purely rational! Certainly the safe path for the economist is the easy path, laissez-faire, if only we can specify it. Since we do not know what to do, how reassuring it is to fall back on the foundation that no advice is the best advice! "He knows enough who knows not to learn" presumably is the way Henry Adams would have expressed his opinion had he been an economist. If one makes positive recommendations of what to do in specific circumstances, on occasion one is certain to be proved wrong and be uncloaked. Simply crying laissez-faire enables the economist to assert that the results, whatever they may be, are simply the natural outcome of forces, the best of all possible worlds. Any tinkering can only make things worse, and bring us disregard.

Three Thirds of the Century

In the capitalist world, the Western world, or what Veblen called Christendom, the twentieth century divides to good analytical purpose into three equal parts. If we focus on the United States, the first part extended to the inauguration of Franklin Roosevelt in 1933. Until then the orthodox economic model held sway almost unquestioned, although it rested on Say's Law of Markets, an underpinning that later was knocked out. "Supply creates its own demand" is a good summary of the crucial aspects of economic doctrine of the period.

The Second Third, of course, extends from the 1933 changes that became the New Deal, to Lyndon Johnson's withdrawal from politics in the spring of 1968, brought about by his recognition that he could not win the presidential reelection that year. Events of the Vietnam War during the previous year or two had made his reelection seem impossible, and the outcomes of the presidential primaries were clear enough to penetrate Johnson's colossal ego. The dominant economic doctrine of this Second Third of the century could be interpreted as being just as mechanistic as the earlier dogma, but without the same type of self-adjusting automaticity. Capitalism and market forces failed; government and central bank actions may or may not be interpreted as having failed also. There is no chicken-egg question as to which was a response to the other. Political pressures brought governmental responses.

The United States and all of Christendom were severely depressed during every year of the entire decade. Keynes's core advice was simple, and was to use governmental fiscal and monetary policy to assure demand adequate to purchase what could be produced at full employment of resources. This principle reversed the previous formulation by Say, and often is interpreted as "demand creates its own supply." Manipulate demand and private businessmen will look after supply of what can be sold, right up to full employment. Governmental activity of almost any kind was resented and opposed by propertied classes if the scale was large, but nobody, including businessmen and bankers, liked a depression of such length and depth. Other nations were turning in despair and revolution to the far left forms of socialism or communism, or to the far right form of society called fascism. Governmental meddling with the system of laissez-faire natural liberty mechanism might be better than either of those, especially since it was being lauded as a temporary phenomenon called "pump priming."

However, by the time of Johnson's political withdrawal, war, militarism, inflation, racism, poverty, sexism, alienation, environmental destruction, national humiliation at losing the war, disgust with high taxes, and a few other dimensions of despair marked the end of an era. At both beginning and end, the age of Keynes is coterminous with the Second Third of the twentieth century. As one might expect in the topsy-turvy world of economic doctrine, it was the next president, Richard Nixon, who popularized the slogan, "we are all Keynesians now." He only meant that governmental programs to save American capitalism would be used as needed, in a pragmatic way that did not confront Keynes's philosophy. There certainly was no official endorsement of Keynes's pronouncement of the desirability or necessity of "euthanasia of the rentier."

Keynes's Law of Markets ran into problems of inflation, production bottlenecks, and so on, long before full employment was achieved. It overtly rejected automaticity of an important type, that of aggregate demand, and it implied ugly things about tax systems and property. Therefore it is not surprising that economists would try to return to Say's formulation.

This is also dangerous doctrine, however. If inadequate demand were a problem only during downturn phases of a business cycle, one could boost demand via fiscal and monetary policies, which would not directly involve governmental or public ownership takeovers. The problem could be acknowledged and solved, perhaps, within the framework of market capitalism. Liberals, for example, Paul Samuelson as a long-time leader of what are called "Fiscal Keynesians," see the point in general. But a reversion to "supply creates its own demand" supports the doctrines called "supply side economics." One reduces tax rates, enlarges loopholes, finances research and development with funding from the public purse, removes regulations and controls—and anticipates a surge of private sector activity, especially investment. What assurance is there that Say's Law, demonstrated by Keynes as not always applicable, was now correct and demand will come along nicely? Business activity can never surge for long if demand lags.

One might suggest governmental supply manipulation in ways other than tax breaks and the failed incentives programs, most notably via economic deregulation. The full problem of demand lag dragging down prosperity and profits has been avoided in the United States so far in the 1980s, in part via the enormous surge in the federal deficit. Ideologues continue the assertions that the deficit is indeed a problem, but only in the sense that households and businesses still are having to pay high taxes, which stifle both incentives and the availability of loanable funds. It is assumed that a reduction of government spending would be at least matched by a surge of private spending. Will we ever really reduce government spending, balance the budgets, and run the risk that Say was wrong? Economists may breathe a sigh of relief on recognizing that we likely will never, ever, make the test. Too much is at stake.

Pressures for military spending plus nondiscretionary civilian programs of public funds spending make it possible to talk of reducing government without risking such a shock. Everyone knows how we explain the failure to at least balance the budget if we are not going to reduce it. Higher taxes interfere with incentives, so we must not raise taxes. The outcome predictably is a major breakdown of the economy sometime soon, from overexpansion of debt. This Final Third of the century is notable for perplexity and uncertainty, with the foundation doctrines having failed.

The stock market surges as the rich play games with tax savings, big governmental investment incentive boondoggles, rapid money supply increase, and the large-scale "throwing of money at problems" called defense spending and space programs. Manipulators garner quick fortunes, but economic growth has not responded well to the stock market froth. What the fluctuations in petroleum prices will do remains to be seen, but we may be assured that the developmental impacts will be mixed, undesirable along with the desirable.

First Third supply side philosophy is no more likely to succeed in a fundamental sense in the Final Third than it did in the First, and the same is true of Second Third demand side philosophies. What we have done in the 1980s might best be categorized as "debt-side" policies. The gods have tricked us. Does capitalism have more than two sides? Not within the framework of mechanism, where there were only mass and motion when God hurled the planets into fixed space. Supply and demand are all there are, and scientific procedure means forcing all phenomena into categories of analytical functions. Evolution and change are not central parts of the picture.

It should be borne in mind that it is Keynes and Keynesianism as rejection of laissez-faire that are under assault by supply siders, not debt expansion as the mode of demand guarantee. Big government and big public deficits must be frowned upon for several reasons, but they cannot be eliminated on pain of collapse. Speaking metaphorically, it is capitalists who sit on the supply side of a great table called economic doctrine, and it is the public who sit on the demand side. Whose case is to be rationalized? Who is to be favored? From the evolutionist platform for observation of our society, to ask the question very nearly is to answer it. Surely proper spending levels can be contrived without redistribution of income, progressive taxing and spending programs, euthanasia of the rentier, or any other of the ugly suggestions made by Keynes. It seemingly will be pollution of air and water that will constitute the almost insuperable barriers to endless growth and expansion, the view that whatever is desired is desirable. It seems definitely the case that the hedonistic or Utilitarian philosophy will have to be transcended.

The evolution of human cultures continues. Which is more likely to collapse first during the final decade of the twentieth century: Leisure Class capitalism or Leisure Class socialism? Each is more likely to flounder and stagger on rather than collapse cataclysmically. A strict adherence to the concept of business cycle involves closer affinity with determinism and mechanism than our model permits, and the downturns of a business cycle proper are not to be construed as collapses. Since we are skeptical of strict usage of business cycle, we are free to label what happened throughout the capitalist world at the end of the First Third of this century as "collapse," a rare event that might be repeated in some different form.

Details of the Great Depression have been presented in bits and pieces so commonly that we will not belabor them. American industrial output dropped to half or less of rated capacity, and a fourth of the labor force became unemployed full time. A few million more persons peddled apples and committed other such acts of desperation. Farm output dropped hardly at all, but prices fell by half and worse. Oligopoly and monopoly industrial output dropped by roughly half, but prices hardly fell at all. Some people took these facts to mean that certain people had power but others did not. Economists believed what they had always chosen to believe, that business firms simply respond to market signals and no one has power.

In the scholarly discipline of economics, one response to the collapse at the end of the First Third was an assault on the pure competition model that was done by two persons separately but simultaneously. The first year of the Second Third saw the publication of Joan Robinson's *The Economics of Imperfect Competition*, and also Edward Chamberlin's *The Theory of Monopolistic Competition*.[1] Both books used algebra and Cartesian quadrant diagrams in much the same way. The Britisher, Robinson, saw and emphasized the wastes of imperfect competition, whereas the American, Chamberlin, perceived advantages. In both cases, however, the business firm has some degree of power in the market and influence on demand and price. Such recognition is devastating to a Newtonian world-view, except where dogmatism is pronounced enough to fend off all facts. Several points need to be made and do not require lengthy treatment:

1. In all such models the firm is the center of attention, and the demand curve it confronts has slope, in conformity with law of demand realization that quantity demanded is ordinarily an inverse function of price.
2. It is quite impossible to know either the position or the slope of the firm's demand curve, however. Even if we were sure of data for this product industry-wide, we cannot be sure just how rivals would react to a price change by our firm under analysis.
3. Qualitative change of product, known as product differentiation, is a feature of many situations, and intrudes additional elements of uncertainty. Is a substantial degree of differentiation in fact a new product? Is a Cadillac one product, a Rolls Royce another?
4. For reasons of convenience, functions are assumed to be well-behaved, meaning continuous and geometrically rational. Cost curves must be U-shaped. Demand functions are usually treated as linear, partly as a simple matter of convenience.

5. The law of supply states that quantity supplied is a direct function of price. Hence the cheaper by the dozen concept and anything else that seems to contradict the principle of profit maximization (at the quantity at which marginal cost is equated with marginal revenue) must be regarded as a special case.

6. An example of the problem just referred to is the phenomenon known as mark-up pricing. A firm is perceived as calculating cost, in any of several ways, and then applying a percentage markup established in part by custom in that industry. This gives price, and in such models price is set by supply cost rather than by demand, separate and apart. The firm produces whatever quantity it proves able to sell at this price. Demand thus has its role, that of determining quantity. This algorithm, that supply determines price while demand determines quantity, clearly yields an equilibrium situation in the short run. If profit seems satisfactory, the procedure may be followed indefinitely, meaning a long run equilibrium with investment or capital changes being made to continue the situation.

7. The example mentioned may be a problem for this type of modeling. The usual argument is made that if the firm tried this simplistic mark-up pricing algorithm, unless it maximized profits by chance, a rival would undercut its price and force it into maximization. But we must recall that our firm has a differentiated product or market, or source of inputs, or some such feature, which gave it the sloping demand curve in the first place.

8. The geometry employed shows conclusively the need to distinguish a logical construction called productive efficiency from another conception called allocative efficiency. The former means operation with lowest possible cost of inputs, which is the low point of the total unit cost curve. The latter means operation with price equal to marginal cost. The former happens only by chance, while the latter can never be the case with the profit-maximizing oligopoly firm. Somehow capitalism is seen as highly efficient even if most production is under conditions not achieving either allocative or productive efficiency in the use of resources, even in terms of the accepted models. Somewhere religion or dogma must have crept in. Some economists have turned to the concept of "contestability" to avoid this embarrassment. Contestability acknowledges monopoly or oligopoly

power, but insists that potential competition is always the case and serves just as effectively as does actual competition.

9. Some economists are circumspect in the use of models to describe the operation of an oligopoly firm, where there is competition of a few, but what are college sophomores to be told? The standard procedure is to beg questions of identification of the demand curve of one firm, and also to assume that supply is the same thing as cost. The diagrams invariably show the oligopolist maximizing profit, which may appear to be a large "pure" profit. Then the argument is advanced that rival firms will be attracted, and long-run economic profits are about zero, which is "normal." This is easily done, by drawing the demand curve tangent to the average total cost curve, at the quantity at which marginal cost and marginal revenue are equated. This is drawn with no problems, and the presumption is that somehow market forces cause this to happen. Allocative and productive efficiency are simply forgotten about, since neither could even possibly result in such a case.

10. If the oligopolist is reduced to zero or normal-profit operation, his unit costs necessarily are higher than the low point that is defined as productive efficiency, and his output and his use of inputs are suspect as well. We fall back on the notion that the market takes care of these things rather well even if not perfectly, and what we have is more efficient than what the socialists have ever managed.

11. Joan Robinson presented algebraic equations which show unmistakably that price elasticity of demand is co-determined along with price and quantity in all of these models, and this is also the case with respect to the markup of price over marginal cost. (This is the case even if no mark-up pricing procedure is alleged.) Shortrun profit is indeed maximized at the point where marginal cost equals marginal revenue, in terms of standard definitions. The Robinson equations can be rearranged as $Ed = 1/1-(MC/P)$. This makes the model embarrassingly overdeterministic, too mechanistic for anyone to believe. When a firm follows the invisible hand to the quantity where $MC = MR$, this simultaneously establishes or reflects the price elasticity of demand. Economists deal with this embarrassing fact by not mentioning it. Empirical studies simply do not reveal elasticity coefficients that are of a magnitude similar to that required by proper functioning of the model.

12. To quote a paragraph published by this author a few years ago: "The central meaning of neoclassical economics as price theory emerges here with stark clarity, however. If elasticity is -3, markup over MC is 50 percent, no more, no less. If a firm markets a product for which elasticity is -2, then the equilibrium markup is 100 percent. If one believes that a reasonable markup is for price to be 133 percent of MC, then elasticity has to be -4. Or, to use [a cited expert's] ratio, if one considers that a 50 percent markup is as much as equity and avoidance of exploitation permit, then the elasticity must be -3. Stated differently, is there any reason to believe that elasticity coefficients for products of individual firms range closely between -3 and -4? A more rigid formulation of theoretical implications is difficult to imagine, and yet economics treatises do not call attention to these deterministic ratios. Quadrant diagrams of this type in *Principles* and *Intermediate Microeconomics* textbooks almost all presuppose markups of approximately 100 percent."[2]

Hence the mainline doctrines of economics have been pushed to a point of mere formalism. Business schools, with purposes slightly different from theoretical economists, use the double-entry bookkeeping concept, which they share with economics-as-dogma, but they find it necessary to yield to realities at least a bit, and turn to managerial and organizational theories in attempts to understand something of the actual operational methods of the giants. There is an abundance of non-Newtonian managerial literature, and we mention only economics Nobel laureate Herbert A. Simon.

A topic for comment here would be what is called public utility regulation. Economists long have recognized that what they call "natural" monopolies cannot be expected to yield efficient production at desirable quantities and with reasonable prices. Only one electric power line, gas line, rail line, or water line into an area makes much sense, because duplication of facilities would be cumbersome and costly. How the rationality for hybrid cases such as telephone and airline services will run remains to be seen.

The monopolist is in a position to demand high prices for the good or service. Most countries in the world have long since turned to public ownership of most utilities, and have included telephones, telegraph, bus lines, airlines, and often medical services. Educational facilities and teaching, plus roads and highways, are publicly owned and operated, or as mixed ventures, in almost every country. Housing and agriculture are controlled and subsidized almost everywhere. Banking, money and credit, and insurance of many varied kinds are not left to free market forces, and no one leaves basic scientific research to the mercies of the market. No sharp line can be drawn between private and public, capitalist and noncapitalist ventures. Most of the large output European automobile companies have the government as either an active partner, as is the case with Volkswagen, Renault, Fiat, and British Leyland, or as a financial backer. Chrysler was pulled back from certain bankruptcy by the U.S. government a few years back. The price, quality, and quantity questions, including the rates of pay for inputs, have almost always been answered on an ad hoc basis. How could it be otherwise, since a mechanistic theory of "public interest" enterprises is a flat contradiction in terms because mechanism came to us via Newton and presupposes autonomous, nonsocially interactive units or individuals, with the mode of social control specified as competition? Public interest has to mean community, not individuals. The brain or decision making process cannot be viewed as a black box by which individuals maximize. What "the public" does cannot be analogous to the black box; there is nothing reasonably to be called the "public brain."

Procedurally, people struggle and vote to get something put into, or taken out of, the classification of activities known as public utilities. Then the assumption is made, overtly or covertly, that the utility will buy its inputs at prices similar to those that prevail in competitive markets; it will be operated efficiently as to production and distribution of its product; and its selling price of output will be expected to cover costs as a first approximation. Then the question arises of whether any price at all will enable costs to be covered—a common example of this problem being city buses—and should operation at a loss be done? How much can subsidy be, and how will it be financed? These heavily pecuniary problems have been around for a few centuries, and likely are going to continue. Why should they be especially disturbing? Most goods can be sold at prices that cover most or all cost, and some "not-so-goods," such as cigarettes and alcohol, sell under conditions that yield a reward to public agencies as well as private. Education requires heavy subsidy because six-year-old consumers simply will not buy it at prices covering cost!

From our perspective, most production clearly is vested with public interest, and the crucial issues are the ancient moral question of what is to be produced? How do we decide what ought to be? How much research and change, when and in what directions? What is the quality of the public utility we are asked to impose price upon? Natural gas is well standardized as to quality. What if we are deliberating about automobiles or refrigerators? It may or may not be the case that automobile companies the world around are separate and distinct enough in price-quality decisions so that we can use the patterns set elsewhere. What if those others are looking to us for guidance? The point here is that even today there is less monopoly power at the international level than within one country for many product lines.

Therefore any car production will need to be done with a view to matching price and quality considerations, after shipping and taxes, of cars made anywhere else. Or perhaps we decide that we have enough cars already, so we operate just one company, as a public monopoly, and deliberately price the cars high enough to yield a large profit to the public's government, whether or not profit is maximized. But who is going to make research and design decisions? Better public agencies than private. Cars are vested with public interest, a consideration that seems to indicate much more public means of transport for a long time to come.

Orthodox mechanism could never be a vehicle for change nor the foundation of theory that deals with change. Consequently the Great Depression dragged along for three and a half years, from Black Thursday in October 1929 until after the inauguration of F. D. Roosevelt in March 1933, with nothing much being done other than to observe economists' advice that shortly the situation would correct itself. There can be little doubt that if one interferes with a self-correcting mechanism, one has a mess. But this begs the central question: Why think of society as a self-correcting mechanism? Roosevelt had little idea of what to do, but he recognized that hungry people need food, that there were fields and factories in place where unemployed men had formerly worked, and that there was no mechanism established by any god to correct the situation. We will not attempt even a listing of New Deal programs, but we note that they had the effect of lessening private interference with social matters. As would have been predictable and politically necessary, government was put to work supporting private interferences and predations much more often than public operations were set up to replace private schemes. This calls to attention two criticisms of the American experience of the Great Depression, both made from time to time by numerous persons. Why was much more not done? Why was the learning experience dropped or forgotten after World War II had brought on line a new prosperity? The intrinsically conservative nature of American Leisure Class capitalism produces economists who cannot transcend the models of mechanism so that they kept right on rationalizing the status quo, or, much worse by way of appraising their efforts or nonefforts, rationalizing the status quo ante, the assumed good old days.[3]

There was a small subset of American economists on the scene in the 1930s who called themselves Institutionalists and purported to be followers of Veblen, but they did not rise to the occasion with well-articulated theory, explanation, or demands. Specifically, through the l930s they lacked an adequate theory of income determination and thus were unable to do the kinds of things Keynes did. Moreover, being for the most part strongly opposed to mathematical model building and equilibrium systems, they were unable to use Keynes's ideas effectively after they were widely disseminated. Further, for the most part they did not develop leads that Veblen had offered. Clarence Ayres, a leader in what is called neo-Institutionalist theoretical work, departed from Veblen's radical critiques and instead wrote rationalizations of the status quo. This reversal of Veblen came about by Ayres, a philosopher rather than an economist, becoming a "complete materialist" technologist. He then jumped to the conclusion that "truth" relates to the future, not to the past, and means whatever is technologically possible. Furthermore, technology is deterministic of human affairs, meaning that societies will do whatever is necessary to enable achievement of the levels of wealth and prosperity that technology makes possible. Scientific possibilities will be achieved, and without serious struggle. Hence we strongly tend at all times toward the best of all possible worlds. Marginal institutional adjustments are required to permit the sunlight of technology to flow freely, so to speak. Classicists, of course, want the sunlight of market forces to flow freely. For Institutionalists, we have reached the welfare state, which is as close as we need ever be to the "promised land." Hardly surprisingly, one of Ayres's articles bears the title, "The Gospel of Technology." [4]

Institutionalists quite properly reject the Cartesian mechanical philosophy and its dualisms, especially of mind-body. The Cartesian method begins with universal doubt, however, and hence orthodox economics can hardly be construed as fully Cartesian because of the stubborn refusal to reject or "doubt" equilibrium. In fact Classical or orthodox economics not uncommonly is referred to by devotees and critics alike as equilibrium economics. Moreover, another anomaly is brought to life in the writings of Institutionalists. As early as Adam Smith, a clear distinction was drawn between *use value* and *exchange value*, with emphasis that the proper concern of economics is with exchange value. Veblen projected the thought to the conclusion that concern with pecuniary or exchange values has come to dominate or overwhelm attention given to production of industrial or use values. This development of the use value—exchange value dichotomy— became a central feature of his thought. Institutionalists have closely followed Clarence Ayres in his further projection, to visualize the dichotomy as being between technology and institutions, which is a very wide leap from the use value—exchange value origins. Serious problems emerge. If institutions mean customs or traditional beliefs as to how things should be and should be done, and if "institutional adjustment" is a part of progress, then there must be something else allowed in the theoretical apparatus to correspond to "relatively serviceable" institutions. If the categories of technology and ceremonial institutions were to be continued, then serviceable institutions clearly would yield a trichotomy, not a mere dichotomy. This step the Institutionalists have not been willing to take. In short, it appears that the Institutionalists for the most part are quite institutionalized. They repeat doctrines or "keep the faith," but are reluctant to evolve. Their reluctance to use facts, data, and quantitative techniques as required to handle data seems to involve a perception of economics as something of a no-contact sport vis-à-vis the empirical world.

Veblen had a suitable theory of boom and bust as early as his 1904 book. He wrote:

> the explanation here offered of depression makes it a malady of the affections. The discrepancy which discourages businessmen is a discrepancy between that nominal capitalization which they have set their hearts upon through habituation in the immediate past and that actual capitalization value of their property which its current earning-capacity will warrant.[5]

After the elections of 1932 had brought the possibility and even the insistence that government play a positive and greatly expanded role in the economy, followers of Veblen should have been clamoring for government to replace business in industries where power was highly concentrated and where production had fallen the most. Possibly the Institutionalists thought of evolution as something that was going on behind the scenes of human choice, and could not bring themselves to insist on active intervention into social affairs. Veblen had not presented much in the way of programs of what to do. According to

Georgescu-Roegen, it appears that "the American Institutionalists, though hailing Veblen as their prophet, have inherited little from him besides an aggressive scorn for 'theory.' Be this as it may, Paul T. Homan . . . has completely missed the issue raised by Veblen."[6] Homan's error was half a century ago.

Anyone who suggests programs is in trouble because others always can ask, "why that instead of this?" and at best, parts of *any* program prove unworkable. In a situation like the 1930s, activists always had at hand the stinging retort: Are things satisfactory as they are?

Keynes: Transcendence of Laissez-Faire Mechanism

The Britisher Keynes came forward with programmatic explanations. His ideas have been presented so many times that we need not detail them here. A few sentences must suffice. In effect he said that all industrial capitalisms were severely depressed in the 1930s, the situation was not righting itself, and most countries were veering sharply off to either the far right or the far left. In either move the forces of the market were being shoved aside, along with private property and any semblance of free expression and democracy. The days of laissez-faire were over, and something must be done.

Should we take over and manipulate demand or supply? Either case might do, but demand is the better choice. It does not involve property ownership and hence detailed control of productive activities. Governmental programs of fiscal and monetary policy can be managed so as to assure that total demand will equal the price value of total supply, at full employment levels. Production or supply can be left in private hands, and businessmen will be glad to produce, or to dig up old bottles, so long as it is profitable. The takeover of supply is both unnecessary and counterproductive, since nationalization of industry would stir up a revolution of protests, and the businessmen can manage production better than the bureaucrats any way. Say's Law of Markets has proved unreliable, but the obverse law, oversimplified to state that "demand creates its own supply," can be substituted and will bring us to full employment of resources. It is assumed that microeconomic theory and the degree of competition are satisfactory.

Keynes proceeded to identify and analyze what he saw as the subsets of spending or demand done by consumers, by government, by business real investment, and the foreign trade balance. Each of these subsets had been analyzed many times long before Keynes. A keystone of mechanism known as Say's Law had prevented theoretical progress by way of the preconception of thought (custom or institution) that if one or more categories of spending falls longer than just briefly, others rise commensurately. If consumer income not spent is called saving, and if this sector of money movement rises, interest rates paid for it should fall. Lower interest rates make investment spending cheaper so investment rises to offset consumption decline. This is mechanism with a vengeance. If consumption spending falls, are not productive facilities thrown into idleness? If present productive investments are idle, will there be a rush to build more, even if interest rates on debt financing are down from their trend? Mechanism as dogma is tantamount to mechanism as religion.

Why it was Keynes, and not someone else, who formulated the demand-centered view of how to save capitalism from either far left or far right totalitarianism is understandable if one recalls that he had rejected crucial parts of mechanism exactly a decade before *The General Theory* was published. Also, however, it is essential to note that the alternate formulation of "Law" would be perhaps equally mechanistic, and so Keynes's thinking and theorizing is much more complex than just reversing elements within the Law. Be this as it may, in the 1926 publication entitled *The End of Laissez Faire*, he expressed outrage at the philosophical underpinnings of received economic theory:

> Let us clear from the ground the metaphysical or general principles upon which, from time to time, *laissez-faire* has been founded. It is *not* true that individuals possess a prescriptive "natural liberty" in their economic activities. There is *no* "compact" conferring perpetual rights on those who Have or on those who Acquire. The world is *not* so governed from above that private and social interests always coincide. It is *not* so managed here below that in practice they coincide. It is *not* a correct deduction from the Principles of Economics that enlightened self-interest always operates in the public interest. Nor is it true that self-interest generally *is* enlightened; more often individuals acting separately to promote their own ends are too ignorant or too weak to attain even these. Experience does *not* show that individuals, when they make up a social unit, are always less clear-sighted than when they act separately.[7]

Continuing his thought:

> Perhaps the chief task of Economists at this hour is to distinguish afresh the *Agenda* of Government from the *Non-Agenda*; and the companion

task of Politics is to devise forms of Government within a Democracy which shall be capable of accomplishing the *Agenda*.

This is a sharp and pointed rejection of laissez-faire and the idea of a self-adjusting mechanism at work in political and economic affairs made by an accomplished scholar from within the ranks of economic reputability. Keynes's father, John Neville Keynes, was a highly respected economist and logician. John Maynard Keynes was a product of Cambridge, had held high governmental posts, and was famous for having written *The Economic Consequences of the Peace* at the end of World War I. He also had authored a work on Indian currency reform, and in 1930 published the remarkable two-volume *Treatise on Money*.[8]

Since the 1936 *General Theory* came at a time far along into the Depression, when something was already being done in England and in the United States, one might have thought that the Keynesian writ for saving capitalism would have been instantly and joyously received. Such was not at all the case, however. His rejection of the automaticity of mechanism simply was a rejection of all that was important in standard, neo-Classical economics. The economics profession could not and never did really accept Keynes. Certainly his ideas on saving capitalism by assuring adequate spending have early and late been put to use, and presidents and textbooks regularly proclaim that "we are all Keynesians now."

Keynes's thought, like that of Marx and Veblen, is complex. He never specifically formulated what we are calling Keynes's Law of Markets, although that implication is unmistakable. How could Keynes be expected to acknowledge such a Law, since he was in open revolt against mechanism? The possibility of interpreting him in a way that might salvage both capitalism and mechanism has been too appealing to resist, however. After his demolition of Say's obverse Law, Keynes's version is not safe to enunciate because it is now too easy to fault by noting that increase in prices may result from increased spending, rather than the desired increase of output. It is, however, a part of economic doctrine since Keynes that businessmen will not be left to face distinctly inadequate demand for their potential output, at customary levels rather than full employment levels. If the contriving of demand is required as part of the contriving of prosperity, we do it and will keep doing it, dropping the concern for full employment and "foolish" talk by Keynes about "euthanasia of the rentier." Military spending is a delightful phenomenon in this context in that it engenders the entire line of cultural repression that Veblen cautioned about, and in general may be regarded as a mixture of conservatism and reaction. Military and space program spending, research and development spending and tax write-offs, educational spending that shapes philosophies dominating institutions of higher learning into ever more conservative channels: these and other programs are government of, by, and for the rich. Banks, money, and monetarism long have been bastions of conservatism.

The reform ideas of Keynes have been thrust aside, and for that and other reasons power in the economy has been ignored as it has become ever more concentrated, as have its coordinate factors, income and wealth. Hence the economy has not functioned well for two decades. What would be the predictable reaction of the economics profession to this high level stagnation, as it sometimes is called? Some theorists have demanded that we move forward with new ideas, but that implies interventionism even beyond what has thus far been done, and that looks like socialism. The alternate route is backward, and that is far more appealing to anyone imbued with the spirit of mechanism. First, assert that this has been the "Age of Keynes," then that it and he have failed, and that monetarism plus militaristic programs with fiscal deficits will provide the spending we need for prosperity.

Since it is certain that mechanism does not apply to the world of biology, and the humans we economists are concerned with are alive, then the doctrines of orthodoxy are dogma, not science. Keynes took a long look at Marxism during his search for explanation and theory during the 1930s, and did not like what he saw. Marxism linked Hegelian dialectic to English doctrines of natural rights and a large measure of hedonic rationality on the part of workers during a depression. Such a philosophy contains large elements of mechanistic determinism, no more suitable to Keynes than was capitalist orthodoxy. Why merely jump from the frying pan into the fire, Keynes might have mused.

His break with the past was considerable for he turned to propensities, tendencies, expectations, uncertainties, and even animal spirits in explaining or listing motivations underlying both investment and consumption. He recognized the importance of the fact that consumption spending necessarily relates to income as the prime source of purchasing power, but that as real income changes, nearly everyone will change consumption spending in the same direction, up or down, but by a smaller amount than the income change. Household saving, meaning income not spent right away on consumption, was a readily observable fact. Keynes, having rejected mechanism, was able to see the meaning of the facts at hand: only the well-to-do did much saving, and neither parsimony nor the appeal of interest rates had much to do with it. We must not inject Veblen's language, but the rich saved because getting richer is honorific or a means to status, and their high level consumption spending in quest of status did not exhaust their available funds. There was nothing noble or even constructive or beneficial about saving as such. If the economic requisites of supply were short, meaning that demand was pressing hard against supply, then a reduction of consumption spending offered a good prospect of being compensated by an expansion of spending on additional means of production, called investment. But during depression, total spending is demonstrably too low to buy all that could be produced with facilities already in place. All four of the major subsets of spending (consumption, investment, governmental, and exports net of imports) are suspect of being low, one or several. Saving as nonconsuming will further restrict total demand, and thus tend to reduce investment spending still further, not raise it. Who would build new factories in an era when those already in place are running at half capacity?

Keynes's consumption function definitionally is mechanistic in its conformity with Cartesian mathematical approaches and those of Newton's great mathematical invention, calculus, without Keynes himself becoming entrapped in mechanism. Newton's problems and his solutions were nothing without equilibrium, in the sense of what universal gravitation does. The planets indeed stay in orbit, but Keynes rejected even equilibrium in its Newtonian sense. Economic actors in motion might tend to bring a balance of supply to accommodate total demand. The system, however, is perceived by Keynes as continually in change, and never is there any natural force whatsoever that leads to a satisfactory or even stable condition. Newton's God ''hurled the planets,'' but Keynes has no God.

What are the Keynesian determinants of the amount of investment spending? The formal model is fairly simple and straightforward. First, investment spending is not a function of income, viewed either individually or in some macro sense. Automatic adjustment of consumption and investment (one rising when and because the other falls) is the conception most emphatically to be avoided, because that is Say's Law, automaticity and mechanism. Investment spending depends upon the marginal efficiency of capital, which is the comparison of interest rates that would have to be paid to get additional capital money, and the anticipated rate of return from the operation of additional (marginal) capital. If earnings expectations are at higher rates than the interest cost of capital, investments are feasible. This combines with consumption spending (a function of income) to yield a prediction or calculation of how much production is justifiable in terms of sales or demand.

Government spending goes into the model and is the source of possible salvation of capitalism, ironic though that may sound. Government spending clearly is not a function of income—a glance at data shows that, nor is government spending closely tied to either interest rates or profit expectations. Therefore government spending can be altered in magnitude to compensate for what the private sectors (households and businesses) are doing. The foreign trade sector is not highly manipulable because foreigners are not totally under our control (even if domestic residents were).

In the formal model one may or may not take the functional relationships as linear. Such an assumption greatly simplifies the analysis, and with respect to investment spending, it is easy to throw in the provision, "linear at quantities near what is actually observed." Keynes's consumption function is more problematic in this respect. He needed linearity for simplicity, but that is not the major issue. The problem was that even a modicum of concern for reality requires that this function have a large intercept value, recognizing that at moderately low incomes people spend as much on consumption as their income, and at still lower incomes they dissave, or spend from past savings as well as going into debt, so that consumption is larger than income. But how much would consumption be in the absence of any production at all in the economy? Such a condition is not realistically imaginable, but the formal model strictly mandates the need for a value or magnitude of such "autonomous consumption." Nobody can know what consumption would total at zero production—beyond a one-day holiday or other such anomaly, useless in this context. Thus, the non-Keynesian assumption frequently is made that the consumption function is linear but as a "ray" through the point of origin of the diagram axes. Or, if the Keynesian marginal propensity to consume is manipulated appropriately, one gets a small intercept value, which seems not to offend anyone. The assumptions yield an equilibrium, and on its own terms, the model is a success, but theories of the consumption function remain confused.

However, as one of his better students, Joan Robinson, remarked, Keynes "does not take his own formal model seriously."[9] This statement is both true and false, because for Keynes "animal spirits" determine investment activity in the long run much more than do such things as interest rates and that "great unknowable," profit expectations. In standard interpretations, however, that is not part of his model, and he is interpreted as another mechanist. One can get past Keynes's own complexities and plug some pseudodata into the model. In a sense this is the strength, vitality, and relevance of Keynes. Out of uncertainties he pulls the relevant tendencies and shapes them into mathematically manipulable form. Thus he gets useful, workable answers, but always on a tentative basis. The model is a creature of his thought, but his thought never becomes a creature of his model. Very few indeed are the economists of whom as much can be said.

Keynes's open rejection of mechanism meant that his thought could never be accepted by the orthodox. He wrote:

> The object of our analysis is, not to provide a machine, or method of blind manipulation, which will furnish an infallible answer, but to provide ourselves with an organized and orderly method of thinking out particular problems; and, after we have reached a provisional conclusion by isolating the complicating factors one by one, we then have to go back on ourselves and allow as well as we can, for the probable interactions of the factors amongst themselves. This is the nature of economic thinking. Any other way of applying our formal principles of thought . . . will lead us into error.[10]

He rejected the idea of a machine for blind manipulation, but that is what orthodox, Robinson Crusoe mechanics seeks. Hence it is disingenuous to declare that Keynes has been proved wrong. He was "wrong" in this sense from the beginning, and anyone who does not follow the holy writ of mechanism is also wrong. Our own rejection of mechanism possibly stems from Keynes as much as from Veblen or Einstein, but be that as it may, would we apply to Keynes his own dictum that in the long run we are all dead? Was Keynes right or wrong? We find little fault with his methods. Granting him legitimacy in his concern to pull capitalism out of the Great Depression, we see his model as highly successful, and the failure lay in not applying it forcefully or on large scale. Was his concern for increasing investment spending as a high priority well grounded? In a pragmatic sense that was feasible. The top capitalists are the ruling class and a revolution in the United States during the pre-*General Theory* first half of the 1930s did not happen. Programs to stimulate investment placated at least some of the ruling capitalists, and enabled the adoption of several leftist reforms such as Social Security, aid to agriculture, labor laws, welfare grants and spending, and public works spending. Keynes's ideas helped prevent the possible death of capitalism and several millions of destitute persons as well.

No one labels *The General Theory* mere nontheoretical, ad hoc pragmatic expediency. In the longer run, how may the appraisals run? The vast governmental spending occasioned by the resurgence of war from the late 1930s on for a decade at least, and through the Korean War (1950–53) in the case of the United States, insured adequate demand. The American economy faltered in 1948 because of weak demand, but there was no doubt at all concerning the applicability of the new economics as providing the prescription for the cure. American entry into the Korean War in mid-1950 is not credible as a deliberate move to assure prosperity or to cope with contradictions of capitalism, but it is credible as a move to protect the scope of the far-flung American empire, the nature of which was at the time very much in flux. Keynes died in 1946. What theoretical adjustments he would have made in his own model, and just what he would have urged as a public policy adviser, consequently are unknowable. We have, to be sure, his statements rejecting both laissez-faire and a "machine for blind manipulation." No one doubts that he would have learned and adjusted his thought, theories, and recommendations.

Large-scale investment spending in most circumstances is a two-edged sword, dangerous to play with. Keynes wanted investment spending primarily as a mode of increasing total demand during the worst of the Great Depression. Factories and other apparatus of production were sitting idle by the hundreds, and multitudes of others were running on reduced schedules. Why build more, except to increase spending and bring the famous multiplier into action, in effect putting previously existing productive apparatus into active service? Neither Keynes nor anyone else can argue that investment spending necessarily creates a market for the potential product of the unemployed machines sitting idle when the investment projects are undertaken, *plus* market demand for output of the machines presumably embodied in the investment currently being done. Investment-spending-as-demand is not unthinkable for a brief time period, a way to start a climb out of a depression. But once built, we have investment-spending-as-supply, and this additional capacity requires additional demand. This becomes a challenge and an opportunity. We pose the issue this way in order to emphasize the differences between Keynes and the neo-Keynesians. Strictly speaking, in the model by Keynes there could not be a major problem because he built in an elaborate supply function that envisions investment taking place only in response to businessmen's supply-side calculations of demand.

Keynes's warning was stated clearly: "Each time we secure today's equilibrium by increased investment we are aggravating the difficulty of securing equilibrium tomorrow."[11] Here he obviously was using the term equilibrium to mean a satisfactory state of affairs that we do not urgently seek to change, not a depressed state equilibrium. Recent decades have witnessed the development of multiplier-accelerator models that purport to deal with the problems, but they are almost wholly formal exercises only.

If things went as projected, the capacity built up by supply-side capitalists thus would not be expanded beyond demand expectations even if tax write-offs provided satanic lures. One might well ask, but what if businessmen, in their exuberance characteristic of the boom phase of the trade cycle, or in their quest to outdo each other, made estimates that were overly ambitious? Keynes admitted assuming accuracy of businessmen's projections, and it is clear that he did so for the worthy reason of demolishing Say's Law.[12] Orthodox thought admitted that demand might falter temporarily, but only until "undertakers" could make adjustments to accommodate realities. They might err on the side of caution, not spend enough on investment, and thus not use all of the savings that were envisioned as preceding investment. Keynes set up his supply and demand functions in such a way that perfect insight or projections still left unemployment as the general case. Hence we do not wish to quarrel with Keynes on this point. In the real world of capitalisms, Keynes's supply function has been shunted aside and interest thrown almost exclusively onto demand considerations. Consequently, investment has been aided and abetted purely as a spending or demand phenomenon, to which upward shift this concept (the multiplier) could be applied, and hence output and income impressively enlarged. One standard procedure has been to use tax incentives to encourage investment spending. Accelerated depreciation schedules and other programs have led businessmen to bypass considerations of adequacy of long run demand for the output of their new equipment. In the money-capital markets more equipment is not necessarily the result or even the aim. Takeovers are the way to make profit for the manipulators. Keynes, and Veblen before him, saw the froth of the stock market gambling casino as a ludicrous means of operating an economy. The validity of such assessment is simply undeniable. Programs of mere pecuniary manipulation therefore are not Keynesian, even in the very short run.

We must note that even the idea of a supply function has been dropped by most neo-Keynesians. They find it convenient to use quadrant diagrams that merely substitute a forty-five degree line or ray, giving "the Samuelson cross." The procedure is mathematically correct in that all points on such a reference line are equidistant from the axes. Thus a point on the line where the aggregate demand schedule crosses it identifies an equilibrium of output equal to sales, properly construed. This is not mathematically incorrect, but it certainly is not Keynesian and such procedure underlies the promulgation of "Keynes Law of Markets" as being adequate. This type of neo-Keynesianism has failed to solve problems during the last two decades, especially those of stagflation. Keynes's ideas, properly formulated, could hardly have failed completely since his full system has not been used.

Two in number are the broad fronts of Keynes that are especially congruent with our philosophical views. Negatively, he strongly renounced not just laissez-faire but the doctrine of mechanism. Affirmatively, he worked out a system of theory that used mathematical and analytical techniques without becoming ensnared by illusions of eternal truth. Keynes asked, consistently and repeatedly, how do people actually behave, and what are their motivations? What is the nature of the actual setting? His entire model is a system of double-entry accounting, but it must not be assumed purely mechanical on that account. The accounting is a tool of great convenience not to be cast aside by anyone. He apparently saw little point in asking himself the question of whether he was at heart a socialist or a capitalist. Those are rigid and antithetical ideas, and as systems both are mechanistic, doctrinaire, and inflexible. They are also failures in a major degree. His own society was capitalist for the most part, and there were many things about it that he thought would continue and were worthy of being continued. Keynes (or anyone else) had but to look out the window any day of the 1930s to see that we live in an imperfect world. It will not be made perfect by any person arguing for laissez-faire, nor by any country merely becoming socialist. Socialism could be attempted only after bloody revolution. What could he, one man, do? Did he call for bailing out the banks? Or saving businesses from bankruptcy for the sake of the owners? Or for maintaining the claims of the rentier? None of these; his clear priority was jobs and the production of useful things for a rational and peaceable world, for "establishing an aggregate volume of output corresponding to full employment as nearly as is practicable."[13]

Keynes's use of wage-units, the wage of unskilled labor and hours of common labor-time, as his basic measure throughout the model along with several other considerations made it look as if he indeed was a traitor to his class and was trying to entice us into creeping socialism. Perhaps so, but he would have us proceed openly and democratically at all times. His purpose was to try to save capitalism from a turn to either far left or far right, as other countries were doing in the 1930s. He saw the need for public programs and enactments to get the system back to full employment. Entrepreneurs, banks, stock markets, private property, enforcement of contracts—all of these foundations of capitalism were to be modified, then left in place until society in some democratic forum or process should choose to further alter or discontinue any of them. Having rejected mechanism and laissez-faire, Keynes took change and yet more change, as time passed and conditions altered, as fundamental to his view. He was in no sense a dictator as some of the later abusers of his thought tend to be. The modern neo-Keynesians seek both to restore the old doctrines of mechanism, and rationalize a degree of concentration of wealth, income, and power that Keynes found appalling and unworkable. That the industrial capitalisms of this Final Third of the century do not function well, but have seemingly intractable problems of militarism, slow growth, inflation, unemployment, and debt that soars out of control is more nearly testimony of the unwisdom of turning our backs on Keynes than of the unwisdom of Keynes himself. It is much more nearly the case that the IS-LM type of neo-Keynesian counterrevolutionary modeling has failed rather than the ideas of Keynes.

One may think back to the statements by Albert Einstein. The doctrines and laws of mechanism do not apply to human social relations, and that is a point we simply need not feel obliged to continue arguing. What we have maintained in our society, have kept staggering along by trying to keep those doctrines alive, is what Einstein and Veblen called "the predatory phase" of human development. As we previously quoted Einstein, the facts of our age "belong to that phase and even such laws as we can derive from them are not applicable to other phases." Keynes threw out such laws, and tried to help us get past the predatory phase in the sense of seeing to it that full employment of persons and the coordinate full output of goods would be achieved. This would be a giant step away from preying upon workers by thrusting them into the harsh world of unemployment and by chance pulling them back out of this reserve army of the unemployed at the whims of capitalists. Our practices in the Third World gruesomely illustrate the point. Accordingly, Keynes saw fit to start building a postpredatory world. If he had planned to stop all social change once the capitalist system was back on its feet, or if, to the contrary, there were in fact a beautifully functioning system of democratic socialism somewhere to be inspected and modeled after, we could be severely critical of Keynes. His entire model of social accounting, forward-looking in the sense of being based on uncertainties and expectations, instead of the backward facing after-the-fact mechanistic models of almost everyone else, is the type of theorizing we need. Instead of relying on blind manipulation, Keynes sought, as was mentioned previously, "to provide ourselves with an organized and orderly method of thinking out particular problems" that change through time.

What do we consider to be Keynes's major contribution? Our answer is his undeviating break with mechanism and its corollary, laissez-faire. This opinion is antithetical to that of orthodox economists, who see the major contribution of Keynes as his ideas on the consumption function, or perhaps the multiplier, or certainly some mechanistic, mathematical formulation by him. They miss the most important point entirely, and are unable to interpret Keynes except on their own grounds of doctrines of mechanism.

Keynes's break was complete during the 1920s, but we must bear in mind that such a view did not nor need not prevent him or anyone else from using mathematical and logical tools. This Keynesian revolution is the one we all need to make, even though most social theorists do not see the point, or the possibility of mathematics used tentatively. The idea of "zeroing in on the truth," establishing or discovering relationships that endure forever, is still the common image of what science is about. As Arthur Koestler observed more than two decades ago, during the heyday of success and fine-tuning by economists:

> our vision of the world is by and large still Newtonian. . . . If one had to sum up the history of scientific ideas about the universe in a single sentence, one could only say that up to the seventeenth century our vision was Aristotelian, after that Newtonian.[14]

This statement does not do full justice to Einstein's contributions, but since we are not pretending to know how to apply relativity to social affairs except as merely "evolution," we emphasize the truth of the observation. It appears that Koestler intended it to apply to philosophy and the social sciences as well as in physics, astronomy, and cosmology. Progress has involved a shift from Aristotle to Newton in most of our everyday thinking, but not much more. Keynes was one of few who transcended Newtonism. Veblen and Georgescu-Roegen were others. Marx took a side street, trying to combine science *à la* Newton with dialectics *à la* Hegel.

To observe that Keynes broke from Newtonian views in and of itself does not credit him with much, to be sure, so we must repeat the positive contributions that he made. Hoping to avoid tediousness in our repetitions, we note that he set up theoretical categories of analysis that were designed to cope with the issue of how people do, in fact, behave. Household consumption and business firm investment were the two sets of factors from the demand side, and householders as laborers share attention with businesses on the supply side. Labor units and wage units tie together, and make it feasible to view consumption as a function of this same labor-and-production process. But labor units—wage units, user cost, and the bearing of consumer spending on the marginal efficiency of capital—all tie workers and capitalists together on the supply side. Supply and demand are welded together by Keynes, and the conception of utility-disutility, pleasure and pain, fades away. A utility function as such is not part of Keynesian furniture, and this is the case with his microfoundations as well as the more obvious macroviews. Orthodox economics is still essentially utilitarian as the mode of utilization of Newtonian philosophy. That we must take care to sharply distinguish supply considerations from those of demand is the orthodox view, or else we will not come out with the results that we postulate in advance that we must reach. When supply and demand functions, limited resources with which to cope with limitless wants, are assumed, we unmistakably are to construe economics as the science of rationing, the making of "rational rationing choices."

What does orthodoxy, in the older Classical versions, have to say about macroeconomics? In a sense there was none, because there was no need for one. In a macrosense the supply function and what Keynes treated as the demand function previously had been implicitly perceived as being mirror images or concurrent, following Say's Law. Modern macro-orthodoxy has ignored Keynes's formulations regarding supply by merely using the forty-five degree reference line, or submerging the whole system in the rationalistic constructs called IS-LM modeling and multiplier-accelerator analysis. This has the effect of establishing the obverse law of markets that we have noted several times previously. What has been learned from Keynes by practitioners embued with the spirit of mechanism and steadfast rationalization of the status quo certainly is not Keynesian!

Debt and Saving in a "Debt-Side" Economy: Evolutionary Perspectives on a Perplexing Problem

Adam Smith was correct when he addressed his concern to the issue of ethics or what we mean by moral conduct. This was no less true with the second famous book, *The Wealth of Nations*, than it had been with the earlier *Theory of Moral Sentiments*. Today it is a truism statement that our national or macroproblems are more nearly political than economic, usually meaning that value questions stubbornly persist. As either problem type, the roots run deeply into philosophical issues of morality. How shall resources be created and used? What is worth doing? How much concern should we have for the future, and for the environment? Should we be deeply concerned about poverty? Why does it persist, even after multiple enlargement of per capita income? Would we be better advised to seek to minimize suffering, rather than trying to maximize pleasure? How do we best deal with externalities that lurk behind every move? Is the best possible advice that of trying to rely closely on market forces for solutions? Rather than avoidance of questions of "should," it becomes more obvious every day that science perceived as a method for gaining either understanding or control requires normative or "where are we trying to go" judgment, and hence wisdom instead of technique alone.

Several major changes that affect household saving have occurred in recent decades in the United States. We can identify five such changes:

1. Growth and alteration in the Social Security system;
2. Absence of major depression or notably high inflation for any prolonged period;
3. Rapid rise of debt financing of consumption spending;
4. Differentiation of savers from investors and the accompanying shift of saving to primarily a purely financial transaction except for education and health services;
5. Rising relative importance of investment in human capital in the form of spending on education and health service and hence implicit categorization as saving rather than consumption of portions of funds thus expended.

We propose an alternate method for calculating a saving rate that attempts to take into account the overall impact of the Social Security and Federal Employees Retirement systems on the household saving rate. Also we enumerate nine additional saving rates by way of comparison.

By orthodox measure, household saving in the United States fell by half during the 1980s, from about six to three percent. An impressionistic explanation comes readily to mind, and no doubt is largely accurate. During the 1970s Americans were coming out of the traumas of the Vietnam War, were confronting scarcities occasioned by oil and other shortages, were stunned by revelations of environmental damage, and were frustrated by inflation that hit double-digit rates. In 1980 they elected a federal administration that told them the cause of most maladies was "government on our backs," with grossly suppressed individual opportunities and gratifications. Accordingly, the 1980s witnessed an upsurge of self-aggrandizement, here-and-now material gratification, with further enlargement of buy-now-pay-later consumer debt to help finance it.[15] Status in the United States is demonstrated via consumption of conspicuous or luxury goods and services, but not by building up savings accounts. It is problematic for orthodox economics that its emphasis continues to rest upon individualistic perceptions of decision making and behavior, à la "economic man" modeling, whereas status intrinsically involves group interactions. Accordingly, economists tend to regard status as a concept appropriate to sociology but not economics.

Technological changes in the fields of mass media, especially television and radio, have been widely accepted and institutionalized. Advertising and other sales promotion effort has been enormously expanded as to scope, intensity of effort, and success as a selling device. Hence the status race has been greatly intensified, and conspicuous consumption remains the primary mode of expression of the concern for status. Wealth and income, the traditional means of affording high consumption, have been supplemented by massive use of consumer debt.

Since increased emphasis on conspicuous consumption is much the same thing as reduction of saving or nonconsumption, nothing analytical is achieved by stating the fact, and we must go on to some of the numerous complexities concerning meanings and measurements of saving. In recent decades, U.S. society has evolved in important respects. Some major changes that bear on saving have been within the social security system. This has been widely acknowledged but poorly understood.

The perplexing nature of the changes can be appreciated by briefly considering orthodox theories of the consumption function or relationship between the changing amount of disposable income and corresponding changes in consumption spending. Modigliani's Life Cycle model and the Permanent Income model of Friedman are the standard interpretations and are rather similar for most purposes. Each model envisions saving as a device for spreading consumption to a smooth or even rate over a person's lifetime. Inflation, income growth, sex and age composition of population, aspirations for bequests to heirs, uncertainty as to life span, and a few other complexities are abstracted away in the modeling.

The models recognize the fact of an interest rate available to savers in making time-preference decisions to save (not spend on consumption), and the long-term results are intriguing. For example, compound interest at seven percent results in interest accruals equal to the original principal in just a decade. Hence the working years of the average household, three or four decades in length, result in accrual of pay back claims due at retirement possibly totaling several times the amount saved and paid over to banks, government, corporations, or other financial intermediaries. Although most households achieve very little net saving, we see that in the long run the household sector receives more pay back per time period than it is setting aside as saving.[16] Only an explosive model in which saving as a percentage of income continually was rising could "avoid" the problem. One could differentiate gross saving taking place, on the one hand, from receipt of pay back and enjoyment of the fruits of deferred consumption gratifications, on the other, and thereby disclose that such a (gross) saving rate has not fallen, or perhaps has risen. Our orthodox measurement consists of subtracting consumption spending, however financed, from disposable income, and then taking this saving datum as a ratio to disposable income. Whatever the degree of uncertainty, this is a measurement of *net* saving.

Herein arises a paradox. If the Life Cycle types of models were strictly accurate, after a lengthy time annual pay back from financial intermediaries, etc., would exceed transfers to them from households. From the point of view of the intermediaries—government, corporations, and banks of various types—household saving would have become negative. The financial institutions would be in a genuine crisis concerning liabilities of payments due. This would be the case unless their income growth rate—and presumably that of the economy—exceeded or at least equalled the interest rate at which household claims were growing. Through most of our national history such a relationship prevailed, but during the 1980s our real interest rates were more than double the real growth rates. Although it is not our purpose to attempt the quantitative study necessary as proof, we offer the hypothesis that if interest rates substantially exceed income growth rates, then money and credit growth rates also must substantially exceed income growth. From this situation arise serious implications concerning repayment of claims, for prices, for income and wealth distribution, etc. The issue is treated further in the next section of this chapter.

Since the model would be explosive or unstable if the proportion of national income going to households steadily increased, limiting factors must prevail. Over the long run, pay back to households may equal but not greatly exceed total transfer of savings from households. Interest rates on savings of approximately the magnitude of income growth rates would accomplish this result. Historically what has happened is that the economy has always disposed of the problem of unmanageably large debt by, first, either depression and bankruptcies, so that much debt has been canceled without payment being made, or second, the economy has gone through lengthy periods of severe inflation, for example, in conjunction with war, so that much private debt is paid off with grossly inflated money. Hyper inflation is sometimes referred to as the Latin American mode of adjustment.

The economy of the United States has suffered neither severe depression (with a high rate of bankruptcies), nor prolonged rapid inflation during recent decades. Does this fact contradict or falsify the principles stated above? The answer is no, but the debt totals have continued to grow, and accordingly the likelihood of serious collapse has also increased. However, an institutional adjustment of gigantic magnitude has been made in a subset of the system, and was made to cope with exactly the problem outlined. The Social Security system (SS) was established in 1935 on the presumption that a fund would be accumulated from the mandated tax plus accrued interest. By the 1970s it was certain that obligations of the system due to be paid back to system participants, in terms of the fund approach then in place, were much larger than could be repaid from monies realistically construed as available. The solution to the crisis—which it was—consisted of discontinuation of the accrued fund nature of the entire SS system. That is, Social Security disbursals henceforth are being

made from current tax or "contribution" receipts, plus interest derivative from the relatively small fund that still exists. The tax or contribution rate has been raised several times, and rates and eligibility
criteria for beneficiaries have been made subject to change. These facts
constitute drastic alteration from the original funded methodology for
financing repayment. Other pension and debt systems do not have
such prospects for alterations to cope with their problems. In ordinary
language, the SS system for the most part has been put on a pay-as-
you-go basis.

The Social Security system came to the point of insolvency during
the 1970s because of funded claims or "entitlements" rising more
rapidly than means of repayment. It should be clear that any system
that operates in such funded fashion will face the same fate unless
growth of its means of repayment approximately matches the growth
rate of its indebtedness claims. Government is the debtor or else the
guarantor of much of the funded debt in the United States representing
pension claims, bank deposits of various types, and vast additional
quantities of debt claims. The claims are assumed to be secure because
of the governmental guarantee or underwriting of debt. Since the
federal government has been running huge budgetary deficits throughout the 1980s, and will have enormous difficulty in reversing this
situation, one must conclude that enlargement of governmental debt is
the mode of liquidity or solvency assurance that exists in much of the
economy. Further enlargement of governmental debt is being protested
for many reasons and is becoming problematical. The orthodox fiscal
policy prescriptions no longer are readily available options. Hence the
soundness of the system is in doubt.

We cannot draw definitive conclusions concerning all ramifications,
but our major point seems certain. Repayment claims have become so
large that net purchasing power transfer as saving, from the household
sector to business and/or government, is no longer possible as a reliable
phenomenon. In a real sense, net saving already approximates zero,
and the worst in this regard is yet to come; the claims exist, and
inflation or depression adequate to the task of canceling much of the
debt will be catastrophic. It is easy to point out that most of our
pension claims and other debt would be more manageable if altered in
a fashion parallel to what has been done to the Social Security system,
but how could such a thing be accomplished? Collapse and either
bankruptcies or extended periods of inflation will be difficult to avoid.

The funded-debt Social Security system was a close approximation
of the Life Cycle models in that a fund was built up as means of

repayment, and social security beneficiaries necessarily take their benefit entitlements as rapidly as eligibility permits, on penalty of losing them. Benefits cannot accumulate, nor can they simply be transmitted to heirs. The rate of consumption spending of social security benefit payments is quite high.

Most financial intermediaries and other corporations have not suffered the impacts that result from strict application of life-cycle models because part of their capital or investment funds have originated via equity, such as stock shares, rather than debt. Moreover, partly as a consequence of utilization of ownership claims, major proportions of accumulated claims are bequested to heirs rather than being liquidated. Hence other (corporate) recipients of household saving have not been forced to the point of insolvency as was the Social Security system.

The alterations forced into being in the Social Security system have drastically altered the nature of overall household saving. The tax rate has been raised to 15.3 percent, half from employee, half from employer. With high probability that benefits will be continued at or near the present high rates, all rational participants in the system construe the 15.3 percent tax rate as saving from their gross pay at that rate. Funds that might otherwise be put into private accounts of various types thus are preempted by Social Security, and *pari passu* the need for other saving is greatly reduced.

It is a peculiarity of our orthodox methodology of measurement of saving to stipulate that Social Security taxes, like all taxes, will not be counted as saving for reasons of tradition involving the preconception that saving means private transactions, not public transfers such as taxes. The benefits pay back from Social Security are not deducted from consumption purchases, however. Hence saving as the numerator in the saving ratio is not adjusted to include the tax impact of Social Security, but the denominator of that ratio, consumption spending, does bear the enormous impact from the operation of the system. Not surprisingly, the saving rate still calculated by the method used before Social Security became such a gigantic phenomenon shows precipitous decline.

The Social Security system and the Federal Employees Retirement system, state pension systems aside, each presents an important anomaly in the analysis of saving because in their functioning they involve a mixture of government and private funds flows. Money going to the government for the system is called taxes, and applies to gross individual pay up to $51,300 or so. The rate has been subject to frequent change. The percentage rate of contribution to Federal Employees Retirement is essentially similar. The crucial consideration is that moderately rational householders are aware that large charge rates are being assessed them, and that they will draw sizable retirement benefits from whichever program applies to them, or both in sequence in some instances. The programs take a large slice out of pay, and accordingly are a large portion of total saving effort of the individual participant. Social Security taxes do not merely alter saving; they *are* saving. The nature of the economy has evolved.

In recent years, total SS taxes have somewhat exceeded benefit payments, and the same is true for Federal Employee Retirement system receipts and disbursements. Since we lack precise tax rate stipulations for total contributions to the Federal Employee Retirement system, to add to SS taxes and treat as a form of saving, and because it may be less confusing to avoid calling any taxes "saving," we have chosen to go at the matter the other way around. Data is readily available for SS benefit payments and for Federal Employee Retirement benefits. We combined these, and then assumed that ninety-five percent of this amount is spent on consumption within a short time after it is received. Then we reduced the figure for total consumption spending in the economy by this amount (.95 times the sum of those two benefit payments), and then calculated the saving rate in the usual way. Data for 1985 in billions of dollars were as follows: Social Security benefits, 253.4; Government Employee Retirement benefits, 66.6; sum of these benefits, 320.0; .95 of 320.0 is 304. Aggregate consumption spending was 2581.9; adjusted consumption (less the 304) was 2277.9. Disposable Income was 2801.1; DI minus adjusted consumption, which is apparent *amount* of saving, was 523.2. Therefore, the saving *rate* was .1868 (18.68 percent). Using a different ratio for marginal propensity to consume retirement benefits yields a different saving rate, clearly, but the trend for the rate, meaning its rising tendency in recent years, is what is far more important.

Our method gives "saving rate accounting for certain government-mandated programs" as 9.88 percent for 1960. It rose fairly regularly to 16.39 percent in 1973, and has held moderately steady ever since. It was 16.12 percent in 1983. For the high GNP growth year of 1984, not surprisingly this saving rate was up to 19.81 percent. The growth rate of GNP receded in 1985, and so did this calculation of saving—but only to 18.68 percent. Since retirement pay backs have grown rapidly in recent years, it is not surprising that a time series that copes with the public taxes, private consumption characteristic of this aspect of savings money flows would yield both a higher rate and much greater stability than does the peculiar orthodox conception. Of interest in certain contexts, this rate approximates the saving rate of many other industrial nations, especially if part of orthodox saving is added.

In contexts where the focus is on saving as a source of loanable funds, one could readily use the orthodox calculation of saving for the *amount*, while using the procedure outlined here as one of several methods for calculating the *rate* of saving and its changes through time. This ratio is by no means a perfect measure of saving. No such thing can be specified because of the complexity of elements, problems of measurement, and different purposes for which the rate is to be used—for example, comparison with that of other industrial countries.

We have noted two major features of evolutionary change in the U.S. economy in recent decades: the growth and alterations in the Social Security system, and the absence of major depression or periods of notably high inflation. The rapid rise in the use of debt to finance consumption spending is an additional change of great importance. Expansion of Total Consumer Credit, a time series provided by the annual *Economic Report of the President*, was at rates less than five percent during the early 1970s. From 1975 through 1979, such credit or debt expanded at annual rates varying between 11.45 percent and 16.95 percent. No doubt the high rate of inflation and low rate of real interest of these years underlay the rapid expansion.

Between 1979 and 1980, consumer credit fell slightly, and from 1980 to 1982, the rate of increase was only 6.07 percent and then 5.23 percent. But for 1983, consumer credit was up 14.23 percent; for 1984 it was up 20.22 percent; for 1985, up 19.59 percent, for 1986 it was up approximately 20 percent.

The impact of the rise in interest payments stemming from a combination of high rates and growing indebtedness can be emphasized as follows. In 1950, "interest paid by consumers to business" was 18.25 percent as large as the official personal saving total; for 1975 the relationship was 23.33 percent. But for 1985, interest to business at $87.4 billions was 67.39 percent as great as the official saving datum for that year, $129.7 billions. This juxtaposition of data shows interest payments up, saving down, in an illustrative manner. Personal consumption was 255 percent as large in 1985 as in 1975, but consumer interest payment was 358 percent as large ($87.4 billions compared to $24.4 billions).

Another major evolutionary change may be noted. In the United States, savers and investors were strongly overlapping sets of people during most of our national history prior to the 1920s. People invested in land, farms, or small businesses, and most people did not retire with pension claims, but today the overwhelming part of saving is purely financial operations—pensions, insurance plans, saving and loan accounts, CDs, government bonds, checkable bank accounts, etc. The great bulk of real investment, meaning resource-using activity to enhance further production, is done by corporations, who get the majority of their funds from profits of on-going operations. Increase of money and credit supply much funding, and conceptually these are quantities without specific bounds.

Saving in no sense need be prior to investment. The fact that federal governmental borrowing approximates the magnitude of total household saving can be construed as "crowding out" investment only if one makes the weird assumption of a fixed money supply. In fact "money comes out of the barrel of a fountain pen," and interest rates are more a matter of Federal Reserve decisions than market supply of loanable funds. Whether money and credit have been increased more rapidly during the 1980s than "should" have been the case (our opinion) is hardly the point with reference to actual quantity and use.

If we recall our statements in chapter 3 regarding macroeconomics and the nature of the consumption function, it is readily seen that concentration of wealth and income is the root of many of our problems. By 1985, the lowest decile of income recipients in the United States received only 4.6 percent of total income, down from 5.4 percent a decade earlier. The top 5 percent, by contrast, received 16.7 percent in 1985, up from 15.5 percent at the earlier date. The distribution of income-earning wealth (i.e., excluding home ownership) showed the top decile (not quintile) owning 83.2 percent of the total in 1985, leaving 16.7 percent for all other families comprising 90 percent of the total. Given this extremely top heavy distribution of wealth and income in a highly status-conscious society, and given our self-assigned role of "world demand creator of last resort," it is hardly a matter justifying complaint that our households have not achieved a high rate of voluntary money saving. Inadequate demand is a ghost that persistently haunts the capitalist world, and we, as a nation, have turned to massive increases in debt as the escape route. A phenomenon shocking to the orthodox world-view is that if we visualize a strict life-cycle model and all saving going into funds (including social security even if made private), in a few time periods *net* saving rate must turn negative, since interest rates exceed growth rates.

Through most of our history we suffered panics, crashes, wars, and depressions that periodically wiped out much of total monetary assets and simultaneously destroyed debt obligations. Businesses, banks, insurance companies, etc., thereby got out from under much of their accumulated debt. By the mid-1930s, notably, most families saw forced reduction of whatever assets they previously owned, and few people were able to retire at pension of significant size.

Nowadays we have numerous people retiring each year and drawing upon savings claims that commonly have accumulated with compound interest for three or four decades. The total annual pay back to the overall saving process has grown large and hence has lowered the saving rate on its orthodox definition and method of measurement.

If one is concerned with the issue of whether Americans are a nation of spendthrifts who set aside very little of current income as provision for the future, then it is crucial to consider the phenomenon known as investment in human capital, which concept has become firmly entrenched in economic thought. Such investment centers on spending to improve productivity by enhancement of health and educational standards, and in parallel with other segments of economic accounting methodology, spending for investment is matched by saving in some sense. Spending on health and education has grown rapidly in recent decades, relative to most other categories of spending. It is beyond our purpose to offer a proposal for determining what proportion of such spending should properly be categorized as saving, but suffice it to observe that the magnitudes are enormous and would result in major alteration of saving rates. Every parent who pays the bills for the college education of a son or daughter knows this full well. Educational expenses of offspring are not mere family consumption items! Tax law changes of recent years for financial relief to burdened families have been based in part on recognition of the investment characteristics of educational expenditures. In lesser degree the same is true regarding medical expenses. It is fully in accord with our philosophy that delineation and measurement of such phenomena cannot be precise.

It is deceptively simple to contrive data time series for household saving. We will list nine and give a representative, near-mean rate for the entire post-World War II era in each case. It is not necessary for our purposes to study the details of any of them.

1. The orthodox saving rate. Disposable income less consumption spending, even if financed by debt or credit, gives the amount of saving. This divided by Disposable Income gives *rate*: (6–7 percent) down by half in the ostentatious 1980s.
2. Change in household mortgage debt: (3 percent).

3. Change in total household debt: (6–7 percent).
4. Change in total household financial assets: (12–13 percent).
5. Saving by individuals (Federal Reserve series): (12 percent).
6. Orthodox rate adjusted to include net purchase of Consumer Durables, plus net contributions to government life insurance and pensions, two lesser adjustments, and use of disposable labor income rather than Disposable Income as the denominator for taking the ratio: (11–15 percent before the 1980s, down sharply since).
7. Saving by individuals plus Social Security taxes: (15-25 percent, trending up until 1981, down since).
8. Saving by individuals less purchases of consumer durables: (9 percent).
9. Saving by individuals plus Social Security taxes less purchases of consumer durables: (12–23 percent, trending up until 1981, down since).

Notably, none of these series clearly sorts out or differentiates saving as nonconsumption out of current Disposable Income apart from the spending of savings accounts during retirement years. The last three series are our concoctions, as was the series outlined for the purpose of judging the total impact of the Social Security and Federal Government Employees Retirement systems.

The Concept of "Debt Ratio Constancy" Budget Balance

Relationships among debt, interest, and economic growth in the United States have changed or evolved greatly in recent years, especially during the 1980s. Tim Congdon recently worked out some algebraic equations that enable calculation of the changing magnitude of budget deficit that would maintain the constancy of debt-to-income ratio for various sectors of the economy.[17] For each sector—households, business, foreign, and federal government—the ratio of debt to income or revenue, appropriately formulated, has been rising in the 1980s. There is no intention here to argue that any of the ratios is of appropriate size, but with the federal government deficit reaching $200 billion in recent years, while legislative, constitutional, and other means are pursued to require budget balancing, the constancy concept might be a helpful guideline. However, because of the abrupt rise of interest rates and debt in recent years, an historical sketch with background data may be necessary for clarity.

Total debt owed by nonfinancial sectors in the United States increased at annual rates averaging 7.0 percent during the 1960s, but for the 1970s the growth rate of debt was 10.5 percent. Moreover, during the 1980s the rate has risen to as high as 14.5 percent, and has averaged 11.0 percent annually.[18]

Early in the 1980s a new factor came into play that, perhaps shockingly, causes more of the rise of debt than do budget deficits in a narrow sense. This new fiscal nemesis is the rise of interest rates to figures much higher than rates of economic growth. It is not improper to assert that any analysis of our debt situation that ignores this departure from our national trends is ill-based and invalid. Furthermore, the prospects seem bleak for either lowering interest rates or raising growth rates adequately to reestablish the former long term tendency toward rough equality of magnitude for these two key variables. Hence our conclusion is immanent in these primary facts: the interest rate—growth rate divergency is far more critical than debt and deficits themselves. A short-term spurt of deficit financing nowadays may be beneficial, with longer-term implications almost catastrophic. Brazil and Mexico are examples of the "trap" nature of overextension of debt, however much their situations differ from that of the United States.[19]

The rapid rise of *federal government* interest costs is shown by the following data. For publicly held, nontrustfund federal debt, in 1980 $50.8 billion was paid as interest, which equalled 1.9 percent of GNP. By 1988, interest for this purpose was $151.7 billion, which was 3.1 percent of GNP. The deficit, consistently defined, was $193.9 billion in 1988, (i.e., on-budget spending $861.4 billion, on-budget revenue $667.5 billion). By our calculation, the 1980 real interest rate was 1.65 percent, whereas for 1988 it was 6.65 percent. (See table 1 and figure 1.)

Any reasonable manipulation of data shows the critical role of the rise in interest rates. Interest costs would not have grown to almost the size of the deficit if interest rates had not increased enormously.[20] Total debt rose rapidly during the 1970s, but the debt-to-income ratio changed only slightly, from 1.372 to 1.406. (See table 2 and figure 2.)

Although the parallel is not exact, overall debt has grown at rates approximating nominal interest rates. For household or consumer debt, where income growth does not ordinarily result from the indebtedness process, this fact is hardly surprising, because families com-

Table 1: Real GNP Growth and Implied Real Interest Rates, 1969–88, United States

	(1) Prime Interest Rate	(2) Producer Price Annual Change	(3) Implied Real Interest Rate	(4) GNP Growth Rate (deflated)
1969	7.96	3.8	4.01	2.4
1970	7.91	3.4	4.36	−0.3
1971	5.72	3.1	2.54	2.8
1972	5.25	3.2	1.99	5.0
1973	8.03	9.1	−0.98	5.2
1974	10.81	15.4	−3.98	−0.5
1975	7.86	10.6	−2.48	−1.3
1976	6.84	4.5	2.24	4.9
1977	6.83	6.4	0.40	4.7
1978	9.09	7.9	1.10	5.3
1979	12.67	11.2	2.24	2.5
1980	15.27	13.4	1.65	−0.2
1981	18.87	9.2	8.86	1.9
1982	14.86	4.1	10.34	−2.5
1983	10.79	1.6	9.05	3.6
1984	12.04	2.1	9.74	6.8
1985	9.93	1.0	8.84	3.4
1986	8.33	−1.4	9.87	2.8
1987	8.22	2.1	5.99	3.4
1988	9.32	2.5	6.65	2.9

Calculated from *Economic Report of the President, 1989.*

$$\text{Real rate} = \frac{\text{prime rate } (+100)}{\text{producer price changes } (+100)} - 1 \text{ times } 100.$$

Price data for 1988 were preliminary and were extrapolated.

10-year means:	1969–78	1979–88
GNP growth	2.82%	2.12%
real interest	0.91%	7.32%
therefore, growth =	3.10 real i;	0.289 times real i;
or, real i =	0.323 growth;	3.45 times growth
	g>i by 1.91%;	g<i by 5.20%

Figure 1. Real Growth and Interest Rates, 1969–88, United States

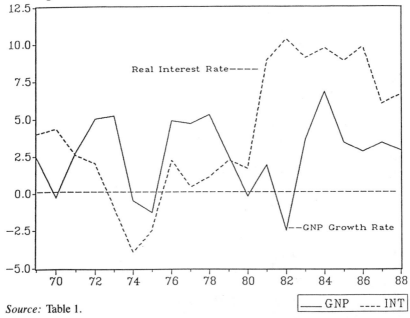

Source: Table 1.

monly turn to enlarged borrowing in part to forestall reduction of purchasing power by income having to be turned to interest payment. Prior to the 1980s, low real interest rates made it possible to manage the rising debt totals without great stress. For each major economic sector, however, the debt-to-income ratio has been rising in the 1980s, after having displayed surprising constancy for thirty years prior to 1982. Total debt equaled around 138 percent the size of GNP with little variation during the entire period, and was 1.39 in 1981. By 1988 the ratio had risen to 1.85, and it shows strong signs of continued rise at least for the next decade because of high interest rates. (See tables and figures.)

While the debt ratio for the United States is not larger at present than that for certain other industrial nations, its recent growth averaging almost 4.5 percent per year (1.39 in 1981, 1.85 in 1988) constitutes one prong of the debt problem.[21] Significant increase in the debt/income ratio cannot be sustained indefinitely, for eventually debt and its servicing would overshadow everything else. Several Latin American nations have approached such a situation. Apparently there is no brick wall that the economy would abruptly encounter, speaking

Table 2: Total Debt, GNP, and Their Ratio, 1960–88, United States,
($ billions)

	(1) *Total Debt*	(2) *GNP*	(3) *Debt/GNP Ratio*
1960	696.8	515.3	1.352
1961	738.7	533.8	1.384
1962	790.7	574.6	1.376
1963	846.1	606.9	1.394
1964	909.1	649.8	1.399
1965	977.5	705.1	1.386
1966	1044.5	772.0	1.353
1967	1120.5	816.4	1.372
1968	1215.0	892.7	1.361
1969	1303.9	963.9	1.353
1970	1393.1	1015.5	1.372
1971	1525.7	1102.7	1.384
1972	1681.2	1212.8	1.386
1973	1868.4	1359.3	1.375
1974	2040.9	1472.8	1.386
1975	2222.9	1598.4	1.391
1976	2462.2	1782.8	1.381
1977	2775.3	1990.5	1.394
1978	3146.9	2249.7	1.399
1979	3527.6	2508.2	1.406
1980	3868.2	2732.0	1.416
1981	4244.3	3052.6	1.390
1982	4627.9	3166.0	1.462
1983	5161.1	3405.7	1.515
1984	5910.1	3772.2	1.567
1985	6719.9	4014.9	1.674
1986	7576.8	4240.3	1.787
1987	8282.2	4526.7	1.830
1988	9027.6	4870.7	1.853

Calculated from *Economic Report of the President, 1989*, Tables B–1 and B–67. Data for 1988 were extrapolated.

Figure 2. Total Debt/Income Ratio, 1960–88, United States

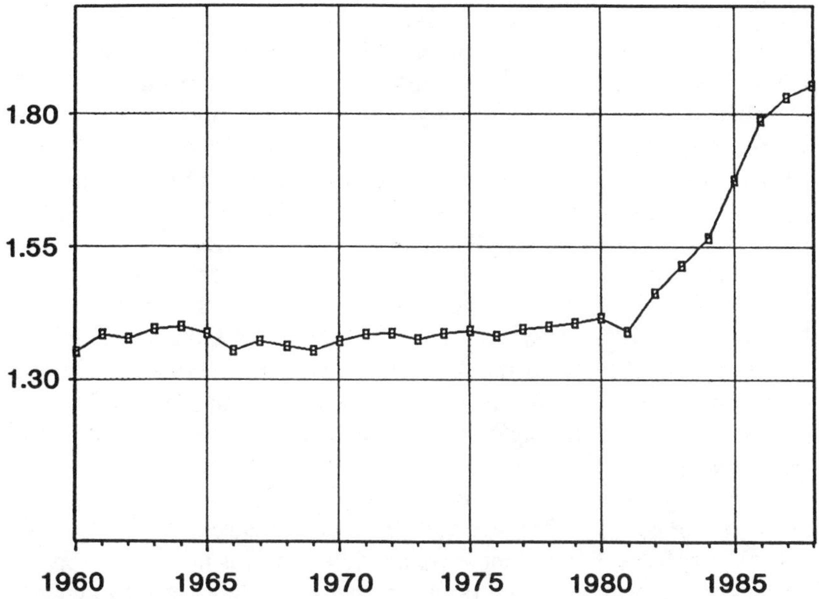

metaphorically, but comparison to drift into a swamp or quagmire seems appropriate in that extrication becomes ever more difficult.[22]

High interest rates are the most basic cause of the rapid rise of the debt/income ratio, and this fact makes servicing of debt particularly onerous. Within another decade, for example, the portion of federal tax revenues that would have to be devoted to mere interest payment, if recent trends continue, would rise from 16.5 percent in 1988 to 19.2 percent in 1998. The figure was only 9.8 percent in 1980, but rose rapidly because of some notably unfavorable relationships during the first Reagan presidential term. It is quite uncertain what will happen during the next several years, but we used the more favorable trends of the second Reagan term for the extrapolation to 1998. Rising interest costs are one factor increasing pressure for taxes to be raised. More-over, the overall process of debt and its servicing redistributes income upward, a fact that might eventually be resented by numerous people.

As debt rises in the household and business sectors, rates of bank-ruptcy and default likely will continue to rise, possibly heralding a real crisis of confidence and a major recession.[23] Worse yet, as we will detail below, high interest rates coupled with faltering growth rates have come to mean that the balancing of budgets alone would not always stop the rise of the debt ratio. Moreover, mere regulations or edicts cannot correct the problems.[24] Economic growth is as difficult to push up as interest rates are to bring down. Each is about as difficult to achieve as is government budget balance. Enormous efforts have been devoted to quests for solutions for all three, but success has been elusive. The difficulties are urgent, especially for a time perspective longer than one presidential term, for example, and it is problematic even to envision a scenario that copes with the varied aspects of the debt problems and at the same time could be called realistic.

To forestall confusion, we must emphasize that it is total debt in the United States with which we are most concerned, and debt or deficits of any subset sector is a matter of less national urgency. In billions, total debt as defined here increased from $4,627.9 in 1982, to $9,027.6 in 1988, which is a multiple of 1.95. During the same period, federal debt held by the public increased from $919 to $2,050 billions, a factor of 2.23. Growth of GNP (billions) was from $3,166.0 to $4,870.7, a factor of only 1.54. For various reasons, including its more rapid growth, the federal government public debt receives far more attention and comment than does the preponderant total debt. In part because the governmental accounts do not distinguish capital or investment accounts from current or operating accounts, analysis often centers on this and other differentiating characteristics and concludes that federal debt and deficits are no cause for alarm. From opposite ends of the political spectrum, one finds Milton Friedman and Robert Heilbroner strongly in agreement with that argument.[25] Herein we take a longer view than what is implied in their analysis; we call attention to total debt as well as the governmental subset; and we focus on the critical impact of sharply increased interest rates. Accordingly, their position might be valid temporarily and not totally in conflict with ours.

Heilbroner and Bernstein concluded in their 1989 book that, "In normal times we favor a 'deficit,' by which we mean growth-promoting expenditures on a capital budget, of 2 to 3 percent of GNP—perhaps $100 to $150 billion at today's values."[26] For emphasis, they italicized the sentence and presented it as a paragraph. It is interesting that their suggested magnitudes roughly approximate those actually realized during the Reagan presidency.

It appears, however, that they did not take proper cognizance of the impact of high interest *rates* upon *amounts* of interest to be paid. The governmental interest obligation rose from $50.8 billion in 1980, to $151.7 billion in 1988, and will rise to $333.9 billions in 1998 if even its slower growth during the second Reagan term, 8.3 percent, should prevail. That is, interest cost per year itself will *increase* by more than their recommendation for magnitude of deficit, and total amount of interest will be more than double the upper limit of their suggested appropriate deficit, which was $150 billion. The debt process requires ever larger absolute increments each year just to maintain stable purchasing power, let alone increases of purchasing power for the agency involved.[27] From calculations presented in table 1, during the 1979–88 decennium GNP growth averaged only 2.46 percent per year, whereas the real interest rate was 7.32 percent, which is a multiple of 2.98. Stated differently, since interest paid in 1988 was $151.7 billion, if their suggested maximum deficit, $150 billion, had prevailed, purchases would have had to be less than taxes, with the debt process reducing fund availability. Purchasing power benefits of debt use cannot long endure in the face of high interest rates. The Heilbroner–Bernstein stipulation would need to be approximately as follows: "the Federal government should run deficits somewhat larger than the projected interest on its debt each year." Over a period of years that is what is required for the spending they wish to accomplish, but the resultant surge of debt would be astonishing and unsustainable. We agree that the productive infrastructure investments they wish to finance are highly desirable, but long-term enlargement of debt is a self-defeating process unless interest rates can be brought down to approximate equality with income growth rates.

A distinction needs to be asserted. If households *never* increased their income as a result of their use of the debt process, they would need to increase annual borrowing at a rate equal to the annual interest rate on their debt in order to avoid reduction of purchasing power because of required repayment. Although the magnitude varies greatly depending on type of spending and other factors, government spending increases national income, which increases tax revenues. Accordingly, to provide the purchasing power Heilbroner and Bernstein urge, governmental deficits need not rise at a rate as high as the applicable interest rate, and it is impossible to stipulate a required rate of rise of deficit because income growth rate is not determinate by these factors alone. Annual deficit equal to annual interest cost is the basic relationship, and with the interest rate exceeding the growth rate, debt growth would be almost exponential at a clearly unsustainable rate. As was learned during the "limits to growth" debates during the 1970s, it is crucial to avoid near exponential growth of unfavorable economic factors.

Keynesian spending and emphasis on demand-side manipulations came to full blossom only with the advent of World War II, but with war bond sales moving briskly, patriotism strongly in evidence, and price controls firmly in place, inflation did not require the routinized banking niceties that in fact were continued and faithfully observed by tradition and recognition of the power and influence of our bankers and their banks. Money, credit, and debt were greatly enlarged during the late 1930s and the first half of the 1940s. Entities that create money are not said to incur deficits in so doing, and a basic principle could be that the federal government would create but never "borrow" new money. The majority of new money and credit (expansion of its supply) could come only via government spending or spending plus lending.

After the Great Depression and World War II, the earlier "fiscal religion" of balanced budgets was generally reasserted through all sectors. Foreign trade surpluses came automatically, in practice, to the one virtually undamaged industrial power. Businesses in general exercised care that productive assets would grow *pari passu* with debt. State governments ran fiscal surpluses as mandated by statutes and constitutions. After the end of the Korean War in 1953, the Eisenhower 1950s were characterized by fiscal restraint and overall surpluses. Households and their creditors alike were cautious in a degree that would now be regarded, even if mistakenly, as quaint, unimaginative, timid, ludicrous, or downright un-American. Through the 1950s, 1960s, and even most years of the 1970s, total debt held rather steady as a proportion of income, whether appropriately compared with GNP, household disposable income, or government revenues.

Further Data and the Appeal of Rapid Debt Expansion

Almost nobody, then or now, has paid much attention to the taken-for-granted fortuitous circumstance of income growth proceeding at rates that almost every year exceeded, or at least equalled, real interest rates. (See tables and figures.) Except in connection with wars, price inflation was nonexistent or mild until the oil embargo of 1973 set off an amazing chain of problems. The central fact is that debt was not a serious problem for the United States until the 1980s, which is when, for complex reasons, interest rates rose and growth rates slumped. The peculiar belief that a massive federal tax cut would "get the government off the backs" of Americans and release productive energies so great that revenue collections would soar and balance the budget by 1983—the Reagan-interpreted Laffer curve—in a sense was the source of our current debt quagmire. Debt and interest rates in the United States have come to be a vast topic indeed, but what we want to do is to consider the history and analyze certain dangers by use of algebraic tools.

In a short-run spurt, any sector can boost resource use via debt, and "live beyond its means," meaning doing things that are not sustainable if conditions even roughly approximate what is usual in the contemporary scene. This is the basis for the great appeal of deficit financing by any sector. Debt always affords short-run benefits. We should hold few illusions on the point. Budget deficits and other aspects of debt ratio expansion are likely to continue in the United States until a major calamity (such as severe recession) occurs. One reason for this is that "debt overhang" and rise in proportion to income would continue even if all sectors balanced budgets on Congdon definitions—*if* interest rates continue to exceed growth rates.

Debt of all the major economic categories fits within the scope of our basic model. Let us ask, what could be wrong with incurring debt as the means to enlarged purchasing power during a given time period? The answer is that borrowing generally can be done only with secured promise to repay later, and with interest. Since more is to be repaid than was borrowed, we need to indicate the basis of benefit. The answer may be easy. Borrowing may be done to enhance income, so that repayment is from a larger pool of wealth claims than would otherwise have been possible. If income rises faster than the interest rate charged on the debt, benefit seemingly is self-evident.

Here consumer or household debt runs into trouble, in that seldom is income of the borrowing householder directly enlarged by uses made of the debt money. Time preference for consumption apparently is enhanced, since by using debt the householder can consume more in a given year than his income for that year. But even this is deceptive because after a very few time periods the fact of interest rates higher than growth rates will bring a reduction, not enlargement, of annual purchasing power unless borrowing grows at a rate approximating that of the relevant interest commitment. If expansion is continued, debt obligations become overwhelming in relation to income. There is general agreement that consumption debt should not become excessive. None of us, however, can specify a convincing rule of reason for an upper limit on such debt.

Algebraic Demonstration of Problems of Debt and Interest

Governmental use of debt often is perceived differently since government theoretically can increase tax revenues to meet commitments. In

most industrial countries tax rates are roughly proportional to householder income (not notably regressive or progressive), and if government spends wisely, or only avoids spending foolishly, its expenditures
enlarge the income base and hence its own revenues, although likely
by a much smaller amount. Opinions vary among both experts and
laymen as to the merits and demerits, wisdom or folly, of governmental
deficit financing.[28] An evasive if proper answer may be that it depends
on circumstances. One should bear in mind that the mathematical
principles apply for all economic sectors. It is in relation to consolidated data that the greatest significance resides, but data for government is more complete and manageable. Presumably everyone is aware
of the bearing of fiscal balance, meaning revenue compared to spending, as the obvious determinant of whether debt increases or de-
creases. But why must 1) the interest rate, 2) the growth rate of
income, and 3) the debt-to-income ratio all go into the equations? First,
amount of interest to be paid is a function of two variables: amount of
debt and the rate of interest on it. Second, since much of tax revenue
is a function of tax rate and the amount of income, the rate of income
growth is critical to the amount of tax collection through time. Third,
since tax collections vary with income and hence its growth, adequacy
of tax revenues depends in part on how large is debt in relation to
income, one base for taxes. A very large debt-to-income ratio would
mean that, with interest rate specified, a large part of tax collections
would be required for interest on debt.

Let us present Congdon's algebraic formulation with slight modifi-
cations in terms of federal government public debt. A possible obscu-
rity in the analysis comes from the fact that our government, like most
others, always meets its debt obligations, both principal and interest.
Hence debt growth, dD, equals and derives from budget balance,
which could have been labeled B in the model.[29]

Further algebraic formulation and analysis is made possible if the
fiscal balance is struck on the basis of expenditures *other than for
interest on debt*. This means revenue minus total expenditure minus
interest payments. Then change in debt is presented as

$$dD = B^* + iD, \qquad\qquad \text{[eq 1]}$$

where B^* (not equal to B) is the specified fiscal balance *net of interest
payment*. Interest *as a sum* is omitted in B*, but appears in the final
term *at its rate* applied to the cumulative debt total which of course
involves the same sum.

Now we can employ a second equation, using i for the rate of
interest, and formulate the growth rate of debt:

$$dD/D = B^*/D + i \qquad \text{[eq 2]}$$

That is, the rate of growth of debt exceeds the rate of growth of income, Y, if

$$B^*/D + i > dY/Y \qquad \text{[eq 3]}$$

The ratio of debt to total income would be D/Y (*if notation is kept appropriate for the sector*). This value is stable if:

$$dD = D/Y\, dY \qquad \text{[eq 4]}$$

Rearranging terms, we have $B^* + iD = D/Y\, dY$, or

$$D/Y\, dY/Y\, Y = B^* + iD \qquad \text{[eq 5]}$$

Since dY/Y is growth rate of income, if we call this g we get

$$D/Y\, g = B^*/Y + i\, D/Y\text{, or}$$

$$D/Y\, (g - i) = B^*/Y \qquad \text{[eq 6]}$$

Since our first term, D/Y, had a meaning of its own, i.e., the debt-income ratio, we can call this term "a" for clarity, so

$$a(g\text{-}i) = B^*/Y \qquad \text{[eq 6a]}$$

This equation gives conditions for point-in-time stability of (sectoral) debt-to-income ratios. If the relevant rate of interest exceeds the income growth rate, the sector must run a calculable "Congdon surplus" (small ordinary deficit). Another term would be "constancy deficit," meaning the maximum amount of deficit that would keep the debt ratio from rising, assuming constancy of the usual macroeconomic variables. For the United States, the constancy condition involves a calculable deficit smaller than an annual federal government interest obligation. Alternately, this means a surplus on purchases—less value of purchases than of tax revenues. The permissible deficit constantly declines because interest rates greatly exceed growth rates.

Recent data show B^*, whether positive or negative, to be quite small in relation to total income (or tax revenue), since the deficit approximates total interest. Hence even a small differential of interest rate above income growth rate causes the debt/income ratio to rise. The larger the debt-to-income ratio, the larger the B^* surplus required for constancy. In practice, emphasis shifts from the algebraic tool B^* to more ordinary budgetary balance concepts.

We inserted data for 1988 into equation 6a and calculated that the federal government would have needed a negative in the algebra of

$66.2 billion *for B** to have prevented a rise in its debt/income ratio. Actual B^* was positive in the amount of $43.5 billion, readily calculable as budgetary deficit minus interest payment ($861.4 spent, less $667.5 revenue, less $151.7 net interest). That is, a fiscal shift of $109.7 billion in on-budget items would have been necessary, or, stated in more ordinary terms, the deficit on publicly held debt needed to be reduced from $194 billion to no more than $85.5 billion. A convenient generalization easily borne in mind is that with the growth rate, interest rate, and governmental debt-to-revenue ratio being as they are, the government can run a deficit, but only of a magnitude much less than its current annual interest obligation, and maintain constancy of its debt-to-revenue ratio.

There are uncertainties as to how the data should be interpreted. The publicly held debt was $2,050 billion and tax revenue was $667.5 billion—hence debt/income ratio was 3.07. On-budget revenue growth, 1987 to 1988, was .0417. Since interest was $151.7 billion, the apparent rate was .074. There were minor problems of rounding of numbers, and different interpretations yielded different results.

The overall debt situation is of greater importance, of course, but the data and its interpretations are far less certain. In 1988 the total debt of nonfinancial sectors was $9,027.6 billion, while GNP was $4,870.7 billion. Nominal GNP grew by 7.6 percent from 1987 to 1988 (calculated from table 2), while the 1987 prime interest rate was 8.22 percent (table 1). Insertion of data into equations 1 or 3 yields actual B^* as $64.6 billion. By use of equation 6a, we calculate that B^* would have had to be an algebraic negative of $55.0 billion for the total debt-to-income ratio to have remained unchanged. Hence the required "fiscal shift" would have been $119.6 billion using this procedure choice.

It is noteworthy that *total debt* "fiscal shift" for debt ratio constancy is proportionately less (in relation to total debt magnitudes) than the required governmental fiscal shift, $109.7 billion. This is because governmental revenue growth was at the rate of only .0417 (because of tax cuts), whereas overall GNP growth, which is relevant to total debt, was at the much higher figure of .076, and moreover the governmental debt-to-revenue ratio was 3.07:1, while the total debt ratio was only 1.85:1. Because using any one average rate for either growth or interest is not fully satisfactory and interpretations of data are uncertain, conclusions clearly are indicative only. Moreover, maintaining the present debt/income ratio is merely one possible policy goal.

Equation 3 demonstrates more simply the conditions for stability in the debt-to-income ratio. We repeat the observation that these principles are valid for all economic sectors. One could retrace the modeling example with data for other sectors to gain different perspectives. Although repetitious, for convenience and clarity we note that the constancy equation might be presented in various forms, including the following:

1. amount of interest less B^* equals appropriate deficit;
2. amount of interest equals B^* plus appropriate deficit;
3. appropriate deficit equals amount of interest less B^*.

The definition of B^* is fiscal balance for a specified sector, net of interest, but it is neither purchases, interest, revenue, budget balance nor amount of debt change.

Economists and laymen alike have been little inclined to take into account that it is the growth of income that must make possible easy servicing of debt, and therefore if the interest rate exceeds the income growth rate, there is a budding problem. Likewise, usually ignored is the fact that the magnitude of the problem is also a function of how large debt is in relation to the size of income (the debt/income ratio). Furthermore, contrary to blythe unexamined assumptions that appear to be widely held, that near-miraculous state of affairs called balancing the federal government budget, even if attained, would not constitute a solution to the problem of debt growth in this country.

We will not go into detailed statement of causes of the quagmire, but a few points merit emphasis.[30] Amount of total debt began rapid growth during the 1970s, real interest rates soared in the 1980s, and both phenomena continue in the late 1980s. Mere reworking of Reagan economics would not be adequate corrective therapy. The sharp tax cuts put into place by the Reagan administration brought about huge budgetary deficits, especially if the Social Security system is left aside, since no adequate spending cuts were contrived. With fiscal policy thereby totally wrecked, fighting the battle against inflation, which has been no mere skirmish, fell to monetary policy. A major tool has been high real interest rates. Although growth rates have been high in certain years of this decade, overall the record is lower than for the 1970s, and high interest rates have been an impediment to growth. Weakened growth rates combined with high real interest rates have been a recipe for major trouble. High interest rates have attracted foreign funds and thereby made the dollar strong, which has boosted imports and restrained exports. Foreign debt has soared.

Recommendations: The Need for Our Traditional
Interest Rates

Comment here must be limited to issues of debt, growth, and interest
rates. What would be the outcome of continuation of the present rapid
growth of debt? No one really knows. First, recall that there are four
major sectors involved, and consequences might differ substantially
among them. For business and households, we generalize that a surge
in rates of bankruptcies and other forms of default would be likely.
One might anticipate that extension of new credit, and renewal of old,
might slacken. Total demand seemingly would slump, and recession
would be upon us. Because of its large debt totals and deficit imbal-
ances, the federal government would be constrained in rescue efforts.
Taxpayer revolts might materialize. What foreign creditors would do is
largely guesswork. Japan, for example, might offer to buy a state or
two, which in economics literature is colorlessly referred to merely as
"asset transfer." Aside from partial settlement of debt accounts, such
a move probably would be done more in a quest for living space than
for raw material availability. Alaska, Hawaii, or Oregon would be
likely candidates. Or perhaps the Japanese would try to move away
from the dollar, meaning reduction of their dollar holdings. Such a
trend would be quite unsettling to the United States.

What can we recommend? How much power are we to have? We
have already stated our opinion that the appeals of deficit financing
will overwhelm other concerns for at least a few more years. A few
minor changes would accomplish little or nothing. By way of perhaps
obvious pronouncements, let us assert that as national policy we
should recognize the limits likely for medium term growth rates as
roughly 2.5 percent, which is lower than the historical trend in this
century, itself a bit better than 3 percent. Then we would insist that
real interest rates must be kept down to near 2 percent, which is not,
in fact, lower than the trend in this century. Both inflation and what
Keynes derisively called "the rentier" would require to be firmly
brought to rein or conformity with overall necessity. Inflation would
have to be fought with tools other than the raising of interest rates.
The glib but realistic answer is that qualitative controls on extension
of debt would have to be imposed, and with a vengeance. Taxes could
be contrived for imposition on new debt or loans, in some circumstances only, so additional payment would go to the tax collector
instead of being funneled to bankers and the rentier. Also, the federal
government could pay some of its bills by running the printing presses

for money and credit expansion more than it customarily has been doing, instead of permitting banks to do the job and pick up the community's "loose change," as Veblen once remarked. The magnitudes of interest payment "take" have become unconscionably large because of high rates applied to enormous total debt.

The federal government needs to raise taxes and reduce spending. We suggest a twenty-cent per gallon increase in gasoline taxes, and the creation of a third income tax bracket, at around forty percent. Entitlement transfers could be subjected to a means test and to progressive income taxation. Military spending readily could be reduced one-third within a year or two, and half of the saving shifted to the building and repair of infrastructure, the present condition of which is a major impediment to production.

These suggestions might roughly balance the federal budget on orthodox measures if income growth continued at recent rates, but balance of this budget would still leave the (long-term) unsustainable situation of rising total debt ratio because of debt problems in other sectors as things now stand. The crucial consideration is to project a realistic growth rate, perhaps 2.5 percent, and then do what is necessary to reduce real interest rates to near equality.

Notes

1. Joan Robinson, *The Economics of Imperfect Competition*, and Edward Chamberlin, *The Theory of Monopolistic Competition*.

2. Floyd B. McFarland, "Markup Pricing and the Auto Industry: A Reason for Stagflation." *The American Journal of Economics and Sociology* 41, no.1 (January 1982): 11.

3. See the chapter entitled, "The Decline of the Mechanical View," in Albert Einstein and Leopold Infeld, *The Evolution of Physics* (New York: Simon and Schuster, 1938). Revolution and evolution both were rampant before as well as after Einstein and his work. Economists refused to be the first, but should not be last, to abandon mechanism.

4. Clarence E. Ayres, "The Gospel of Technology." In *American Philosophy Today and Tomorrow*. Edited by Horace Kallen and Sidney Hook (New York: L. Furman Inc., 1935). Ayres was a prolific writer who served for years as an associate editor of *The New Republic*. In total, he wrote several books and a multitude of articles and short commentaries. This writer completed three degrees in economics with Ayres and others at The University of Texas, Austin. I think they have not accomplished much evolution or progress for evolutionary economics, and accordingly I have chosen not to give detailed attention to the work, some of which has real merit.

5. Veblen, *Theory of Business Enterprise*, 237.

6. Georgescu-Roegen, *Entropy* . . . , 321 n. His reference is to Paul T. Homan, "An Appraisal of Institutional Economics." *American Economic Review* XXII, 1932.

7. Keynes, *End of Laissez-faire*, 39, 41.

8. John Maynard Keynes, *A Treatise on Money*. 2 vols. (New York: Harcourt, Brace and Company, 1930).

9. Joan Robinson, *Economic Philosophy* (Garden City, N.Y.: Doubleday & Company, Inc., 1964), 108.

10. Keynes, *General Theory* . . . , 297.

11. *Ibid.*, 105.

12. Chick, *Macroeconomics* . . . , chap. 4, 71–72; chap. 5, 111–21.

13. Keynes, *General Theory* . . . , 378–79.

14. Koestler, *The Sleepwalkers*, 496–97.

15. The most convenient source of data on numerous aspects of the United States economy for many people is the annual *Economic Report of the President*, published by the Government Printing Office. Most of the data in this section are from that source.

16. Duesenberry, *Income* . . . , 42.

17. Tim Congdon, *The Debt Threat* (Oxford: Basil and Blackwell, 1988), appendix.

18. Calculated from data in *Economic Report of the President 1989*.

19. International Monetary Fund, *World Economic Outlook*, Annual editions (Washington: IMF); Organization for Economic Cooperation and Development, *Economic Outlook*, Annual editions (Paris: OECD). David Lomax, *The Developing Country Debt Crisis* (London: Basingstroke and Macmillan, 1986).

20. Congdon, *The Debt Threat*; Benjamin M. Friedman, *Day of Reckoning* (New York: Random House, Inc., 1988); Joyce Kolko, *Restructuring the World Economy*. (New York: Pantheon Books, 1988).

21. Congdon, *The Debt Threat*; and *Economic Report of the President*.

22. Congdon, in *The Debt Threat*, argues vehemently that such is the case. Most of the other authors we have cited share the concern, if in less pronounced degree.

23. Congdon, *The Debt Threat*.

24. In a time of emphasis on economic and political deregulation, nearly all writers emphasize the inefficacy of edicts and regulations.

25. Robert L. Heilbroner and Peter L. Bernstein *The Debt and the Deficit* (New York: W. W. Norton, 1989).

26. *Ibid.*, 138.

27. Again it is Congdon who makes the point with greatest emphasis.

28. The Heilbroner-Bernstein book, *The Debt* . . . , is one of few in which the author specifically favors increased or continued debt and deficits.

29. Congdon, *The Debt Threat*, appendix. It is perhaps a bit curious that

Congdon presented his algebraic formulations in detail in this book, but never presented actual data employing or illustrating the mathematical formulations.

30. Benjamin Friedman, *Day of Reckoning*, is especially good on statement of background causes.

8

Conclusion

What do economics professors profess? This is the query with which we began the book, and it may be helpful to restate it as a reminder of the intended scope of coverage. It is difficult, if not impossible, to specify the limits of what people do that might be included as economics. There are numerous areas of specialization in every university department of economics, to speak only of academia. We have attempted to limit our inquiry mainly to "core" courses that are stipulated as degree requirements in American university economics curricula. This means micro and macro theory at the intermediate level, plus concern for interconnections with other topics. A major concern in this book is to suggest the desirability for economics to alter its underlying philosophy to conform with certain aspects of other social sciences, especially cultural anthropology. It sometimes is alleged that economics has been concerned with interdisciplinary approaches in the social sciences, but with economics "imperializing" via the message of mechanism. There is merit in the accusation, but such a development would be decidedly unwise because of issues of qualitative change.

The Legacy of "Economic Man" Equilibrium Economics

It has been our contention that this central core of knowledge is the economist's version of Classical mechanism. This is the theory and view of the world synthesized by Isaac Newton from prior work by Kepler, Galileo, Descartes, and others. Newton invented calculus, separately from the different notation system of Leibnitz, as the required tool with which to expound, measure, test, and sustain his conclusions. Classical mechanism envisions the world as having been created, rather than evolved, so that history is irrelevant. All phenomena consist of interactions of forms of motion with forms of mass. From macro to micro, planets and stars to atoms and molecules, gravitation and uniform attraction of units of mass is the key factor holding everything in its place, in balance or equilibrium. The incredible, and still poorly understood, phenomenon of gravitation acts at a distance—sometimes of enormous magnitude—via a postulated medium called the ether, a construction about which Newton was dubious but from which he could never fully dissociate his theories.

Newton rejected the orthodox religions—Protestant and Catholic Christianity—of his English homeland, and was Arian instead. He believed in God, but his God was outside the universe and affairs of mankind, having created the world system and stepped back to interfere but little. God had created a nearly perfect self-adjusting mechanism. There was a hierarchy, of larger and thus more gravitationally powerful bodies along with small mass bodies. In human social affairs, to which Newton devoted limited comment, the power or influence that is involved in this hierarchy does not rest upon the mass of persons, to be sure, but rather wealth, political affiliations, family tradition, customs such as royalty and divine right of kings, and other socioanthropological phenomena. Newton believed that God established a hierarchical structure of human interrelationships or *world politic* that closely paralleled the relationships of the *world natural*. There were characteristics of the hierarchy in human affairs that established and maintained an equilibrium or balance, so that societies did not fly apart or continually struggle violently one against others. This was God's foreordained system for the functioning of human affairs. Mass interacting with, or against, motion (in the postulated ether) constituted the essence of *world natural*, we have noted. What were comparable factors in human affairs of *world politic*? Newton did not elaborate.

It was Adam Smith who made the giant step of systematic application of Newtonian principles into sociopolitical affairs. Men are led by an invisible hand, comparable to universal gravitation (also quite invisible), to promote an end that was no part of their intention. The individual intends his private gain, what the later Utilitarians called maximization of pleasure. The unintended result is simultaneous maximization of the public good. Market forces of supply and demand are the specific directive factors bearing on human behavior, comparable to mass and motion, and the ambiance, setting, or atmosphere that parallels the ether is what economists formalized as pure competition.

Since the mass-motion phenomenon is unrestrained by other than its self-constituted forces, human action likewise will require to be unrestrained in the form known as laissez-faire. Accordingly, orthodox economics, a subset of Classical mechanism, holds to a world-view that does not merely conclude that free private enterprise capitalism is the only logical way to run an economy, but instead this conclusion is assumed into the premises and postulates employed. Do not worry about, or even ask, what humans "ought" to do; merely observe what they in fact do, as they are singly and severally led by the unseen hand.

Felicific calculus is the mode by which we humans make our calculations for maximizing pleasure and finding "bliss points." Since it frequently is the case that we economists do not know what to do, it is indeed reassuring that the best advice is no advice. Merely leave it alone and let the market forces lead us forward. Though he credited him little, Adam Smith borrowed much from Newton, "the greatest philosopher that ever was," in Smith's stated opinion. We modern economists have learned much from Smith, in turn, and have credited him fully. In fact, during more than two centuries we have departed little from Smith's vision. Virtually any or all of our mainline, orthodox economic theory treatises could quite well bear the title, "Economics Construed as Mathematical Principles of Natural Philosophy." Much has been done in mathematics, physics, and other realms of science since Newton's time, but our embellishments in economics are squarely within the paradigm that Newton did so much to establish. To label it "inadequate" probably is better than to say "wrong." Since the model presupposes conditions that theoretically yield maximum efficiency of resource allocation, and thus rationalizes the status quo of power and wealth with the "each man for himself, cried the fox in the henhouse" policy implications, there is little reason to think that the model will be given up until after a recognizably disastrous turn of events. The Great Depression of the 1930s was severe, numerous reforms were discussed, and a few were made, but as soon as recovery based on government spending was achieved, reform was cut to a skeleton, while massive government spending remained. Thus the system has been continued with surprisingly little change. Orthodoxy works!

Our criticisms of orthodoxy are set at several levels. The model is not satisfactory as science or theory because it is committed to a mechanistic framework that is essentially static and cannot confront qualitative cultural change. Moreover, the results in practice are a highly stratified or hierarchical society, with pronounced poverty alongside unnecessarily large holdings of wealth and receipt of income. It is now well demonstrated by experience that this stratification continues. Third, the mechanism model has no clear mode of dealing with externalities and environmental concern. Fossil fuels, for example, "should" be used at the most rapid rate that via sales promotion people can be encouraged to consume them to maximize growth of GNP. Enough is never enough. A fourth criticism is commonplace: booms followed by busts, whether or not meriting the label business cycle. It is usual during the post-World War II era to argue that governmental tax-and-spend interventions have satisfactorily overcome the fluctuations that seemed intrinsic to the free market model. Our conviction is that because of the enormous surge of debt expansion, public and private, the entire economy has become hopelessly overburdened by debt and soon will collapse or at least be severely constrained by debt overhang. Demand has been made to soar via debt increase, and further expansion of debt is required to make payments on prior debt, and to assure the urgently sought strong demand. A major obstacle is the fact that interest rates now are at least twice the rate of growth of real income. Economists assume that free market forces of prospective borrowers interacting with prospective lenders automatically bring proper expansion of debt, just as uninhibited forces bring the right amount of everything else. The economists' advice on what to do always must be "nothing." Increase the money supply 4 percent annually and, like God, stand back!

Is there nothing positive to be said about mechanistic equilibrium economics? The response has to be "not much" for model or underlying philosophy. It is extraordinarily normative in demands for policies of laissez-faire. Since little advice for positive policy action derives from the model, its proponents insist that it is purely positive, value-free, and objective. What is true, if confusing, is that mathematics and modeling are useful tools. Since these tools are readily employed in the mechanistic model, there is a false preconception that their use is dependent upon allegiance to orthodoxy. Nothing could be further from the truth, and in fact it is in centrally planned types of economy that deterministic modeling could best be employed.

John Maynard Keynes used the expression "Classical economics" to refer to what we are calling orthodox or equilibrium economics, correctly perceiving that the distinction employed within the profession of Classical versus neo-Classical is not well grounded philosophically. Orthodoxy is Classical mechanism, the central preconception being that of equilibrium, not evolution, and accordingly the entire body is Classical economics. There has been no genuine paradigm change because the world-view is that of atomistic individuals and firms maximizing pleasure, minimizing pain, in equilibrium and behaving as "economic man" rational calculators devoid of genetic instinct-remnants, emotion, or tradition. Publication date of Newton's *Principia Mathematica* was 1687. Economics has rested on one peculiar base for three hundred years.

That this base is not satisfactory has been obvious for a century and a half, recognition having been forced by Karl Marx and associates after the labor exploitation intrinsic to the early suppy-side model was argued by the Ricardian socialists during the 1830s. Indeed, the response to Marx's assault took the form of subjective demand-utility modeling employing the concept of decision making at the margin. This was the origin of what is called neo-Classical economics, but change was only expansionary and mechanistic equilibrium continued as the philosophy and paradigm.

Marxism constitutes one alternative to the received truth. Marx was appalled at the scientific pretenses of the objective labor-cost school of British Newtonian philosophy intruded into social affairs, which taught that Adam Smith had brought the light of laissez-faire market capitalism as the final stage of rational economic thought and action. The Prussian was trained in the Hegelian dialectic, and following Feuerbach, shifted his interpretation of the dialectic to what he thought was a materialist base in human affairs centering on changes of modes of production. Marx sought theoretical understanding of the entire process of change in human history. Continental Hegelianism was idealist-spiritualist in method and outlook, and glorified the German-Prussian state as the manifestation of God's will being achieved or "becoming" on earth. Feuerbachian materialism shifted the entire philosophical world-view to a push-of-the-past, *causa materialis* base. The British Smithian–Newtonian labor theory of value models were taken by Marx as appropriate, properly restructured, for economics and the entirety of historical human behavior. History for Marx consists of socioeconomic class struggles, leading from slavery, to feudalism, to mercantilism, to laissez-faire market capitalism—and on to socialism and communism. How superficial the rationalization of the capitalist status quo to pronounce it the last stage of rational economic organization! Since labor and capital stand in opposition, the struggle necessarily will continue. Capitalists win battles, decade after decade, and after whipping labor down each time they continue the exploitative system because it serves their quest for capital accumulation. Crises and depressions necessarily worsen, however, and laborers finally make a genuine revolt that they win. One win by labor brings abolition of the labor-exploiting system. This is the highest of drama! Thorstein Veblen remains one of the few persons ever to appreciate the significance of Marx's "lessons . . . on how to transcend the static framework effectively," as Georgescu-Roegen expressed the point,[1] while at the same time considering Marxism more romantic than scientific. Marxism is a mixture of untenable mechanism with untenable dialectic. In the epoch of its origin, however, it was progress, since it intruded qualitative change into scientific discourse. The Marxist approach still enables, and almost mandates, attention to crucial questions that adherents of Classicism prefer to ignore. Included are issues of wealth and income distribution, as well as alienation and exploitation.

Through use of the dialectic, Marx achieved his goal of developing a theory of history that accounts for qualitative change in human affairs. To adherents, the Marxian is the only valid theory of history, with perhaps even stronger and more inflexible commitment to the system than is the case for most practitioners of Classical mechanism. Marxists, like orthodox economists, "know that they are right," but in the United States, especially, adherents of orthodoxy are accustomed to public acceptance of the principles as above all challenge. Marxists do not share this comfort.

Labor ends class struggle by ending class stratification. Socialism and dictatorship of the proletariat work the way on to communism, the true final stage. Theoretical formulations vary, with modification being forced by successive failures to realize promise and expectation. Marxism transcends Classicism and accounts for qualitative change, but not satisfactorily. Capitalist societies all have their intractable social problems and instabilities, but there has never been an instance of an advanced capitalist system being overthrown by a proletarian revolution. Where forms of socialist states have been established, none has moved on to communism. Instead, all have been beset by deep-rooted problems for which solutions thus far have not been achieved. People may make a socialist revolution, as did the Fidelistas in backward Batista Cuba, but it is misleading to argue that "history" made the revolution. Rather, conditions became bad, and other factors developed in certain variable ways, so that revolutionary activity gained strong support. An obvious corollary is that revolutionary efforts might gain wide support in the USSR or other so-called communist countries. Such an event cannot be dismissed as impossible on grounds that such a development would constitute "history running backward," as some Marxists argue. China, in the post-Mao era, has been an example of a shift from communist ideology and practice to considerable reliance on individualism, greed, and market forces. What can be said truthfully is that change constituting cultural evolution continues, although frequently it is warped, frustrated, ill-suited, suppressed, and delayed.

Activities of "Real Man" Instead of "Economic Man"

Neither equilibrium philosophy nor Marxism is satisfactory as social theory or methodology for such theory. What remains to consider is theory compatible with the work of Clausius in thermodynamics—the Entropy Law—and Darwin's work on evolution. Both bodies of theory and data brought recognition of qualitative change in nature, and thus the need for incorporation of such change into scientific discourse. We must move past Darwin because of his virtually exclusive attention to genetic, heritable traits, which is the type of principle well illustrated by Mendellian specification concerning inheritance of dominant and recessive genes. The theory of cultural evolution is an adaptation of Lamarck's belief in the genetic transmission of acquired traits, modified as cultural transmission of acquired *cultural* traits. Lamarck's work per se was incorrect because acquired (biological) traits are not transmitted genetically. Since acquired cultural traits take the form of customs, beliefs, and know-how, revised Lamarckian evolutionary principles are more basic than the Darwinian to theoretical constructs in the field of cultural evolution. Human action utilizes and relies upon rational processes, but at the same time it is strongly influenced by historical developments, environment, know-how, customs, beliefs, emotions, and genetic instinct-remnants. Idealism, rationalism, and spiritualism, jointly or separately, do not constitute an adequate basis for social theory.

Hence there persists the question of "moral sentiments," in Adam Smith's language, meaning what should be and what should be done. Mechanism counsels to ignore the question and simply be positive or value-free in observing what people in fact do. The procedure presupposes that what is desired is desirable, with no question concerning the historical basis of desires, sales effort involved, social pressures from concern for status, impact of income and wealth distribution, available productive potentials, various structural characteristics of a population, or possible consequences. Persons as consumers in fact are heavily influenced by a ubiquitous concern for status, not impinging equally upon everyone, it is true, but always in evidence in degree. At all times concern for status is a group phenomenon rather than individualistic, and it is largely a zero-sum game. For someone to gain status, someone else must lose, for it is a matter of ranking. The mechanistic philosophy assumes that consumer decisions are adequately perceived as rational, and hence resource use is maximized. But since decisions do not rest exclusively on rational calculation, maximization is falsely concluded.

Business firms might try to maximize sales value or gross revenue, or maximize volume of production within the constraint of paying bills and staying in business, or short-run net revenue (profits), or long-run net revenue, or any of several other factors. Pricing and production procedures would vary to fit the chosen purpose. However, there is little reason to believe that all firms seek the same goal. The choice of goal might depend upon the vagaries that determined the composition of the board of directors and the officers of the firm. Studies by Herbert A. Simon and others conclude that the common goal is satisficing, not maximizing. The decade of the 1980s, especially, has witnessed an enormous surge of merger movements, hostile takeovers, leveraged buyouts, and other financial manipulations. The standard rationale is that the takeover, whatever its form, results from vulnerability of the subject firm occasioned by its failure of maximization of full profit potential.

This is a startling admission. Hundreds of firms, giants and pygmies, have been swallowed up because their managements were failing to maximize profits! *Now* we are to see resource allocation come to social maximization. Everything *now* is to be set straight. Of course this is farcical. What was wrong previously? Does the model work, or does it not work?

What is going on is societal evolution, albeit in this instance in highly warped form. As we have observed previously, there occur many instances of deleterious change. Experience demonstrates that takeover promoters usually gain large benefits for themselves, which is adequate motivation to explain the takeovers. In addition, the degree of monopolization generally is increased, a development hardly to the public good where monopoly power, by design, is poorly regulated. In 1983, the richest ten percent of American families owned 83.2 percent of all wealth other than homes, and the buy-out, takeover mania commonly turns to manager ownership called "privatization." What is involved, of course, is further concentration of ownership.[2] Only true believers in classicism can fail to see undesirable and unworkable tendencies involved. It is self-deceit to assume maximization of social benefits or anything else, and one thing revealed is the ideological nature of blind faith in the mechanistic laissez-faire model. Much of this chicanery doubtless will be blown away, temporarily, by the next crash. The history of evolution of organizational forms in our economy strongly implies the necessity of reforms in postcrash reincarnations. What we learn slowly we seem to unlearn rapidly.

American agriculture provides an example of evolutionary change at its worst, or at least of thoroughly deleterious character. For decades, farmers, being small-scale producers, appeared to confront demand functions that were horizontal (i.e., perfectly elastic), before resultant disasters to them brought change. For many decades, farmers as the rugged individualists *par excellence*, "bought their inputs at retail prices but sold their output at wholesale prices," so to speak. Farmers engaged in self-exploitation in staying in the game. Eventually, screams of protest by those who did not migrate out of agriculture brought implementation of gigantic governmental programs. These simultaneous production limits and production enhancements, credit easement programs, price supports, export promotion programs, and the like *ad nauseum*, have eliminated scientific merit in the use of most agricultural activity as examples of the beneficent and efficient working of mechanism. Ideology is preserved, or attempts at preservation are made, by the ruse that in general, governmental interferences into markets were made prior to emergence of problems, and programs caused the problems. It would seem to follow, therefore, that the proper advice is merely to return to the "Golden Age" of the status quo ante, the good old days. Classicism abounds.

Our suggestion for agriculture is government ownership of about one-third of all high-grade agricultural acreage. Land would be divided into moderately large family farm parcels, with considerable size variation. Parcels would would be leased to farmers at moderate charge, one parcel per family, with leases renewable indefinitely with satisfactory performance. The proportion of total farm land in this program could be altered to contrive reasonable prices and so that most young people who wanted a lifetime career in agriculture could readily afford it. Farmers would not have to buy farmland and thereby become hopelessly enmeshed in debt and financial or pecuniary machinations. They would not be encouraged to endulge their status-seeking inclinations, nor could they become land speculators. There would be heavy reliance on market forces to set prices. If overproduction caused market prices to drop to unreasonable levels, land would be pulled out of production and assigned to other uses such as open space, recreational use, and conservation programs. Government banks would finance most machinery, but little debt by these farmers would be necessary or permitted. International movement of commodities and products would be permitted on a much more nearly free-market basis than now is the case. Mechanical modeling of supply and demand would be more useful here than in less competitive sectors, and it is likely that market forces would in fact be given freer play than is the case with our present confused system.

Public ownership of a substantial portion of farmland would be the sharpest departure from received practice. This is necessary to prevent speculation and large-scale use of debt. The latter has commonly been a trap into which farmers have entered in efforts to obtain leverage for land and machine purchases to permit expansion of operations. A mere glance at historical data enables farmers to see that profit per unit of farm output has been low, if not negative. To realize much profit they accordingly must produce enormous quantities, and hence there has resulted the usual capitalistic drive for expansion.

A theorist of considerable significance relative to land and resource usage and problems was Henry George. He gained a large following in his own time, the final third of the nineteenth century, with his recognition of the widespread incidence of economic rent. Pure rent in economics long has meant a price higher than would be required to call forth specified production. Henry George proposed a one hundred percent tax on rent.[3] The proposal is highly meritorious, then and now, whether the government's rent-collector takes it all, or only the major part. We consider George an example of a good evolutionary economist. His argument that the rent tax would be the only tax necessary of course is totally a nonsequitur. It is a credit to the genius of Henry George that the principle of economic rent as a widespread phenomenon is being recognized by contemporary economists, and the feasibility of coping with the problem via taxation applies in most sectors of the economy, not just with respect to land. Let us note with all due emphasis that supply-demand analysis using tools from the mechanism paradigm is highly useful in this type of situation. Tools are one thing, while mechanism and equilibrium construed dogmatically as the vehicle for automatic maximization of benefits is something else.

For confronters of sloping demand curves, the almost ubiquitous case, efficiency and welfare implications are astounding. If firms follow the $MC = MR$ short run profit maximization algorithm, they would not even theoretically achieve allocative efficiency, price equal to marginal cost, because the demand curve lies above the marginal revenue curve. There are no market forces causing the following outcome, either short- or long-run, but if by chance the marginal revenue curve passed through the lowest point of the usual total unit cost curve, operation would logically be done at the corresponding quantity resulting in "productive efficiency." Pure or economic profit would be taken, long-run as well as short, and in terms of the model long-run pure profit is unwarranted. Accordingly, there is less than maximum social efficiency in resource allocation. Marginal cost pricing is requisite for this form of perfection.

Zero economic profit would result if competitive forces resulted in output at the quantity at which $MC = MR$, if by chance the demand curve was tangent to the total unit cost curve at this quantity. No long-run profit or loss might be thought to imply efficiency until we note that in this instance, neither allocative nor productive efficiency could possibly prevail.

For various reasons, including convenience and lack of full information, firms appear commonly to resort to forms of mark-up pricing, meaning that unit cost is estimated and price is marked up, perhaps fifty or one hundred percent above the cost figure. Only by chance does this procedure maximize anything whatever. It may be presumed, however, that the decision makers perceive the operations as "satisficing." This means yielding, or thought likely to yield, results that are deemed satisfactory. The 1978 Nobel Prize for economics went to Herbert A. Simon in part for work on development of the concept of satisficing.

Status-seeking, group-oriented, personal productive and consumptive behavior, like mark-up price satisficing by firms, would be neither maximizing nor in equilibrium of the mechanistic *genre*, except by chance. Such behavior is not subject to theoretical rationalization as resulting in "the best of all possible worlds." Economic activity thus is no longer merely a matter of allocating given limited resources (means, supply, production) among given limitless wants (ends, demand, consumption). Means and ends are manipulated. Real world decision makers appear to be following decision algorithms, now and for a long time past, greatly at odds with those of Classical mechanism.

Recognition of this fact is more a matter of "observing how people in fact behave" than a plea for altered behavior.

Perhaps it is we economists who most definitely need to alter our behavior: "The question is why a science interested in *economic* means, ends, and distribution should dogmatically refuse to study also the process by which new *economic* means, new *economic* ends, and new *economic* relations are created."[4] Aside from sheer weight of tradition, we economists cling to our mechanistic model because it is the only thing we have with a claim, however spurious, to our customary conception of scientific validity, simultaneous maximization of social welfare, little call for policy programming, and simultaneous rationalization of the activities of the rich ruling or elite class. These considerations admittedly have their appeals, which are broader than careerism alone.

Even when there is recognition of evolution or change, we are reluctant to accept that

> the evolutionary pace of the economic "species"—that is, of means, ends, and relations—is far more rapid than that of the biological species. The economic "species" are too short-lived for an economic husbandry to offer a relevant picture of the economic reality. Evolutionary elements predominate in every concrete economic phenomenon of some significance—to a greater extent than even in biology. If our scientific net lets these elements slip through it, we are left only with a shadow of the concrete phenomenon.[5]

Therefore we are enabled to offer a point of advice: alter the paradigm of economics from Classical mechanism to cultural evolution to enable the "professing" being done to catch up with what business schools long have been professing as managerial, organizational, and behavioral theories of the firm. Also, we should try to catch up with the findings of some of the more progressive work in cultural anthropology, political science, and social psychology. Then perhaps we could even pull ahead. In addition, we should treat all theoretical formulations as tentative, not the sort of thing that might be regarded as "zeroing in on the truth." The suggestions are meant as a starting point of a major philosophical change toward closer conformity of theory with apparent reality, not in any way a final position since we are concerned with continual cultural change.

How Much Can We Use the Market Mechanism?

The answer is, very much indeed. But it is our conviction that little can be done as science in economics without getting past the remnant of positivism that insists on a sharp distinction between what is and what ought to be, the positive versus the normative. If science can study only what is, then it is clear that the social sciences cannot do other than rationalize the status quo, for clearly that is "what is." Traditional economists, fairly stated, try to opt instead for the never-never land of the status quo ante—the "Good Old Days" of unimpeded operation of market forces. We must remind such practitioners of Classicism, however, that it was Adam Smith more than two centuries ago who not only invented their science but cautioned against governmental red tape and mercantilist obstructionism and against sharp business practices as well. Closely paraphrasing Smith, businessmen seldom meet even for social occasions without the conversation turning to efforts at monopolization or market-rigging. It is true that most rent-garnering schemes, the current euphemism for monopolization, involve aspects of collusion with governmental agencies. This is as true of military procurement that bypasses competitive bidding for esoteric machines as it is of agricultural boondoggles or tax write-offs or accelerated depreciation for office building construction, etc. The other half of the scheme is the business promoter, capitalist, or perhaps organized labor. Corrupt practices often involve both private and public functionaries. An equally important point is that policies to "let the market forces work freely" are apt to serve, even if unintentionally, as a veil for obstructionist or antisocial practices. As punsters remarked concerning Galbraith's book on countervailing power in American markets, "the concept veils more power than it counters."[6]

Within the paradigm of cultural evolution, by contrast, social science thought is formulated for the purpose of understanding how we are, how we came to be this way, what are the problems and faults, and, therefore, which way is forward. We all recognize profound and recurrent change in human conditions and affairs. It is true that physicists can hardly do other than accept much of the status quo of nature, and for that reason models and methods taken from physics are not appropriate to the biosphere. Incidentally, the old positivist adage might well have appended to it a statement acknowledging that even in physics, the prince of sciences, *purpose* has its place—certain elements, for example, are man-made, not found in nature. Thus, "what is" itself is no simple matter.

We have insisted that in modern times there have been only three full-fledged paradigms in economics. These are Newtonian–Lockeian Classical mechanism, Marxian dialectical materialism, and Darwinian–Lamarckian hybrid evolution. Only within the latter two is qualitative change confronted and dealt with, and of these the dialectic has failed in the sense that its deterministic historical stages pronouncements have not been realized. Our work is within the paradigm of evolution, and accordingly the price mechanism, with or without equilibrium, is a tool to us but not the core view. We will never have models or formulations that come to a final term, and particularly not with equilibrium as the criterion of successful specification of models. Our advice, accordingly, is not constrained to rationalization of present forms of society.

All of this may be stated in many and varied ways. The nonlife part of the physical universe may be treated as itself learning very slowly if at all, and most of the biosphere learns, adjusts, and changes at rates that can be treated theoretically as moderate. Economics is an affair of humans, where thought, experiment, learning, and adjustment or need for adjustment are, in comparison to the remainder of our world or reality, very rapid indeed. Regarding some aspects of physical sciences, effort may reasonably be regarded therein as seeking "The Truth," to get things straight once for all, to axiomatize, to zero in on the truth, to formulate abstract functional relationships as laws that hold for all time and place. Rational principles thereby are seen as ruling the world or controlling events rather than reliance on forms of cause and effect that evolve and thus vary.

Let us comment briefly on U.S. foreign trade as an example of confusion regarding both theoretical and policy reliance on principles of Classical mechanism rather than evolving cause-effect push of past sequences. All through our national history, academic theorists have argued consistently for free trade as an unassailably proper principle. But during most of our history prior to World War II, business interests and their allies in the conservative political party of the time insisted upon and got strong protectionism in the form of high tariffs and other trade impediments. Prices and profits were pushed upward in pronounced degree, with pecuniary concern decisively outweighing allegiance to philosophical or theoretical principles. Meantime, householders, laborers, and the progressive or liberal opposition party demanded free trade. The clamor for free trade likewise arose not from commitment to abstract principles espoused by academics, but rather as a consequence of the wish to avoid paying higher prices for goods because of the effects of tariffs and protectionism.

Applying party labels, in the twentieth century prior to World War II, the Republican Party of the conservatives was staunchly protectionist, while the Liberal-Labor Democrats called for reduced trade impediments. Subsequently to World War II, however, the positions totally reversed. It is the Republicans who, for some fifty years, have been arguing the case for free trade, whereas Democrats insist on various forms of protectionism. Why the reversal of roles, and who has been "correct"? The U.S. economy was so much more powerful after the War, especially with respect to manufacturing and finance, that there was little immediate need for protection; our firms could outdo anyone else. Democrats, not surprisingly, were not protectionist for some two decades. The most significant change or evolved factor was the rise to prominence of the multinational firm. Technical improvements in shipping had enormously reduced transportation problems and costs, and means of communication had improved even more dramatically. With satellite radio and television methods, operations in a limitless number of countries could be monitored and closely controlled by management personnel located at any chosen point on the planet. The big appeal of far-flung operations has been cheap raw materials in some cases, and cheap labor in virtually all instances. It has been learned that "high tech" production methods and machinery can readily be shifted to any chosen locale, and indigent labor can rapidly learn what it needs to know to do the jobs. So—why pay workers a total of ten dollars an hour, say, to produce consumers' electronics goods in the United States, while more compliant workers can be hired in Hong Kong, Korea, Taiwan, Singapore, or even next-door Mexico, at one or two dollars per hour? If those labor sources are all put to work and more personnel are needed, there lie Indonesia and India—absolute giants of labor pool potential. Overall, Third World population growth continues to exceed any likely amount of their employment by multinational firms. In cases for which governments or political factions are recalcitrant, partnership with local interests is the obvious way to take on political protective coloration, and obtain additional funds and market channels.

What remains to be considered is the necessity of free trade or an approximation thereof on the part of the big consumer demand sink, the United States. The sophisticated products involved in overseas productive ventures, almost without exception, are far too expensive to sell in large quantity to the indigenous population, as everyone knows. Good quality and good price are readily achievable, and make possible a reliance on the American market. The capitalists get profits, the Third World country gets much needed jobs, and American consumers get good products at good prices. Moreover, American exports are assumed to rise because the foreigners would now have higher incomes than before, including expanded dollar earnings. What possibly could be problematic with the scenario? Is not the Law of Comparative Advantage valid and immutable?

Briefly stated, the principle is valid granting all of the necessary assumptions of the Classicists, but there is little reason to believe the world ever fulfills the assumptions. First, where did anybody come up with the idea of international trade being trade between nations? The language sounds that way, but the trade involved would have to be trade between the governments of the two nations, which is quite a different thing. Actual trade is almost exclusively between companies with facilities of some sort in the countries involved. By way of example, ponder the following scenario. A Japanese firm sets up productive facilities in Malaysia to produce a car, perhaps called the Proton, to be sold in the United States. Cheap labor in Malaysia, strong markets—sometimes—in the U.S. are the basis of the operation. Do both the United States and Malaysia "gain" from this trade? Some Malaysians get jobs, likely at relatively good wages. They may or may not have to pay more taxes, tolerate more congestion, confront additional pollution, etc. The population and its growth rate are large enough that wage rates are not likely to rise noticeably, and Malaysia might follow the Korean lead and prohibit labor strikes or other major disturbances against operations by multinationals. In the United States, consumers get a wider choice of new cars, but is this actually worth very much, particularly since we have dozens of models from which to choose already, and the nation has an overcapacity of car production approximating five million cars per year?

Will American automobile workers suffer reduced employment totals? We must assume so, for the facts of such developments are ready at hand. Perhaps more hamburger frying or government service jobs will be created, probably via the pull of additional expansion of debt and credit, both public and private. Will our exports, and hence the jobs involved, expand? The Japanese businessmen and banks have more dollars, not necessarily the case for any Malaysians. Why does anyone think that Japanese purchases from the United States would rise? The trend has been strong for Japanese-owned dollars to be invested in the United States in major portion, especially in money market types of securities, with direct production investment lagging weakly. The Japanese-owned dollars have served well as the basis for expanded governmental deficit financing, and private sector debt expansion as well. Does either the United States or Malaysia really gain from this expansion of international trade? What the United States has achieved thus far from several decades of trade and investment operations has been shocking degrees of deindustrialization or loss of high-productivity jobs and output, and vast outpourings of "red ink" or indebtedness. We conclude that possible beneficial results from operation of the thoroughly famous Law of Comparative Advantage depend upon many factors. Following Friedrich List, we argue that wisdom dictates keeping close attention to growth of "the productive powers" rather than cosmopolitan trade without question. Ever since World War II, our relevant slogan should have been "high and balanced trade," rather than just "free trade." The comparative development of Japan and several other nations, including ours, would have taken a very different form, and many of the institutionalized bad habits we have engendered would not be plaguing both ourselves and the Japanese today. They would not have developed their great overcapacity for automobile production, or for consumer electronics. And it is simply not the case that we had to doom ourselves to destruction and nondevelopment of a United States's consumer electronics industry. That we have desperately needed national labor policy, instead of permitting ourselves to be left to the mercies of labor unions interacting with corporate giants, for automobile and electronics production and many other things as well, appears an inescapable fact.

We are convinced that American society currently is exhibiting dominant behavioral characteristics or a "life style" that demonstrate that what evolves is not necessarily or even probably able to withstand critical analysis. "Needless to say, tradition, just like biological heredity, often transmits institutions that are indifferent or deleterious."[7] The evolution of our society has occurred within bondage to our worldview, philosophy, and preconceptions of Classicism. Therefore it is well within the bounds of predictability that we have reached the present time-point as a notably predatory and jungle-like culture, beset as a consequence by violence, frustration, drug use, crime, corruption, and the most crass and inhumane forms of greed. We have managed to submerge even the best characteristics of our highly mixed multiple religious heritages, which might have provided adequate moral guidance had we not permitted ourselves to be lured into the traps of materialistic greed. The statement that "we have met the enemy and it is we" would be only slightly more accurate as "we have met the enemy and it is some of our traditions."

We have been cranking the mills of credit and debt at rates that can no more be sustained through the 1990s than was true for the 1920s. Not surprisingly, we wave our flag and proclaim ourselves the leader of the Western world. We are, in fact, rather an absurd mess, with mountainous debt as the most obvious pecuniary manifestation of profound malaise. From an evolutionary perspective, our traits and behavioral modes of the present certainly do not merit emulation. No culture or people is ever worthy of the world leadership role of type and degree we have decreed for ourselves, which is something analogous to that of "stallion of the world." A moment's reflection brings recognition that we altered our best traits that were worthy of world emulation at the time of, and because of, our ascension to world dominance after World War II. The allusion to biblical teaching of ascension meaning the bodily passing of Christ from earth to heaven is, of course, deliberate.

Which is more likely, that we as a nation will reform ourselves by deliberate action before a major collapse, or after the fashion of our "binge" in the Roaring Twenties, will serious reform be possible only after the system crashes? One cannot formulate recommendations without specifying which scenario is postulated. History is not a vise from which no escape is ever possible prior to smashing the bonding device. However, we believe that efforts at reform, for example to break our addictions, to debt expansion (public, private, and international), to thoroughly corrupt money-grubbing, to drugs (including alcohol and tobacco), to violent acts in efforts to see that "our will be done, abroad as it is here at home and in heaven," will fail until after a shock enables deep-reaching institutional change. There is a fall in our future! Then we may achieve a decent "come-back."

Many Americans believe there is a core of goodness in the principles and customs that became entrenched or institutionalized in the aftermath of the convulsion that brought termination of our status as a colony of Britain. One must start somewhere, and we are in full accord with the view that the principles of liberties and rights that were embodied in our constitution are sound as such things go in human affairs. Certain elements of culture that were under experimentation in that era have survived the evolutionary tests of time, while others have not. Need we comment, however, that we reject the peculiar view that "our founding fathers were divinely inspired"? There were bits of cultural mutation in the events surrounding our birth as a nation, but it was a matter of humans taking thought and reacting to "push of the past" experiences as well as "pull of the future" opportunities that rationally seemed possible. Neither of those philosophical positions was fully dominant over the other. Our next wrenching crash, likely to come before this century ends, will bring with it the opportunity for change as deep-reaching as that of our early years. It is a mistaken agenda to try to return to the golden past because it was much less than perfect and conditions have changed almost beyond belief, so "you can't go home again, you can't step twice into the same river."

We are not alone in proposing a drastic change of philosophy. Keynes, for example, was an evolutionary economist who wrote half a century ago in some of his most thought-provoking work:

> The object of our analysis is, not to provide a machine, or method of blind manipulation, which will furnish an infallible answer, but to provide ourselves with an organized and orderly method of thinking out particular problems. . . . This is the nature of economic thinking. Any other way of applying our formal principles of thought . . . will lead us into error.[8]

Economists are thoroughly addicted to the equilibrium model, but as we have observed, business schools have followed the empirically revealed practices of business decision makers with such theoretical formulations as organizational, behavioral, and managerial models of firm behavior. Satisficing, rather than maximizing, constitutes a sharp departure from insistence upon equilibrium. The same is true for mark-up pricing models. We endorse such theoretical departures because they employ mechanistic concepts as tools rather than core perception of reality and rational conduct. To the extent that these contemporary models maintain a flexible and tentative stance rather than dogma, and incorporate only limited elements of the price mechanism, we are in accord with such usage. Subsets alone do not comprise Classical mechanism. It is the mental fixation on the adequacy, and even exclusive validity, of Classicism to which we vociferously object.

In standard theory, three categories of markets are distinguished and analyzed. These are, first, factor markets, where resource inputs requisite for production are obtained. Then, second, there are product markets, in which produced goods and services are sold. The third category is financial markets. The latter are extraordinarily complex and varied as to components and functioning. Also it is here that much chicanery and predatory activity is centered, especially if one includes sales effort in this category. A large part of what is done in financial markets and sales effort is wholly or in part unnecessary to rational functioning of a society. This is not to say that these largely predatory activities are not essential to society in the form that has evolved. Rather, these activities, "making money instead of making things," identify an enormous range of conduct in our society that comprises problems more than bringing solutions. Financial manipulation must be sharply reduced if we are to get past the malfunctions of today's system. It remains true, as Veblen wrote in 1904, that

> Modern circumstances do not permit the competitive management of property invested in industrial enterprise, much less its management in detail by individual owners. In short, the exercise of free contract, and the other powers inhering in the natural right of ownership, are incompatible with the modern machine technology. Business discretion necessarily centers in other hands than those of the general body of owners necessarily reduced to the practical status of pensioners dependent on the discretion of the great holders of immaterial wealth.[9]

Eternal vigilance is the price of liberty, decency, prosperity, a livable environment, and continuation of life itself. As a nation we long ago reached the circumstance wherein the five hundred largest of our several million productive units account for fully one-half of total production. Previously we cited the datum that the wealthiest ten percent of American families own fully five-sixths of total commercial income yielding wealth. It is absurd to assume that either methods or purposes of this ruling group, ill-defined though it may be in some particulars, will be appropriate to the needs and wishes of the five percent of humanity who live in the United States. And what is to be done regarding the plight of the other 95 percent? Keynes was correct when he observed during the 1930s that we need to accomplish "the euthanasia of the rentier." Neither detailed specification of what would be involved, nor how it might best be achieved, is within the scope of what we can do here. The pecuniary trappings of "the rentier" are vast almost beyond comprehension:

> Citizens with only a casual interest in finance perhaps assumed that the stock market was the most important enterprise of Wall Street because it always received the most attention in the news media. . . . In fact, the stock market was dwarfed by the credit markets. The year-end market value of corporate equities in 1979 was about $1.2 trillion—compared to $4.2 trillion in the credit markets. Most of that vast sum was dedicated to long-term debt, from mortgages to corporate bonds, but even the short-term lending in the money market was about equal in volume to value of corporate stocks.[10]

The next major restructuring will accomplish some of the necessary elimination of the rentier class and system, and will cast circumstances into hectic confusion from which change and evolution of institutional arrangements must be made. It is our responsibility to see that change is for the better, not deleterious. Hopefully, we as a culture will be willing and able to alter the present system into something more decent and more rational.

Perhaps we should enumerate additional elements of evolutionary change that we envision as desirable. First, a decision must be made, hopefully not merely by default, on our national choice for degree of reliance on free markets, domestically and internationally. A high degree of utilization of free markets also strongly implies free human migration over the planet, which would be mainly from poor countries to rich. Many Chinese likely would prefer to move to the United States, while many Indians, Bangladeshis, Pakistanis, Nigerians, et al., might be inclined to join relatives and fellow countrymen in Great Britain, rather than moving to the Americas. Are these societies ready for this influx? If not, we free traders had better rethink our position concerning the merits of free trade. Even assuming continuation of barriers to free migration of persons—philosophically illicit in a free trade paradigm—are people in rich countries ready to face the wage-rate implications of freely functioning market forces? Thus far the full market logic of essentially equal wage rates internationally has not brought open revolt by industrial workers in rich countries because the issue has not been stated forthrightly and openly. Moreover, debt has been increased rapidly enough to bring the creation of service-sector jobs adequate in number to avoid high rates of unemployment, even if pay rates for such jobs are lower than for the industrial jobs lost to foreign operations. So far we economists have been speaking glibly about our national transition to "the post-industrial society," something we pass off as representing desirable and progressive change. In fact, we American residents continually expand our use of industrial products, and what has changed is that we now import them from low-wage areas. Hence we are more accurately described as a deindustrial-ized economy than postindustrial society. Furthermore, to accompany our deindustrialization we have been able to rely on those imports at much lower prices than our domestic costs of production permit. Workers have to adjust to lower wages from hamburger frying jobs than they received from work in automobile manufacturing, but gasoline, cars, electronic gadgetry, and much else is available in abundance at reasonable price and quality standards. Accordingly, workers benefit as consumers.

A crisis is in the making, however, as it becomes obvious that the enormous trade imbalance is not sustainable. Presumably many Americans are pleased when we economists offer reassuring words of advice on how we can collect payment on the huge debt the Third World owes us by way of assets transfer. Third World basket-case countries thereby can pay much of their debt to us by selling us the best of their productive capital or resource-rich land areas. It seems impolite to ask if the peoples involved will tolerate such actions, or how viable their economies would be after they gave up the most profitable assets—the ones we would want. Worse yet, reassurance may turn to shock when we ask just which of our states the Japanese may choose in asset transfers to pay part of our indebtedness to that country. Why think that asset transfers move only along a one-way street? The market system has more than a few unpleasant features, and it seems certain that we must compromise our principles in the near future fully as much as we have done in the recent past. In its entirety the free trade paradigm simply will not serve adequately.

International solidarity needs to be fostered as the means of granting fuller expression to the needs of "the tired and huddled masses" of several continents. Imperialistic practices of world giants, especially ourselves and the Soviets, require to be broken. We are assaulting people as well as land, environment, and resources the world around in a grossly predatory fashion. The question of "what did the future ever do for me" requires an answer, not merely a shrugging of shoulders and a speed-up in the rate of use of fossil fuels, etc. Man does not live by enlarged GNP alone, and even growth can be thwarted by foolish growth programs.

To be added to our list is an urgent need for immediate reduction of military spending in the United States by about one-third. Within a short time, the Soviet Union almost certainly would match the spending cuts, and the process of reduction could be repeated. All of this as a package is radical, but it is required as movement toward international sanity. What is desired in markets is not necessarily desirable, and as we have known from Adam Smith straight along, monopoly power serves society badly. Acutely different institutional arrangements are required if humanity is to survive and overcome the impacts of our current deleterious and predatory practices.

We repeat that adoption of a sytem of sharply progressive income and inheritance taxation is crucial, as is implementation of taxation of economic rent. Reliance on debt must be lessened. Consumer demand could be enlarged by way of a much more equal distribution of income, apologetics for the status quo to the contrary notwithstanding. Conspicuous consumption and pecuniary emulation as bases for rewarding the quest for social status must be greatly reduced. However reluctant we may continue to be to acknowledge the validity of Veblen's ideas, the fact and functioning of our Leisure or Privileged Class constitute crucial elements for understanding society and its problems.

Let us conclude by going back to the beginning by repeating our earlier quotation from Margaret Jacob to lay emphasis on the still appealing but tragically ill-suited substance of Newtonian philosophy applied to social affairs:

> The ordered, providentially guided, mathematically regulated universe of Newton gave a model for a stable and prosperous polity, ruled by the self-interest of men. That was what Newton's universe meant to his friends and popularizers: it allowed them to imagine that nature was on their side; they could have laws of motion and keep God; spiritual forces could work in the universe; matter could be controlled and dominated by God and men. . . . That, briefly stated, was what the world natural, explicated in the *Principia*, meant to churchmen who were primarily interested in promoting their vision of the "world politick."

Notes

1. Georgescu-Roegen, *Entropy* . . . , 321.

2. Data from Joint Economic Committee of the U.S. Congress, *The Concentration of Wealth in the United States* (Washington: Government Printing Office, 1986), 24.

3. Henry George, *Progress and Poverty* (New York: Robert Schalkenbach Foundation, 1958).

4. Georgescu-Roegen, *Entropy* . . . , 320.

5. *Ibid.*

6. John K. Galbraith, *American Capitalism. The Concept of Countervailing Power* (Boston: Houghton Mifflin, 1952).

7. Georgescu-Roegen, *Entropy* . . . , 359.

8. Keynes, *General Theory* . . . , 297.

9. Veblen, *Business Enterprise* . . . , 266–67.

10. William Greider, *Secrets of the Temple: How the Federal Reserve Runs the Country* (New York: Simon, Schuster, 1987), 29–30.

Bibliography

Ayres, Clarence E. 1935. "The Gospel of Technology." *American Philosophy Today and Tomorrow*. Edited by Horace Kallen and Sidney Hook. New York: L. Furman Inc.

Bentham, Jeremy. 1789. *An Introduction to the Principles of Morals and Legislation*. London: T. Payne and Sons.

Boulding, Kenneth. 1981. *Ecodynamics*. Beverly Hills, Calif.: Sage Publications.

Chamberlin, Edward. 1962. *The Theory of Monopolistic Competition*. Cambridge, Mass.: Harvard University Press.

Chick, Victoria. 1983. *Macroeconomics After Keynes*. Cambridge, Mass.: MIT Press.

Columbia Encyclopedia. 1956. 2nd ed. Morningside, N.Y.: Columbia University Press.

Congdon, Tim. 1988. *The Debt Threat*. Oxford: Basil and Blackwell.

Council of Economic Advisers. (Annual) *Economic Report of the President*. Washington: Government Printing Office.

Daugert, Stanley M. 1950. *The Philosophy of Thorstein Veblen*. New York: King's Crown Press.

Debreu, Gerard. 1959. *Theory of Value; An Axiomatic Analysis of Economic Equilibrium*. New York: Wiley.

Dorfman, Joseph. 1961. *Thorstein Veblen and His America*. New York: Augustus M. Kelley.

Duesenberry, James. 1949. *Income, Saving, and the Theory of Consumer Behavior*. Cambridge: Harvard University Press.

Einstein, Albert. 1949. "Why Socialism?" *Monthly Review* vol. 1, no. 1 (May).

Einstein, Albert, and Leopold Infeld. 1938. *The Evolution of Physics*. New York: Simon and Shuster.

Eisner, Robert. 1987. "The Federal Deficit: How Does It Matter?" *Science*, 237, 25 September, 1581.

Fleming, D. F. 1961. *The Cold War and Its Origins*. 2 vols. Garden City, N.J.: Doubleday & Company, Inc.

Frank, Robert H. 1985. *Choosing the Right Pond*. Oxford: Oxford University Press.

Friedman, Benjamin M. 1988. *Day of Reckoning*. New York: Random House, Inc.

Friedman, Milton. 1953. *Essays in Positive Economics*. Chicago: University of Chicago Press.

———. 1957. *A Theory of the Consumption Function*. Washington: National Bureau of Economic Research.

Fuller, R. Buckminster. 1969. *Utopia or Oblivian: The Prospects for Humanity*. New York: Bantam.

Galbraith, John K. 1952. *American Capitalism. The Concept of Countervailing Power*. Boston: Houghton Mifflin.

George, Henry. 1958. *Progress and Poverty*. New York: Robert Schalkenbach Foundation.

Georgescu-Roegen, Nicholas. 1971. *The Entropy Law and the Economic Process*. Cambridge: Harvard University Press.

Green, Robert W. 1973. *Protestantism and Capitalism: The Weber Thesis and Its Critics*. New York: D. C. Heath.

Greider, William. 1987. *Secrets of the Temple: How the Federal Reserve Runs the Country*. New York: Simon, Shuster.

Heilbroner, Robert L. 1980. *Marxism: For and Against*. New York: W. W. Norton.

———, and Peter L. Bernstein. 1989. *The Debt and the Deficit*. New York: W. W. Norton.

Hicks, John R. 1974. *The Crisis in Keynesian Economics*. New York: Basic Books.

———. 1939. *Value and Capital*. Oxford: Oxford University Press.

Homan, Paul T. 1932. "An Appraisal of Institutional Economics." *American Economic Review* XXII.

International Monetary Fund. (Annual) *World Economic Outlook*. Washington: IMF.

Jacob, Margaret C. 1976. *The Newtonians and the English Revolution, 1689–1720*. Ithaca, N.Y.: Cornell University Press.

Jevons, William Stanley. 1924. *The Theory of Political Economy*. 4th ed. London: Macmillan.

Joint Economic Committee of the United States' Congress. 1986. *The Concentration of Wealth in the United States*. Washington: Government Printing Office.

Keynes, John Maynard. 1926. *The End of Laissez-Faire*. London: Woolf.

———. 1936. *The General Theory of Employment, Interest, and Money*. New York: Harcourt, Brace.

———. 1930. *A Treatise on Money*. 2 vols. New York: Harcourt, Brace and Company.

Koestler, Arthur. 1959. *The Sleepwalkers*. New York: Grosset & Dunlap.

Kolko, Joyce. 1988. *Restructuring the World Economy*. New York: Pantheon Books.

Kuznets, Simon. 1946. *National Income, a Summary of Findings*. New York: National Bureau of Economic Research, Inc.

———. 1953. *Selected Essays in Business Cycles, National Income, and Economic Growth*. New York: W. W. Norton.

———. 1953. *Shares of Upper Income Groups in Income and Savings*. New York: National Bureau of Economic Research, Inc.

Liebenstein, Harvey. 1950. "Bandwagon, Snob and Veblen Effects in the Theory of Consumer's Demand." *Quarterly Journal of Economics* 64.

Linder, Steffan B. 1970. *The Harried Leisure Class*. New York: Columbia University Press.

List, Friedrich. 1928. *The National System of Political Economy*. Translated by Sampson S. Lloyd. London: Longmans, Green.

Lomax, David. 1986. *The Developing Country Debt Crisis*. London: Basingstroke and Macmillan.

Mansfield, Edwin. 1979. *Microeconomics: Theory and Applications*. Shorter Third Ed. New York: W. W. Norton and Company.

Marshall, Alfred. 1920. *Principles of Economics*. 8th ed. London: Macmillan.

Marx, Karl. 1904. *A Contribution to the Critique of Political Economy*. Chicago: Charles H. Kerr & Company.

———, and Friedrich Engels. 1935. *The Communist Manifesto*. (1848); reprinted in *A Handbook of Marxism*. Edited by Emile Burns. London: Victor Gollancz Ltd.

Maslow, Abraham. 1954. *Motivation and Personality*. New York: Harper and Row.

———. 1968. *Towards a Psychology of Being*. New York: Van Nostrand Reinhold.

McFarland, Floyd B. 1982. "Markup Pricing and the Auto Industry: A Reason for Stagflation." *The American Journal of Economics and Sociology* vol. 41, no. 1 (January).

Menger, Carl. 1981. *Principles of Economics*. Translated by P. Dingwall and B. Hoselitz. New York: New York University Press.

Mill, John Stuart. 1891. *Principles of Political Economy*. 5th ed. New York: D. Appleton.

———. 1962. *Utilitarianism, On Liberty, Essay on Bentham and John Austin*. Edited by M. Warnock. Cleveland: World Publishing.

Newton, Isaac. 1952. *Mathematical Principles of Natural Philosophy*. (1687) Great Books of the Western World. vol. 34. Chicago and London: Encyclopedia Britannica Inc.

Organization for Economic Cooperation and Development. (Annual) *Economic Outlook*. Paris: OECD.

Robinson, Joan. 1969. *The Economics of Imperfect Competition*. New York: St. Martin.

———. 1964. *Economic Philosophy*. Garden City: N.Y.: Doubleday & Company, Inc.

Russell, Bertrand. 1945. *A History of Western Philosophy*. New York: Simon and Schuster.

Samuelson, Paul A. 1972. "*Maximization Principles in Analytical Economics*." *American Economic Review* 251 (June).

Sheffrin, Steven, et al. 1988. *Macroeconomics: Theory and Policy*. Cincinnati: Southwestern.

Simon, Herbert A. 1982. *Models of Bounded Rationality*. Cambridge: MIT Press.

———. 1979. "Rational Decision Making in Business Organizations." *American Economic Review* 69 (September).

Smith, Adam. 1937. *The Wealth of Nations*. New York: Modern Library.

———. 1966. *The Theory of Moral Sentiments*. New York: Augustus M. Kelley.

———. 1967. *The Early Writings of Adam Smith*. Edited by J. Ralph Lindgren. New York: Augustus M. Kelley.

Smolinski, Leon. 1973. "Karl Marx and Mathematical Economics." *Journal of Political Economy* 81 (September–October).

Tawney, Richard H. 1926. *Religion and the Rise of Capitalism*. New York: Harcourt Brace and Company.

Veblen, Thorstein. 1899. *The Theory of the Leisure Class*. New York: Macmillan.

———. 1904. *The Theory of Business Enterprise*. New York: Scribners.

———. 1914. *The Instinct of Workmanship*. New York: Huebsch.

———. 1934. *Essays in Our Changing Order*. Edited by Leon Ardzrooni. New York: Viking Press.

———. 1954. *Absentee Ownership*. New York: Viking Press.

———. 1954. *Imperial Germany and the Industrial Revolution*. New York: Viking Press.

———. 1961. *The Place of Science in Modern Civilization*. New York: Russell and Russell.

von Neumann, John, and Oskar Morgenstern. 1964. *The Theory of Games and Economic Behavior*. 3rd ed. New York: Wiley.

Weber, Max. 1956. *The Protestant Ethic and the Spirit of Capitalism*. New York: C. Scribner's Sons.

Westfall, Richard. 1980. *Never at Rest: A Biography of Isaac Newton*. New York: Cambridge University Press.

Whitehead, Alfred N. 1925. *Science and the Modern World*. New York: Macmillan.

Wicksteed, Philip H. 1933. *The Common Sense of Political Economy*. London: George Routledge and Sons.

Index